THE HISTORY
OF THE
CENTRAL BROOKS RANGE

GAUNT BEAUTY, TENUOUS LIFE

Ernie Johnson and Bob Marshall after their fifty-day Alatna-John River trip. Photo taken with Robert Marshall's camera. Courtesy of the Bancroft Library, University of California, Berkeley.

THE HISTORY
OF THE
CENTRAL BROOKS RANGE

GAUNT BEAUTY, TENUOUS LIFE

William E. Brown

University of Alaska Press
Fairbanks

© 2007 University of Alaska Press
PO Box 756240
Fairbanks, AK 99775-6240
888-252-6657
fypress@uaf.edu
www.uaf.edu/uapress

Library of Congress Cataloging-in-Publication Data

Brown, William E. (William Edward), 1930–
  [Gaunt beauty—tenuous life]
 The history of the central Brooks Range : gaunt beauty, tenuous life / William E.
 Brown.
   p. cm.
   Originally published: Gaunt beauty—tenuous life. Alaska : National Park Service.
   1988.
   Includes bibliographical references and index.
   ISBN-13: 978-1-60223-012-5 (cloth : alk. paper)
   ISBN-13: 978-1-60223-009-5 (pbk. : alk. paper)
   ISBN-10: 1-60223-012-9 (cloth. : alk. paper)
   ISBN-10: 1-60223-009-9 (pbk. : alk. paper)
  1. Gates of the Arctic National Park and Preserve (Alaska)—History. 2. Historic
  sites—Alaska—Gates of the Arctic National Park and Preserve. I. Title.
  F912.G36B76 2007
  979.8'6—dc22   2007008865

Cover photograph by Dennis Witmer, from *Far to the North: Photographs
from the Brooks Range*, © 2005, by Far to the North Press.

TABLE OF CONTENTS

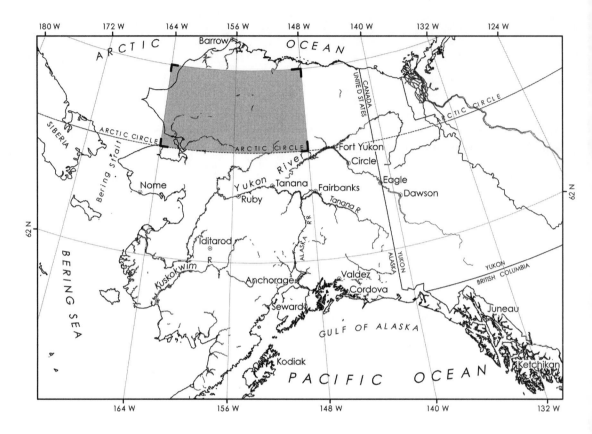

Map of Alaska showing the Gates of the Arctic region. USGS Technical Data Branch, Menlo Park, CA.

Introduction

The first edition of this book, titled *Gaunt Beauty . . . Tenuous Life,* was published in very limited quantity by the National Park Service in January 1988. That two-volume set was a historic resources study done by the National Park Service as part of a multiyear, interdisciplinary cultural resources inventory for Gates of the Arctic National Park and Preserve, performed under the direction of archeologist Michael L. Kunz. The inventory was funded by the National Park Service as an essential element of the planning process for the new park. The project began with archeological surveys in 1983. Most of the historical research, field work, and writing was accomplished in 1984 and 1985.

The original publication was offered as a functional document for the park in terms of (1) recording and evaluating historic sites, and (2) a narrative of historical themes useful for historic site context and interpretation of the park's history. Beyond this, the author hopes that the book will enrich the experience of park employees and visitors to the park by exposing them to the narrative history and making them attuned to the resources and park residents and neighbors.

Before this, no comprehensive study had been done of the history of this remote region. Thus the historical narrative had to build from the ground up, without benefit of prior syntheses, using many original sources. The nature of the history in this region—multicultural, anecdotal, and subject to severe variations of activity and decline—also militated against shortcuts. People and events shone forth here that would be lost in the shuffle in a more populated region. Nearly everyone and everything was unique. Finally, in the original publication the author quoted at length from original sources, particularly Native accounts, narratives of early exploration, and the works of Robert Marshall. There were several reasons for this. First, people working in the wilderness can't carry whole libraries with them, even if they could find copies of the rare and scattered documents that fueled so much of the narrative. Second, it seemed important, in a place that still beckons to the spirit and discovery, that original perceptions of homeland people and early discoverers not be filtered. The historic resources study is therefore partly an anthology of original literature that most readers would otherwise never see.

The book that you are now reading preserves the themes and narrative of the original while leaving out part, but by no means all, of the extensive quotations from original sources and the detailed site descriptions.

The study benefited from many kinds of cooperation, which the author appreciates:

- Project director Michael Kunz provided historical, historic architectural and engineering, archeological, and anthropological information and perspective. Planning and programming preparations were done with help from regional chief of cultural resources Leslie Hart and her staff.

- The NPS's Historic American Buildings Survey and Historic American Engineering Record (HABS/HAER) contributed documentation of historic structures and mining technology, both in the park and nearby. This was a highlight of the study and a splendid example of a park benefiting from a program often categorized as external to park operations.

- The Bureau of Land Management and the National Park Service jointly conceived a regional study that would benefit both agencies by applying the assembled talents for the park inventory to recordation and evaluation of historic resources in both jurisdictions. Archeologist Susan Will of BLM had earlier prepared cultural resources studies of Coldfoot (Will 1982) and Wiseman, and these were eagerly appropriated by the author. Her final inventory of Wiseman historic structures is reproduced in Brown (1988).

- Park superintendent Dick Ring and his always cooperative staff supported the inventory project throughout with bases of operations and logistical help. In turn, the incremental products of the inventory from all disciplines were immediately incorporated into the planning process. Thus, research, field-proofing, and planning melded together as a team effort. In this context, anthropological and historic-use pattern insights from the inventory work may have contributed most to the planning effort.

For the author it has been a tremendous privilege to work with the history, the land, and the people of the Gates of the Arctic.

Note on Sources

Most of the historical quotations and photos used in this book are derived from public domain sources. Quotations from modern, copyrighted sources have been limited to short passages. All sources of direct quotes are credited in the captions and in the bibliography. For a more comprehensive bibliography of original source material about the central Brooks Range, see Brown (1988).

To convey Robert Marshall's special insights, I have drawn heavily on his published literature and from the Robert Marshall Collection—both written and photographic—at the Bancroft Library, University of California, Berkeley.

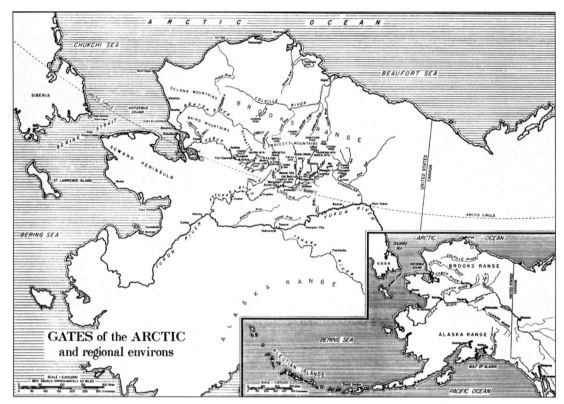

Gates of the Arctic and regional environs. Courtesy of National Park Service Historic American Buildings Survey (HABS) Program.

Acknowledgements

Obviously, much is owed to many after a work of this kind—to the members of the history, HABS, and archeological crews whose work is identified in the pages that follow; to the park, regional office, and Washington office staffs for continuing support and patience; to the archivists of many institutions who helped me dredge up the old documents and photos and maps; and to the people of the study region who gave both hospitality and knowledge unstintingly, most of them named as integral parts of the history. I thank all of these and hope that the work that follows requites their trust and efforts.

For this revised and streamlined new edition, Warren Gardepe scanned and retyped the text. Erica Hill and Sue Mitchell at the University of Alaska Press edited the original National Park Service report and arranged for production. Frank Norris and Grant Spearman provided much-appreciated help with historical photos. And finally, thanks to Jeff Rasic and superintendent David Mills of the National Park Service, Gates of the Arctic National Park and Preserve, for funding this work.

Frigid Crags, one of the Gates. National Park Service photo by John Kauffmann.

Chapter One

Land of Traditional Times

In the central Brooks Range, the Arctic Divide splits descending waters to the Arctic Ocean and the Chukchi Sea or to the Yukon River and Bering Sea. Radiating from the mountain core, the rivers course through canyons and valleys. South of the mountains, boreal forest covers the lowlands and probes the slopes. But toward the mountain crests north winds warp and stunt the last struggling spruce trees. They disappear, replaced by the dwarf plants of the arctic tundra. Trending east to west, the Brooks Range blocks the northern drift of moist Pacific air and marks the transition to arctic deserts dominated by polar air.

The Gates of the Arctic region lies north of the Arctic Circle. Its major draining rivers trace the connections to adjacent regions—west-flowing Kobuk and Noatak, north-flowing tributaries of the Colville, southeast-flowing Chandalar, and south-flowing branches of the Koyukuk. Passes carved by ancient glaciers and eroding rivers allow transit across mountains and through the valleys, where, in summer, lakes of glacial origin reflect crowding peaks and towering clouds.

Each spring, following the natural routes of streams, passes, and portages, herds of caribou migrate north across the mountains from forested wintering grounds in the Kobuk, Koyukuk, and Chandalar drainages. They seek rich upland meadows in the northern foothills of the Brooks Range. There the cows assemble to calve. After calving, the bands concentrate, then disperse to range across the Arctic Slope—even to the coast 200 miles from the mountains. Finally they congregate again in preparation for the fall migration back through the mountains.

For at least 10,000 years, human hunters have seasonally posted themselves in the valleys and passes to intercept migrating caribou. At hundreds of lookout sites, the evidence of their vigils can be found—cores and flakes of stone, finely knapped projectile points and blades. They worked as they watched and waited—hammering, chipping, flaking with bone, antler, and stone—repairing weapons, making spare points, constantly attending to their tool kits. In the variations of form and substance that distinguish these artifacts, a succession of cultures can be inferred. The surface scatter and mixing of artifacts at the typical hilltop lookout station would confound dating and classification were it not for a few stratified sites in neighboring valley and coastal locations. At these fortunate finds, cultural layers reveal the ancient history of this land. A few names of generally accepted cultural traditions give a sense of this progression:

American Paleo-Arctic, Northern Archaic, Arctic Small Tool, Northern Maritime, Athapaskan.

The people who made the artifacts and who lived and hunted at the places discovered by archaeologists were, to varying degrees, ancestral to the modern Indians and Eskimos of arctic Alaska. Population movements have been tracked using artifactual evidence—from Asia to Alaska, south to the interior of North America, east to Greenland. But dispersion of people and traits was not simply linear and one way. Five-thousand-year-old tools of the Northern Archaic Tradition, found at caribou hunting sites on the North Slope, could have been borrowed from Indians far to the south. Perhaps the wielders of these tools were Indians, as archaeologist Douglas Anderson suggests, who were attracted "back" to the Arctic by the unusually mild climate of that period.

Gaps and incongruities in the archaeological record hint at mysteries: people with distinct cultural traditions, seemingly unrelated to those who came before and after them—such as the Old Whalers of Cape Krusenstern, who came out of nowhere and disappeared in a few decades. And the cultural dynamism of some periods indicates the explosive force of new technologies and subsistence strategies—for example, the Denbigh people of the Arctic Small Tool tradition, who 4,000 years ago swept from Alaska to Greenland to pioneer the eastern Arctic. Sometimes called Paleo-Eskimos, the Denbigh people harvested caribou in the interior and seals on the coast with their highly adaptable tool kit (Anderson 1981).

During these thousands of years of migrations, cultural exchanges, and climatic and biotic variations, the inhabitants of northern Alaska perfected their myriad adaptations. Eventually they became the Indian and Eskimo peoples encountered by Europeans two centuries ago.

To survive and flourish for millennia, these people adjusted to each variable of the natural environment. They changed their habits and their habitats as necessary. If caribou failed, they hunted sheep or went to the coast for seals. They spread up the rivers and became expert fishermen. From the materials at hand they fashioned the implements they needed. They borrowed and traded ideas, tools, and raw materials with their neighbors. Their tool kits, both mental and material, allowed rapid shifts from one hunting mode to another, from one place to another. Knowledge of an animal, a place, or a technique, once learned, was held in reserve for the time when it would be needed. Always there was an alternative ready, for inflexibility in the spare and unforgiving Arctic meant famine or death.

Nor did these people—so intimate with their homelands—lack spiritual vision. Rooted as their lives and cultures were in the very bedrock of natural forces and powers, they conformed their individual and social practices to the sacred order of the landscape. From observation and meditation they saw both the obvious and the ineffable in the natural order. They created rituals to reveal and propitiate the powers that surrounded and sustained them. Even in the mute evidence of their abandoned tools, the blending of science and artistry illustrates the balance and vigor of their lifeways (Anderson 1981; Burch 1972; Gal and Hall 1982; Lopez 1984; Murie 1935; Williams 1958).

Until the late nineteenth century, the central Brooks Range remained terra incognita to Euro-Americans. Because the country was buffered by hundreds of miles of forest and tundra traversed by unmapped rivers, the Eskimos and Indians of this northern heartland experienced only indirectly the transitory effects of European explorations along Alaska's arctic coast, which began in the late eighteenth century. Location of Russian and British trading posts on the Yukon River in the 1830s and 1840s, followed by Yankee whalers and traders along the arctic coast in the 1850s, abruptly changed Native societies in these accessible regions. Although events on the Yukon and along the coast reverberated in the Brooks Range, a few more decades would pass before the full effects of Euro-American incursions reached inland peoples. Thus through the mid-1800s, the folk of the central mountains and upper rivers maintained their ways of life (Burch 1975a; McFadyen Clark 1974; Oswalt 1979).

Archaeological evidence shows that ancient Indians occupied both faces of the Brooks Range thousands of years ago, and that early Eskimos filtered into the northern part of the range from the coasts, displacing the Indians southward. In time, cultural regionalization produced a pattern in which the Eskimo inhabited the tundra, mountains, and coast while Indians adapted to life in the forests (Kunz 1977).

Ethnohistorical and historical studies describe a shifting boundary that placed Athapaskan Indians on the upper Kobuk and Noatak rivers and on the north face of the mountains in valleys tributary to the Colville River. Then Eskimo expansions forced the Indians east and south. War alternated with trade along these changing cultural boundaries (Kunz 1977).

Hunting, writ large, lends meaning and inspiration to life; as a way of living it gives participants their sense of identity. A proper, cordial relationship with animals becomes vital in maintaining that sense of identity—that sense of how the world functions and how humans are to conduct themselves within this larger sphere of existence. Animals instruct human beings . . . in the mysteries of life: by giving heed to animals and their ways—by making themselves receptive to their counsel—hunters learn how they must behave (Martin 1980, 44).

Tanana River and Fort Yukon Kutchin (Gwitch'in Athapaskan) Indians on Yukon River, 1867. From Dall (1870). Courtesy of the Bancroft Library, University of California, Berkeley.

Tanana Indian summer encampment on the Yukon River, 1867. From Whymper (1871). Courtesy of the Bancroft Library, University of California, Berkeley.

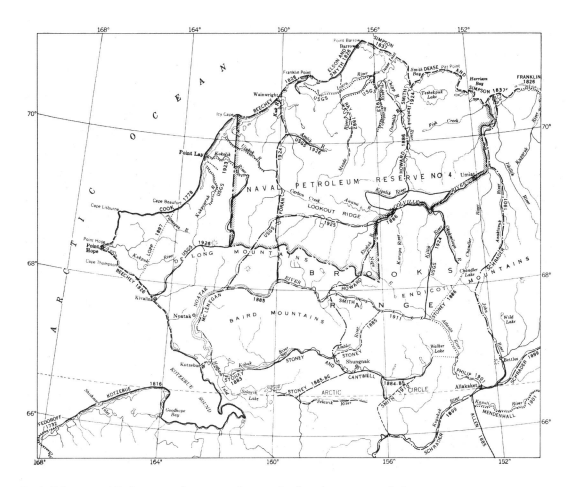

This map shows the routes of early explorers in northwest Alaska. From Reed (1958).

Both Eskimo and Indian were hunter-gatherers. Oral traditions recorded a time in which all creatures appeared as human beings. Occasionally, some creatures donned animal guises. In such a cosmology, animals had souls, power, and the ability to suffer. Yet the hunter must kill the animal to feed and clothe himself and his family. Thus developed elaborate systems of taboo, intricate ceremonies to assure the animal's gift of itself to the hunter, and forms of courtesy to ease the suffering of and show respect for the taken animal. In this way its power would not turn malevolent, and its soul would come back in the guise of another animal, which in turn could be hunted. Disharmony and disease occurred when humans failed in their ethical duties, for example, by killing too many animals or failing to show proper respect. At such times, in one tradition, plants took pity on the hunters and offered themselves (Vecsey 1980).

Embedded in the rituals and oral history of these lifeways were the knowledge and techniques of survival. Stories contained the science of place, season, and animal behavior. They described techniques of hunting, travel, and cold-weather shelter. Languages geared to infinite descriptive detail conveyed every nuance of dynamic and dangerous environments.

The traditional societies of the central mountains and upper rivers in 1850 included mountain- and tundra-dwelling Eskimos, who ranged across the northern part of the Brooks Range and through the foothills and valleys

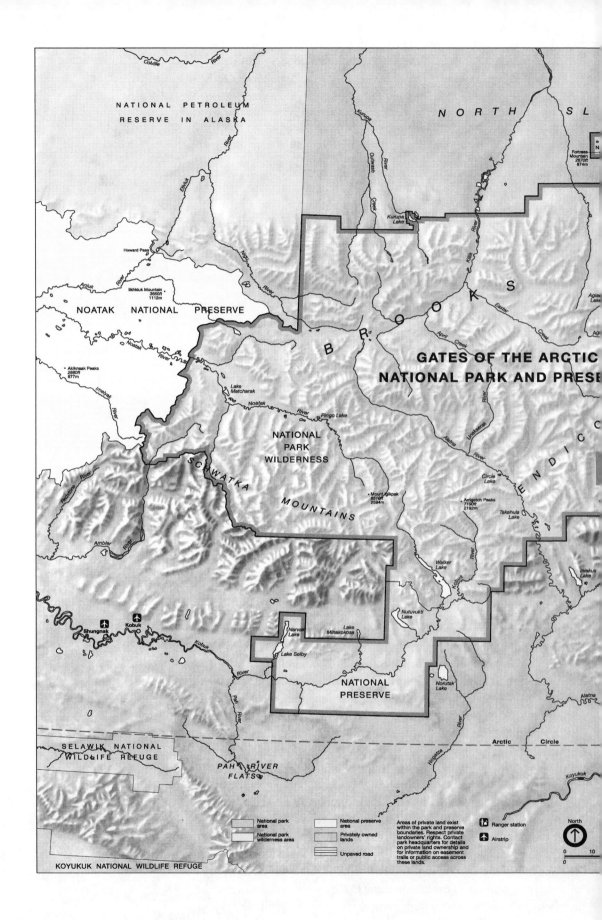

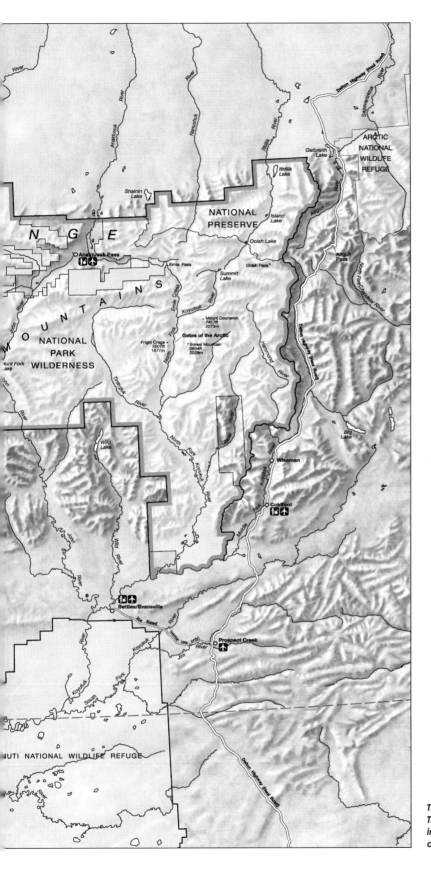

The Gates of the Arctic region. This map gives some idea of the intricate mountain terrain and drainage patterns of the region.

bordering the Colville River; the forest-dwelling Kobuk River Eskimos; and the groups of Athapaskan Indians living in the upper Koyukuk and Chandalar drainages.

Anthropologists of the 1940s and 1950s identified cultural distinctions between coastal Eskimos (Tareumiut) and inland or riverine Eskimos (Nunamiut). Aside from location, the distinctions were based upon the different lifeways and social arrangements resulting from primary dependence upon marine resources on the one hand and terrestrial or aquatic resources on the other. The Eskimos of the Brooks Range—both traditional and contemporary—are generally called Nunamiut. Ernest S. Burch, Jr., cites a multitude of reasons for dropping these terms as cultural distinctions and group names, maintaining that the Eskimos themselves use the words solely in a spatial sense, i.e., any group farther inland than another group would be Nunamiut, or, going the other way, Tareumiut. Burch makes the further point that the imposed Nunamiut/Tareumiut dichotomy disregards the idea of an inland/coastal continuum, for the Brooks Range Eskimos could move to the coast and hunt sea mammals when caribou failed to support them in the mountains. Conversely, people based on the coast forayed inland to hunt caribou as a regular part of their subsistence strategy and in emergencies when sea mammals were scarce (Burch 1976a).

In this volume, the Eskimos of the northern Brooks Range-Colville River area will be described simply as mountain or inland Eskimos, except when terms coined by the people themselves, e.g., the Ulumiut (People of the Ulu Valley) are more appropriate.

One final caution about cultural perceptions—most visitors from temperate regions have described the homelands of northern Indians and Eskimos as cruel and barren wastelands. The people themselves were seen as enduring stoics, constantly at the margins of survival, socially undeveloped, and too primitive and isolated to know enough to choose a better place and way of life. Students who have lived long enough with these people to share their celebrations of life on the land, to enter at least the foyers of their respective societies, have found a different reality. A burgeoning Native literature in recent decades has made this reality available to all.

The northern world is one of great beauty, at times "nurturing and easy" (Nelson 1983, 33). The very demands of its difficult seasons forged compensatory social systems distinguished by intricate kinship ties, visiting, and seasonal rounds of ceremonies, feasts, games, and dances. Trading fairs and potlatches combined all of these, serving as reunions that brought relatives and friends together from across the length and breadth of the country (Burch 1975a; VanStone 1974).

• • •

For at least several hundred years, the central mountains and upper rivers have been places of shifting cultural frontiers between Indians and Eskimos. The long-term cultural evolution of a given group in a given place cannot be assumed, especially given the acceleration of population movements during the last century of Native contact with Euro-Americans (Hall 1984; see also Burch 1976a; Burch 1981; Kunz 1977).

Despite these qualifications, the ties of memory and material remains do allow an approximate reconstruction of traditional societies, locations, and lifeways in 1850. Though there were territorial surges and retreats by various groups of mountain Eskimos and Athapaskans, the broad pattern of recent centuries indicates a demarcation based on the Brooks Range (Kunz 1977).

The situation is somewhat different on the upper Kobuk. Here, Eskimos adapted to inland/riverine life penetrated the fringe of the forest environment and mingled frequently with Koyukon Indians from the upper Koyukuk. Early visitors recorded a bilingual people in this area who blended Eskimo and Indian lifeways (Foote 1966).

Annette McFadyen Clark, in *Koyukuk River Culture* (1974), compares the precontact habitats and lifeways of the Koyukuk, Kobuk, and mountain peoples. Her comparative study, with emphasis on the Koyukon Athapaskan Indians, provides a starting point for the discussion that follows. The works of J. L. Giddings (*Kobuk River Eskimo*, 1961), Nicholas J. Gubser (*Nunamiut Eskimo*, 1954), and Robert A. McKennan (*Chandalar Kutchin*, 1965) provide similar depth for their respective subjects. The upper Noatak people are subsumed in the treatment of mountain, or Nunamiut, Eskimos (Giddings 1952, 1961; Gubser 1954; McKennan 1965).

The similar environments of upper Kobuk and upper Koyukuk, as well as the neighboring Chandalar country, contain a mix of swampy, lake-dotted lowlands and meandering, forest-lined rivers that head as swift mountain streams flowing out of constricted canyons and valleys. Rising above all, craggy alpine peaks overlook mountain lakes and valleys carved by the glaciers that dominated these highlands not so long ago. Intricate vegetative mosaics in the lowlands, terraces, and valley slopes reflect such factors as permafrost and soil conditions, wind exposure, and successional stages in the active floodplains and on the burned areas left by summer storms. Tundra prairies cover large expanses of exposed lowland; open muskeg bogs punctuated by stunted black spruce occupy poorly drained areas over shallow permafrost. Larger white spruce and birch grow on well-drained slopes and on natural levees that parallel the rivers. Willows and alders pioneer disturbed areas, both upcountry burns and river bars and beaches, and cottonwoods colonize the more stable stream banks.

Significant fauna in the lowlands and foothills include species such as caribou, moose, brown and black bear, porcupine, beaver, muskrat, and snowshoe hare. The white sheep of the northlands seldom stray from the high mountains, thus forcing extended hunting trips. Predatory fur bearers include wolf, lynx, fox, mink, marten, and otter. Resident ptarmigan and grouse provide variety and emergency food, and migratory ducks and geese arrive just in time to supplement failing winter food supplies.

Despite the fact that this forested upriver country is north of the Arctic Circle, the climatic regime is Interior Alaskan, more subarctic than arctic, except at higher elevations. The Interior climate has short, relatively warm summers and still, cold winters nearly eight months long. Rapid transitions between these two seasons bring breakup of frozen water in May and freezeup in October.

According to Clark, there are three major differences between the upper Kobuk and the upper Koyukuk: (1) the Kobuk has a greater supply of salmon; (2) until recently, the Kobuk had fewer caribou; and (3) the Koyukuk has more moose than the Kobuk, at least since the contact period. As a result of these differences, the Kobuk Eskimo have relied upon salmon fishing supplemented by caribou, while the Koyukuk Indians subsisted upon salmon, moose, and caribou in roughly equal parts. Both groups supplemented their diets with small game and berries (McFadyen Clark 1974; Giddings 1952; McKennan 1965; Nelson 1983).[1]

Except for occasional forays south of the divide to hunt, trade, and gather wood, the Nunamiut, or mountain Eskimos, lived in a treeless environment. They led a highly mobile lifestyle in search of caribou—their main source of food, clothing, and shelter. Sheep, bear, marmot, and ground squirrels, along with migratory birds and lake fish, supplemented the Nunamiut diet, but caribou provided the key to existence for these people. When caribou were unavailable, starving times loomed, and the people scattered to the forest edge south of the divide or went north and west to the coast (McFadyen Clark 1974).

Ernest Burch conveys a sense of the difficulties facing caribou hunters in traditional times. Given that people cannot follow the herds, for they mi-

grate on average about ten kilometers per hour, they must be intercepted. The problem for the hunter is to determine their route. Once he has made this decision, he must move to the right spot and be ready when the animals arrive. With the stakes so high, knowledge of the prey animals and climatic conditions and refined capabilities for timely arrival at hunting sites were essential (Burch 1972).

A Koyukon caribou corral, 1866. From Whymper, 1871. Courtesy of the Bancroft Library, University of California, Berkeley.

• • •

Meat and fat from mammals, fish, and fowl provided almost all the calories consumed by traditional hunter-gatherers of the central mountains and upper rivers. Berries, wild tubers, and green shoots were eaten raw when gathered or used to garnish stews and pokes of meat and fat. But vegetables alone could not sustain life (McFadyen Clark 1974, 29). Thus, patterns of livelihood for each group of people revolved around a few key animal species. While the Kobuk Eskimos had greater access to fish than the Koyukuk Indians, they had fewer caribou and practically no moose. The Koyukuk Indians had moose and small game. The Nunamiut enjoyed food security when caribou herds were large, but faced starvation when they were not (McFadyen Clark 1974).

Each traditional society in the region comprised a homogeneous cluster of related families, separate and distinct from all other societies in the region, even from neighboring linguistic brethren. Clothing, eating habits, tool kits, and dialectical differences within the broad linguistic groups (Iñupiaq Eskimo, Koyukon Athapaskan, Gwich'in Athapaskan) allowed quick identification of strangers; those who trespassed societal or ethnic

Traditional hunters and gatherers were top predators in the northern Alaska ecosystem. Successful top predators must be opportunistic and mobile. In the cold and spare ecosystems of this region, human predators had to maintain a low population relative to prey populations, and low density within their hunting territories where, except for migratory concentrations, animal life was spread thin (Melchior 1976, 203).

boundaries risked their lives. At certain seasons and under certain circumstances travelers could cross these boundaries for trade, ceremonial, and recreational purposes. But the overriding fact of life in traditional times was fear and suspicion of strangers. Kinship, trading partnerships between individuals of different societies, and intergroup trading fairs and invitational gatherings at appointed times and places relaxed these inhibitions periodically. Warfare, between Eskimo groups or between Eskimos and Indians, preserved societal and ethnic boundaries over time (Burch 1979).

Mountain Eskimos

The Tulugagmiut (People of the Tulugak) band of mountain Eskimos took its name from Tulugak Lake in the upper Anaktuvuk Valley. This band of perhaps fifty people was part of a larger society whose bands roamed through the central Endicott Mountains from the valleys just south of the divide to the northern foothills. Except for summer trade visits via the Colville (Kuukpik) River to the Arctic Coast, the band stayed mainly in the mountains, high valleys, and foothills of its home territory.

A head man, or *umialik*, provided counsel and direction for band activities, based on his proven strength of character and sound judgment. The leadership function was most important when the band prepared for spring and fall caribou drives.

The *umialik* predicted and selected the best place to intercept the migration, supervised construction of the ceremonial house or *qargi*, and

Below: First Eskimos met on Schrader's traverse to the Arctic Ocean, at camp on Goobic (Colville) River, forty miles from the coast. F. C. Schrader photo 1005 of 1901. USGS Historical Photo Library, Denver.

assigned tasks relating to caribou corrals and snares. After coordinating the hunt, he oversaw the butchering and distribution of meat. Then he took an active role in communal singing, dancing, and feasting. His function as political, social, and ceremonial leader extended to settlement of disputes within the band.

The Eskimo camp, with skin boat on side for wind shelter, skin tents, and fish drying rack. F. C. Schrader photo 1006 of 1901. USGS Historical Photo Library, Denver.

Following the successful outcome of the spring drive in March or April, meat was cached and the band began to disperse into family units. These smaller groups hunted and trapped as they made their ways by sled down to the foothills and along the Colville River to await breakup. While waiting, they cached their sleds and refurbished their *umiat* (skin boats). After the rivers were clear of ice, usually in May, the families loaded their craft with children, trade goods, and food and floated downriver to Niglik on the Colville delta. There they engaged in trade, games, and feasting with coastal Eskimos. Many families spent the rest of the summer along the coast hunting and fishing.

As fall approached they began traveling back upstream to the places where they had cached their sleds the previous spring. Waiting for freezeup, they hunted, fished, and trapped. Then they set off by sled to their home territory to prepare for the fall caribou drive. After the autumn hunt, the band once again dispersed into family units to hunt and trap until spring.

These seasonal dispersals of family hunting groups over thousands of square miles, except at times of caribou concentrations, kept the right balance between predators and prey. This necessity made the extended family the basic economic unit of mountain Eskimo society. Most often headed by the wife's father or grandfather, the family functioned as a unit, sharing food, tools, and other goods with all of its members. Children learned the basic skills and responsibilities of their society in this context.

The seasonal round tapped all essential resources on schedule. Caribou—killed in large numbers during migration drives and occasionally after dispersal—provided the basic sustenance: not only meat and fat for food but also bone, antler, and sinew for tools and hides for clothing, footwear, bedding, and shelter. Pelts of wolves, wolverine, and fox became ruffs and trim. The thick fleece of sheep made warm parkas, as did the skins of squirrels and birds.

Trade between inland and coastal Eskimos centered on the exchange of furs and hides from the mountains for oil, blubber, and skins from sea mammals. These transactions represented an essential division of labor across environmental lines (Spearman 1979).

Vignettes of traditional life as related by mountain Eskimos or Euro-American observers add substance to the chronicle of seasons and sustenance. Norwegian explorer Helge Ingstad lived with the Tulugagmiut during the winter of 1949–1950:

As I wandered into this endless mountain world, I often stumbled upon old signs of caribou hunting—traces of vanished times. Along the slopes of the valley where the caribou have their tracks, I quite often came upon rows of little stone cairns. These were to lead the caribou to the spot where the marksman lay in wait with bow and arrows. At some places the hunters had built themselves stone screens, sometimes in a square like a small house without a roof (1954, 49).

Natives at Sheshalik, Kotzebue Sound, 1884. From Healy (1889). Courtesy of the Bancroft Library, University of California, Berkeley.

Elsewhere Ingstad (1954) describes places where caribou were driven into the water and slaughtered from kayaks. He also provides a valuable description of a *kangiraq*, an enclosure made of willow branches into which caribou were driven.

Bessie Ericklook, an elder from the Colville River, remembers the early years:

When the caribou had at last been driven up the slope towards the enclosure, people ran up from both sides, clapping their hands, hooting, and yelling. The beasts rushed in panic through the opening and into the inner enclosure. A number went straight into the snares; others broke through the willows into the other enclosures and were snared there. Some of the hunters sent a rain of arrows at the beasts trying to escape, while others were busy with their flint spears. There was sometimes a large bag, which was divided equally among the families participating (Ingstad 1954, 62).

We did find artifacts from these old house sites. . . . [They] had water dripping into a water bucket made out of bark sewn together. And they had one dipper for all, made out of sheep's horn. . . . They used these for drinking because they didn't have cups. . . . Their tents would be made of caribou skins sewed together when still wet. . . . The people who lived in these old house sites used braided caribou sinew for fish nets . . . They used moose and caribou skin ropes. They would slice them after they rotted the hair off and it would dry in a day. My father used that for ropes too. We all had snow shoes that he made us using skin ropes. . . . My father told us long ago when people used to fight among themselves they used to build their houses in out of the way places where they wouldn't be found so easily (in North Slope Borough 1980, 127–28).

Fall scene on Kotzebue Sound, Natives preparing for ascent of Noatak River. W. R. Smith photo 300 of 1925. USGS Historical Photo Library, Denver.

The Upper Noatak people followed an annual cycle similar to that of the Tulugagmiut and other Endicott Mountain Eskimos—spring and fall caribou hunts, dispersal in the winter. But their summer float to the coast on the Noatak River took them to Kotzebue Sound, where they and other Eskimos hunted beluga whales using skin-covered umiat and kayaks. Later, in separate encampments lining the beach, the various groups joined in the trade fair at Sisualik (Sheshalik), a sand spit north of present-day Kotzebue. Eskimos from as far away as Siberia came to this "major occasion devoted to inter-societal trade, athletic competition, feasting, and alliance making" (Burch 1975a, 17). In contrast to the quick downriver journey, the return up the Noatak with tons of dried meat and muktuk (whale skin with attached blubber) took time and hard work.

Eskimos ascending Noatak River in skin boat. P. S. Smith photo 783 of 1911. USGS Historical Photo Library, Denver.

Sod igloo on Noatak River.
P. S. Smith photo 653 of 1911.
USGS Historical Photo Library,
Denver.

Anthropologist Edwin S. Hall, Jr., got help from a Noatak elder Carl Luther in assembling a tool kit typical of those used by his nineteenth-century ancestors (Hall 1976). Carl's wife, Ellen, made a traditional tool bag of wolf, wolverine, seal, and caribou skins, sewn with caribou sinew. The bag held a mix of tools reflecting the historic combination of indigenous forms and materials with scraps of metal acquired through trade with Siberia. Cutting, drilling, and engraving tools, lashed or set in antler, bone, or wood handles allowed working of softer materials. Hammers and flakers were used for stone and jadeite. Webbing and cordage from bark, baleen, hide, and sinew was used to construct snowshoes and lashings. The bag contained examples of objects in progress (lures, arrowheads, and spear prong) as well as bits of ivory and other raw materials for future use. Substitution of metal cutting edges and points in place of slate, jadeite, or flint illustrated the early stages of the nineteenth-century transition to European goods, but sparely and selectively, given the high value of metal in those days. Such tool kits, with cultural variations, combined with ingenuity and local raw materials, enabled Eskimos and Indians of northern Alaska to fashion all the implements they needed for daily life.

These were the ways of shamans those days. My father once tried a song he was taught on a wolf. The wolf was in a wide open area and he decided to try it out. The wolf had sat down on a small knoll and there was no way it could get out of his sight. He was watching it through his binoculars. He sang a song that was supposed to put the animal to sleep. After he sang it he started walking toward it to see if the song would really work. When he reached it, the wolf almost woke up, but my father shot it (Pete Suvliq, in North Slope Borough 1980, 97).

Native grave, Noatak Valley.
P. S. Smith Photo 780 of 1911.
USGS Historical Photo Library,
Denver.

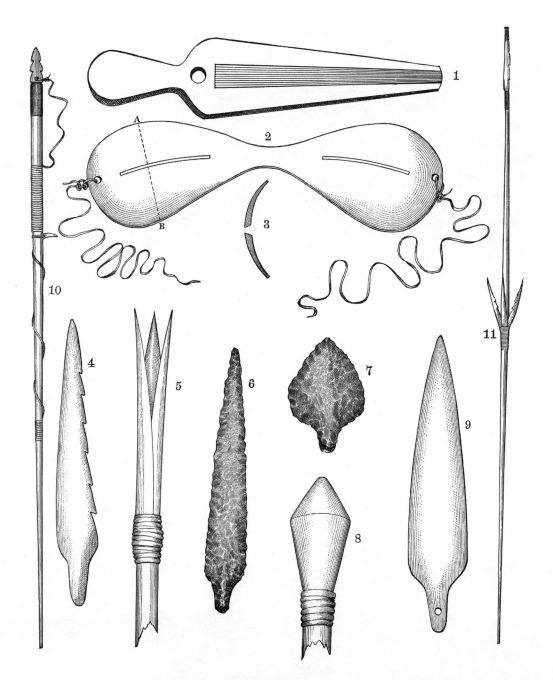

Plate I, implements of the chase:

1. *Holder for throwing spears, one-third size*
2. *Snow spectacles, natural size*
3. *Section of 2 through AB*
4. *Spear-head of ivory for deer, natural size*
5. *Arrow-head of ivory pronged for birds, natural size*
6. *Spear-head of chipped flint, natural size*
7. *Arrow-head of chipped flint*
8. *Blunt arrow-head of ivory or bone for birds, natural size*
9. *Spear-head of polished jade; very rare*
10. *Seal spear with detachable ivory head, one-sixth size*
11. *Bird spear with prongs of ivory, one-sixth size*

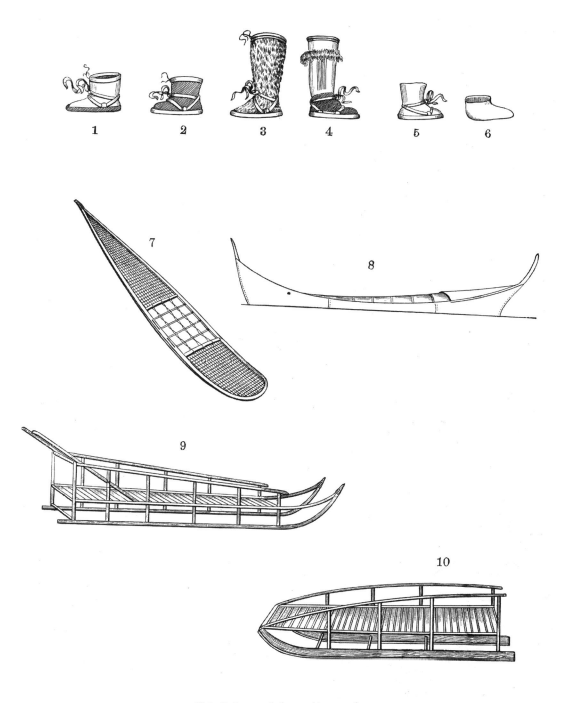

Plate III, Transportation and Locomotion

1. Shoe of deer-skin with walrus-skin sole
2. Shoe of walrus-skin with whale-skin sole
3. Boot of seal skin
4. Boot of deer skin ornamented with fur
5. Shoe of fawn skin
6. Inner shoe or sock of tanned buckskin
7. Snowshoe
8. Birch-bark canoe (Kowak River)
9. Sled (Kowak River)
10. Sled with ivory shoe (coast Natives)

Arrigetch Peaks. National Park Service photo by Robert Belous.

Kobuk Eskimos

During the fall and winter, the Kobuk River Eskimo lived in relatively large settlements at or near the mouths of Kobuk tributaries. Most houses were moss- or sod-covered. The rich resource base of the Kobuk people is illustrated by their diet, which consisted of caribou, bear, fish, and several species of small game. At breakup, Kobuk River Eskimo dispersed to spring camps where they fished and hunted muskrats. In the fall, when the men went north to hunt caribou, the women would catch and dry hundreds of pounds of whitefish and salmon. At freezeup, everyone would return to their winter settlements (Burch 1975a).

Explorers in the 1880s noted that the people living near the Kobuk headwaters around Walker Lake spoke both Eskimo and Athapaskan. Their lifeway combined elements of both cultures, and both Indian and Eskimo place names mark the area. Location of the upper Kobuk people placed them astride traditional trade routes connecting Kotzebue Sound, the Koyukuk River, and the central Brooks Range. Using such well-traveled routes as the Alatna Portage, these people acted as middlemen for the exchange of goods throughout inland arctic Alaska. Before 1840, most

European items came from Russian sources. After mid-century, extended trade links with Hudson's Bay posts to the east brought flintlock muskets and metal traps into the country (Foote 1966).

An old man of the upper Kobuk, Robert Cleveland, has told of traditional life when he was a child, about 1890, before the changes came:

> When I first became conscious of a way of living, this is the way we lived. If the fishing was not good in the summer we did not eat, because in those days there was just nothing else to eat. There were very few rifles. Only the rich people could afford them. The rifles were muzzle loaders (su pu di pak) with either a single or double barrel. They made bullets by rolling foil lead and rounding it out with their teeth. But a lot of the people still used the bow and arrow in those days (in Foote 1966, p. III).

Koyukon Indians

The Koyukon Athapaskans of the upper Koyukuk River are upland hunters of big game. In traditional times they and their Gwich'in Athapaskan neighbors on the upper Chandalar followed a lifeway dictated by a forest and mountain environment deficient in the fishery resources. Big game—caribou, bear, moose—wandered through these boreal territories, and so did the people who preyed upon them. Small kin groups were the rule; only occasionally, during communal caribou drives or at feasts and potlatches when food was accumulated beforehand, could people come together in large groups. Local leaders guided communal efforts during caribou hunts and the fishing seasons. Salmon fishing provided significant food for Koyukon bands of the Hogatza and Kanuti river areas, but for the Indians of the Koyukuk's upper forks and tributaries, fish were secondary resources, with such species as whitefish, grayling, and pike more important than the salmon of the upper reaches. When caribou were few, and before moose moved in large numbers into Koyukuk country in the last century, people might rely upon the smaller forest animals such as hare, beaver, muskrat, porcupine, and squirrel. Migratory ducks and geese and resident grouse and ptarmigan supplemented the diet (Nelson et al. 1982).

Deadfalls and snares, coupled with a thorough knowledge of the behavior patterns of the target animals, allowed men to hunt in absentia and thus extend their predatory effectiveness. It is likely that remote harvesting techniques produced as much or more food and furs than did the activities limited to men and their hand weapons (Nelson et al. 1982, 55).

The dominant food quest, the changing seasons, and the unpredictability of animal populations and distributions prevented settled village life for these upriver Indians. They combined or divided their labors as custom and circumstance demanded to accomplish the tasks of hunting and gathering, processing food, and producing clothes, shelter, and tools.

In summer, except for periodic hunting and trading trips, the people lived along major rivers, camping near stream junctions where men fished with traps at stream entrances and women netted in eddies and sloughs. As berries ripened, they were gathered and stored in birchbark baskets for transport to the next camp. Meat and fish in excess of daily needs was air dried and stored.

Mount Igikpak. National Park Service photo by Robert Belous.

The country knows. If you do wrong things to it, the whole country knows. It feels what's happening to it. I guess everything is connected together somehow, under the ground (in Nelson 1983, 241).

Approaching fall meant relocating to upland lakes where lake and stream fishing took place and, after freezeup, fishing through the ice. Winter house construction or repair anticipated the deep cold to come. These semisubterranean structures, walled and roofed with spruce logs and poles and covered with moss, sod, and dirt, were occupied throughout the winter whenever families returned from hunting trips. Group caribou hunts took place in late October, with several families joining together. Hide tents on willow frames, piled with insulating snow, provided shelter during these outings. Some hunters journeyed north to the mountains to hunt sheep while women hunted small game and ice fished.

When sunlight returned in late winter, some families traveled to the Brooks Range or to the Kobuk for messenger feasts with their Eskimo trading partners; or Eskimos might visit Indian encampments. These gatherings, the invitations carried by runners called messengers, were based on

established intertribal partnerships. They fostered the exchange of material goods as well as the sharing of ideas and techniques.

Springtime brought light, the first flights of returning birds, and a break in the weather. But in years of game scarcity and exhausted food stocks, this was the most difficult season. Some families went to muskrat camps near the rivers. Hunting parties began to look for returning caribou, now gathering for spring migration. Parties of hunters posted themselves near caribou fences and surrounds. Caribou driven into these extensive barriers and flared enclosures, which were fitted with snares, could be killed easily with spears. Old people, left at winter camps to fend for themselves, trapped and snared available small game.

As late-May breakup approached, the Indians moved to spring fish camps on creeks between the lakes and major rivers. Easy cross-country travel ended as the landscape thawed and the ground became sodden. Migratory birds arrived in large numbers and the men spent most of their time hunting them in the marshes. In June the annual cycle closed with return to summer camps along the large rivers (McFadyen Clark 1974).

Among traditional Athapaskans, the potlatch was the central ceremonial event of the year, permeating every aspect of social life. The potlatch was, and remains today, a feast for the dead. The festivities rejuvenated the spirits of the participants and provided an honorific farewell to the deceased. The potlatch also affirmed the prestige and wealth of the one who organized it. Distribution of food, blankets, and other gifts was important ceremonially and functionally as a means of sharing that wealth with other members of the band. Finally, the potlatch offered a rare opportunity for people normally dispersed to come together as a group to entertain one another and renew their social ties.

Moses Henzie, a Koyukon elder of Allakaket, showed the persistence of old ways when he talked of them in 1978:

> We depend on our animals to make our living in this country. We have to treat them with respect. Like when I find a wolverine or wolf in my trap. After I shoot 'em, I rub a little piece of

My father trapped that country before me, and I trapped there all my life. But if you go there now it's still good ground—still lots of beaver in there, plenty of mink and otter, marten; good bear country. I took care of it, see. You have to do that; don't take too much out of it right now or you'll get nothing later on (in Nelson 1983, 200).

When a brown bear has been killed, none of its meat should be brought into the village for some days or weeks; it is too fresh and potent with easily affronted spiritual energy. During earlier years, in fact, it was left in a cache at the kill site until the midwinter potlatch memorializing people who had died in the previous year (Nelson 1983, 188).

Takahula Lake. National Park Service photo by Robert Belous.

moose fat on his nose. Then I make a little fire and burn that fat. Just like feeding them. I always carry that piece of fat in my sled bag (Madison and Yarber 1979, 28).

Gwich'in Indians

Just before contact with Europeans, the northwesternmost bands of Gwich'in Athapaskans—the Dihai and Netsi—lived on the mountain forks of the Koyukuk and Chandalar rivers respectively. In their spare mountain environments, which seasonally included both slopes of the Brooks Range, these big-game hunters subsisted mainly on caribou, with a limited winter fishery in upland lakes. By 1850, under pressure from expanding mountain Eskimos, the Dihai were trending eastward, where eventually they would assimilate with the Netsi along the east fork of the Chandalar. Previously, the Dihai had roamed throughout the Endicott Mountains as far west as the Kobuk and Noatak headwaters.

In contrast to the enduring trading partnerships that encouraged peaceful Koyukon-Eskimo relations, increasing competition between the Dihai and Eskimos over caribou hunting sites in the mountains led to war. Old battlegrounds and stories tell of bloody encounters and raids throughout the central mountains as the Eskimos pushed eastward and southward. About 1850, an epic battle near Anaktuvuk Pass ended in defeat for the Dihai. The Endicott Mountains became Eskimo territory. Burch attributes the movements of Eskimos east from the Kotzebue Sound drainage and south from the Meade and Colville rivers to the decline of caribou around the mountain periphery. This shift of Eskimo populations to the rich mountain hunting grounds forced the retreat of the Dihai Gwich'in back to core Gwich'in territory, and became the primary source of the late nineteenth-century Nunamiut population (Burch 1979; Hall 1975; McKennan 1965).

The Dihai and Chandalar Gwich'in, far removed from the relative riches of their riverine brethren to the south, lived a hard life of constant movement in search of food. Elders who were children in traditional times recalled only hunting, periodic hunger, and hurrying on to the next camp. A single family might cover hundreds of miles in a season, carrying only a skin tent for shelter. People might have to spend a season or a year in another territory, hundreds of miles from home hunting grounds. Dispersal of families was the rule; aggregations were rare and settled villages did not exist. Even today, the highly individualistic or autonomous-family lifestyle of Gwich'in villages contrasts with the greater sociability and cohesion of Eskimo villages (Nelson 1973).

• • •

Considering its power over people's lives and emotions, it is not surprising that weather is the most fully personified element in the Koyukon physical world. . . . But at least its moods can be anticipated. When deep cold approaches, the sun often has a bright spot, or "false sun," on either side. Koyukon people say, "The sun is building fires beside her ears," and if it is midwinter it may soon be −30° to −50°. This sign is caused, outsiders would say, by ice crystals precipitating from chilling air aloft—it is a very reliable one (Nelson 1983, 40).

Kobuk River. National Park Service photo by John Kauffmann.

Narvak Lake. National Park Service photo by John Kauffmann.

The mountain core of northern Alaska foiled European mapmakers until the 1880s—in fact, the more remote reaches of this region remained incompletely mapped until the advent of airplanes and the strategic focus on the region forced by World War II and its Cold War aftermath (Fitzgerald 1951). But traditional people knew the mountains and their riverine environs intimately. Their travel routes by river and portage, through the passes and along the mountain spine numbered in the scores—each route mapped in detail in the travelers' minds; each classified as to appropriate travel technology, seasonality, advantages and dangers, and the necessities of shelter, fuel, water, and food.

The combinations of travel technology and strategy—adjusted for season and terrain to accommodate hunters, family trading and festive parties, and communal hunting groups and complemented by sophisticated shelter, clothing, and provisioning—are triumphs of cultural adaptation. They allowed these traditional people to move rapidly with large quantities of goods over long distances, year-round, through country that today

is inaccessible, short of helicopter transport, to all but the most resolute trekkers (Burch 1975b, 1976b).

Anaktuvuk Pass Village. National Park Service photo by John Kauffmann.

Beginning in the 1880s, these perfected skills and knowledge would be shared, enabling the first Euro-Americans to penetrate this ancient homeland.

Killik River. National Park Service photo by John Kauffmann.

Lower end of Kobuk River Gorge, described by Cantwell. W. C. Mendenhall photo 232 of 1901, USGS Historical Photo Library, Denver.

CHAPTER TWO

EARLY EXPLORATION, 1700–1900

T he coming of outsiders to northwest Alaska was no surprise to local Iñupiat, for around the turn of the nineteenth century a number of Eskimos, including the gifted seer Maniilaq, had foretold that a new race would come and prove a mixed blessing. Some Iñupiat would be made rich, others poor, and amazing changes would follow. According to Maniilaq, it would be possible to travel upriver in a boat with ease without having to use a pull rope or paddle. Men would fly through the sky on iron sleds and speak through the air over long distances. They would write on thin birch bark, and a new kind of clothing would be introduced (Anderson 1981, 182).

Nor was the presence of indigenous peoples in northern Alaska a surprise to Europeans. The Chukchis and Eskimos of eastern Siberia and their Alaskan cousins had been trading for centuries before Russian explorers actually sailed to the Great Land. As early as 1648, Russian ships had neared Bering Strait, within sight of the Alaskan mainland.

Just before his death in 1725, Peter the Great planned a series of voyages that led to Vitus Bering's fog-shrouded passage in 1728 through the strait that bears his name and to his official "discovery" of Alaska in 1741. Bering's course took him to the Gulf of Alaska and the Aleutian Islands, where sea otters and fur seals abounded. This wealth of furs along Alaska's southern rim occupied Russian hunters and traders for many decades, saving delineation of the northern coasts for later explorers (Ray 1975).

The next phase of north Alaskan discovery began with British Capt. James Cook's voyage of 1778. Passing through the Aleutian Islands and Bering Strait to Icy Cape, he was blocked beyond 70 degrees north latitude by ice as far as the eye could see (Price 1971). His venture and subsequent ones by Russians and Britons were driven by the quest for an Arctic Ocean passage between Europe and the Pacific. Imperial rivalries and competition for the lucrative trade in furs also spurred naval exploration. Governments, scientific academies, and companies such as the Russian-American Company and the British Hudson's Bay Company participated in a series of expeditions that by 1837 had charted Alaska's northern coasts and named its capes and bays after European rulers, explorers, and scientists (Webb 1977a).

Mikhail Gvozdev and Ivan Fedorov were commissioned in 1732 to sail from Siberia to explore islands and lands to the east. In their ship *Gabriel* they briefly anchored off an Eskimo village at Cape Prince of Wales. Rising winds drove them back to sea before they could land. Though theirs was the first certain sighting of mainland Alaska by Europeans, their local venture was overshadowed by Bering's official discovery nine years later (Brown 1988, 67).

Journals of official and company explorers mention random encounters with independent traders. For example, in July 1820 at Kotzebue Sound, Capt. Lt. Glieb S. Shishmarev of the Imperial Russian Navy hosted Capt. William J. Pigot of the American brig *Pedler*. Pigot had sailed from Hawaii to trade furs with the Natives (Ray 1975).

In 1833, Russian traders established a post at St. Michael near the mouth of the Yukon. They cautiously probed the lower Yukon and, between 1838 and 1839, they erected a post at Nulato, just downstream from the Koyukuk River junction, whence they traded as far up the Yukon as the Tanana River. Expansion of the Hudson's Bay Company westward via the Yukon and Mackenzie drainages resulted in the founding of the Fort Yukon post in 1847 (Webb 1977b). Thus the middle Yukon marked the transfer zone for European goods flowing northward to the central mountains.

As charts improved and accounts of eager Native traders filtered to the outside world—where they quickly circulated among sea captains at Hawaiian and Pacific ports—the reach and pace of commercial activity increased. Various Royal Navy expeditions associated with Sir John Franklin's search for the Northwest Passage and his disappearance in 1847 opened up the arctic coasts and seas. Coastal Eskimo villages hosted first the explorers and searchers and later traders. Reports from the Franklin expeditions, describing great numbers of whales and walrus in arctic summering grounds, lured whaling captains north. By the mid-1850s, the arctic whaling industry was firmly established. In time, whaling ships would overwinter on the Arctic coast in places sheltered from the pack ice. The ships eventually became winter trading posts. Together with later shore-based whaling and trading stations, these ships irrevocably altered Eskimo lifeways and social arrangements. Dependence on Euro-American trade goods and foods, acquisition of modern rifles, working as crewmen and caribou hunters for the whalers, the devastating impacts of diseases and liquor, and the decline of caribou and sea mammal populations, variously attracted, repelled, and killed Alaskan Eskimos. (For accounts of exploration, trading, and whaling and their effects, see Ray 1975, Oswalt 1979, and Burch 1975a.)

The American purchase of Alaska in 1867 ushered in a series of government-sponsored reconnaissance expeditions, designed in part to consolidate United States authority in the new territory. One of these, led by Capt. Charles Raymond of the Corps of Engineers, wrought portentous changes on the Yukon. In July 1869, he departed St. Michael aboard the paddlewheel steamer *Yukon*. Entering the mouth of the Yukon, he started the era of river steamboating that would dominate interior Alaska transportation until World War II (Webb 1977b).

Far to the north, First Lt. Patrick Henry Ray traveled by sled up the Meade River, reaching the northern limit of the arctic foothills in 1883. This was the deepest inland penetration toward the central mountains up to that time. His account and that of naturalist-observer Sgt. John Murdoch provided a wealth of information about the coastal Eskimos and their relations with inland Eskimos and Indians (Sherwood 1965).

A final significant expedition during this early period of exploration was that of First Lt. Frederick Schwatka. His reconnaissance expedition of 1883 was the first full-length traverse of what became the Gold Rush trail from Taiya Inlet and Chilkoot Pass to St. Michael along the entirety of the

Yukon River. His insistence upon the need for army posts and steamboat-transport capabilities if the army were to effectively operate in the Interior foreshadowed the army's post-and-communication system, which began to develop in 1898 (U.S. Army 1969; Greeley 1970; Bearss 1970).

By 1883, the coastal and riverine fringes encircling the central mountains were known to American explorers and military men. Scattered outposts rimmed the region, serviced by ocean ships and a rudimentary riverboat transportation system. In late April 1854, Cmdr. Rochfort Maguire of the *Plover*, a Royal Navy depot ship based at Point Barrow to aid the Franklin search, took a sled party eastward toward Beechey Point. Along the way he met a party of four Indians, called Ko-yu-kun by the Eskimo, hunting at the mouth of the Colville. Maguire had been told that the Interior Indians did not come to the coast except for summer trading, and he was surprised at their unseasonable presence. He was also a bit anxious, as each of the Indians carried a musket, while Maguire's own party had only two guns. Remembering the fate of Lieutenant J. J. Barnard, who had been killed by Koyukon Indians at Nulato in 1851, Maguire decided to return to Point Barrow after giving the Indians printed notices of the Plover's station. The Indians, in turn, were disappointed that Maguire's party had little to trade (Stein 1978; Dall 1870).

Maguire's main purpose at Point Barrow was to provide succor to Capt. Richard Collinson of *Enterprise*, a search vessel trapped by ice in the Canadian Arctic. In July 1854, Collinson broke free and made his way westward through the leads between pack ice and shore. Near Barter Island, a group of Eskimos accompanied by Interior Indians visited him with letters from the Hudson's Bay Company agent at Fort Yukon: *Plover* was still on station at Point Barrow. Maguire's notices, given to the Indians at the mouth of the Colville in April, had reached Fort Yukon in June. From there, Indian messengers veered north to intercept Collinson on the Arctic coast in July. He rewarded them with ample gifts. The Indians' use of established travel routes to convey messages and their receiving prestigious gifts paralleled traditional practice. In this case golden opportunity beckoned in the form of coveted European goods.

Such prodigies of aboriginal travel were not unusual. For too long Euro-Americans had watched Natives disappear into bordering woodlands or fade from sight over rolling tundra, only to reappear hundreds of miles from their starting points. Russians and Britons, and now Americans, increasingly felt the need to map the Alaskan Interior that the Natives traversed so confidently. By the 1880s, machinery was in place to drive geographic exploration of the region. In the far north, the three military services—army, navy, and Revenue Marine (now the Coast Guard)—competed for the honors of discovery.

Brig. Gen. Nelson A. Miles, of the Northwestern Department of the Columbia, was a competent, vain, and ambitious man with imagination. He advocated a dominant role for the army in Alaskan geographic exploration. Though the army had withdrawn from Alaska in 1877—replaced by the

The Youkon River, Ranges of Mountains, Shores of Norton Sound & many Features of the Interior from a Reconnaissance by W.H.Dall, Director of the Scientific Corps, of the W.U. Tel. Expedition 1865-1868.

This section from the end-map from Dall (1870) shows the state of knowledge of the Gates of the Arctic Region as of 1869. Except for the coastwise segments of draining rivers, the region is a blank, fit only for the map title.

navy in Southeast Alaska and the Revenue Marine along the western and northern coasts—Miles insisted that he must learn about the territory for which he was militarily responsible. Because he was a man of vision, energetic young officers rallied to his standard (Sherwood 1965).

Lieutenant Frederick Schwatka's 1883 trek over Chilkoot Pass and down the Yukon was the first of the expeditions sponsored by Miles. Another, led by Capt. William R. Abercrombie in 1884, bogged down in the Copper River delta, failing its larger purpose to ascend the Copper and cross the Alaska Range to the Yukon drainage. It fell to Lt. Henry Tureman Allen in 1885 to accomplish that purpose and exceed it as far as the upper reaches of the Koyukuk. Allen's trek inspired Morgan Sherwood to characterize it as "the most spectacular individual achievement in the history of Alaskan inland exploration" (Sherwood 1965, 118).

The Allen Expedition of 1885

In preparation for his trek, Lt. Allen first familiarized himself with Russian, British, and American accounts of the Koyukuk. In March 1885

Lieutenant Allen, with two enlisted men and two prospectors, began the ascent of the Copper River from the Gulf of Alaska. Their route would take them north up that river, then on over the Alaska Range to the Tanana River, which flows into the Yukon River about 1,000 miles from where they started.

Transported initially by Indians in their canoes, they traded for canoes or made them from moose or caribou hides as they went from one Indian territory to the next. Often subsisting on roots or maggot-infested meat, they had many adventures and near disasters. By the time they got to the Tanana–Yukon junction, they were sick, destitute, starved, and exhausted from the hardships endured.

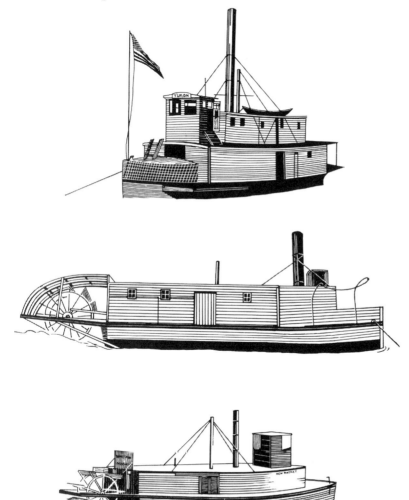

Yukon River steamboats: Yukon *(1869),* St. Michael *(1879), and* New Racket *(1883), after* Schwatka *and* Allen. *From* Osgood *(1971, 7).*

His mission to explore the Copper and Tanana river basins completed, Allen could have hitched a steamboat ride down the Yukon and gone straight home. But while resting and recuperating at the Nuklukayet trading post at the junction, and on a quick resupply trip downriver to meet the steamboats *New Racket* and *Yukon,* he heard of new gold prospects and a great range of northern mountains in the upper Koyukuk River drainage. All this new country and the bustling activities of traders,

Indians, and riverboat suppliers must be investigated, mapped, and reported (Sherwood 1965; Allen 1887).

In late July, accompanied by four Yukon River Indians, Koyukon guides, Pvt. Frederick W. Fickett, and five pack dogs, Allen barged down the Yukon for seven miles with a Russian trader, disappeared through the fringe of trees on the river's right bank, and headed north. The Indians stayed on the ridges as much as possible, where high ground was sparsely vegetated. By the third day they descended from the mountains to swampy ground "where the footing is miserable, the hummocks or tetes de femmes offer a very uncertain hold for the feet. To walk between them is to walk continually in water of uneven depth, which consequently is very tiresome" (Allen 1887, 95). Hordes of mosquitoes and gnats brought more misery but were displaced by the discomfort of cold wind and fog. At night the wind died and the mosquitoes returned in force. To allow them to sleep at night, Allen and Fickett, following Native practice, rigged a two-man "wickyup" covered with strips of cloth and sealed with moss.

Except for an occasional displaced twig or bit, the trail was indistinguishable to non-Native eyes, and Allen admired the Indians' ability to follow it. One incident of the march impressed him greatly; field glasses were lost early in the forenoon and the loss was discovered several hours later. An Indian backtracked many miles over the imperceptible trail to the surmised point of loss. He returned that night to their camp with the coveted glasses.

The next day, after a four-hour march over marshy ground following the outlet of Todatonten Lake, Allen's party reached the Kanuti River. They fired shots to inform the nearby villagers of their approach, and were shortly paddled in canoes up the river to the village. The camp of thirteen people was about 120 trail miles from Nuklukayet. Allen had pushed across the portage from Yukon to Kanuti in six and a half days (Allen 1887).

Within two hours Allen discharged his Koyukuk packers, obtained two birch canoes, and, with Fickett and the four Yukon Indians, started downstream to the Kanuti's junction with the Koyukuk. After a fourteen-mile run they reached the big river—swollen with excessive rains, 300 yards wide, and flowing at four miles per hour. Allen's hopes of reaching the Koyukuk headwaters in six days from this point seemed impossible against such a volume and current of water.

Accompanying the explorers from the Kanuti village were three young men and an old man and his family, en route to the uppermost village on the Koyukuk. The Koyukon men traveled alone in small canoes, with the women and children following in a large canoe of the type that Allen and Fickett commanded. Allen observed how they stayed close to the bank in shallow water where the current was slower, pushing themselves over the firm bottom with a light stick in each hand. The explorers immediately adopted this form of propulsion and soon had the knack of it, steering and moving forward with dispatch. Allen marveled at their swift progress. Fickett and Allen each had a canoe with two Yukon Indians, "hence each canoe had three pairs of sticks for propellers" (Allen 1887, 98).

By August 6, the tandem travelers had reached the mouth of the Nohoolchintna River, the South Fork of the Koyukuk on today's maps. On its bank, a few miles from the main Koyukuk, lay the last settlement on the upper Koyukuk drainage, which Allen estimated extended another 200 miles into the mountains. Before the Indians split off toward the South Fork village, Allen probed their knowledge of the country one more time. The old man told him that two long days or three short days would bring him to the Ascheeshna (John) River. Allen doubted the old man's claim that fifteen days would be required to reach a second tributary, the Totzunbitna, or Wild River, but the old man insisted. So Allen used the old man's descriptions and names to sketch the upper course and tributaries of the Koyukuk beyond his own limit of travel.

The departure of the Koyukuk Indians and continued progress up the river disheartened the Yukon Indians. They became "very timid, worked indifferently, and begged to be allowed to go back" (Allen 1887, 100). They refused to eat until a visit by three South Fork villagers with salmon to barter relieved their dread of intruding upon strange country without local partners. Cold rain the next morning made them again "faint-hearted" and reluctant to break camp. The Indians' sense of territorial limits and Allen's time-and-food supply limits combined to brake the northward journey. But the party pushed on toward the next big tributary,

On August 2, near Tatatontly (Todatonten) Lake, after a long march that would extend into the evening, the Indian packers issued their own challenge to the white men—a running race for a whole half hour, with packs on. Allen and Fickett hung on and finished the race, proving to the Indians that they could "keep apace with them. Though I must confess that it was the most stubborn contest I ever engaged in" (Allen 1887, 96).

the Ascheeshna, which they reached on August 9. Allen named it Fickett River; it was later named John River by prospectors in memory of Allen's former trailmate, John Bremner.

As the party started downstream, "bound for home" (102), they met an Eskimo—resident on the upper Kobuk—who had come down the Alatna. He asked for cartridges for his old-model Winchester rifle, "which had been furnished by the Arctic whalers" (102). He had a bag of iron pyrites, "doubtless imagining he had a treasure" (102). Allen traded some tobacco for the Eskimo's pipe and three dried salmon. This was the epitome of the traditional and early-contact cultural mix.

Broods of young ducks and geese improved their fare; they were taken "with scarcely any delay...while seated in canoes armed with one miserable shotgun and a carbine" (103). At a Koyukon camp on the Batza River they obtained fish "dried during the present season and stored away for winter use" (103). The entire encampment escorted Allen to the fish cache to supervise the bartering.

Twelve miles below the Hogatza River they discovered a poverty-stricken family of Mahlemutes, partially clothed in ragged caribou skins, living precariously on young waterfowl "secured by means of a tri-tined spear" (104). Their pyramidal dwelling, covered by spruce bark, was the only one of its kind seen by Allen in the territory. "They pointed to the high mountains to the north, indicating that they would cross them when the litter of pups they were training had grown larger" (104).

Of the various fish camps Allen passed—usually of only two or three families—the people of only one had such sufficiency of fish, or the inclination, to donate fish to the explorers. At this camp of seventeen souls some miles upstream from the Huslia River, the inhabitants "vied with each other in giving the greatest amount" (105). Reflecting upon the hard condition of the Koyukuk Indians, Allen cautioned against a suggestion he had heard that shipwrecked sailors should be steered over the portages into that region "when unable to reach Saint Michael's by the coast on account of ice" (104). Trusting to food from the Koyukuk Natives "would be fraught with more serious danger than a division of the party and the passing of the winter among the Eskimos" (104).

Three miles below the Dulbekakat (Dulbi River) Allen found "the metropolis of the Koyukuk River" (105). In this village of forty-five lived a famous shaman, Red Shirt, who had been implicated in the attack on Nulato in 1851, when Lieutenant John J. Barnard of the Royal Navy lost his life after expressing his intention to "send" for the principal Koyukon tyone to appear before him at Nulato (Dall 1870, 48).

The next night Allen arrived at the mouth of the Kateel River, thus linking his original exploration on the Koyukuk to that of the Russian Zagoskin more than forty years before. Allen noted the remains of the American trading station established soon after the Alaska purchase. The Koyukons had forced its abandonment, brooking no competition with their role as middlemen in the Kobuk-Koyukuk-Yukon trade.

Finally, on August 21, after "wondering whether there was an end to the Koyukuk River" (Allen 1887, 106), Allen's weary party reached the Yukon, and a few hours later, Nulato. They missed by hours passage to St. Michael on the steamboat, which by previous arrangement was to have waited for them at Nulato until August 23. Allen and Fickett continued their canoe travels down the Yukon, hiked across the Kaltag portage, canoed down the Unalakleet River, and paddled and sailed an Eskimo skin boat along fifty-five miles of Norton Sound's windy and surf-battered coast to St. Michael. On September 5, they departed for San Francisco aboard the Revenue Cutter *Corwin*, Capt. Michael A. Healy commanding (Allen 1887).

Within months, during the depths of the 1885–1886 winter, Engr. A.V. Zane of Lt. George M. Stoney's expedition portaged from the Kobuk to the Koyukuk then proceeded downstream to the Yukon and St. Michael. He returned by essentially the same route, following established Native routes both ways (Stoney 1974).

General Miles compared Allen's journey of 1,500 miles to the achievement of Lewis and Clark. Allen mapped three major river systems, the Copper, the Tanana, and the Koyukuk; his maps served later explorers and scientists for decades under the most trying circumstances and were found to be "marvelously correct" by a later explorer who retraced parts of his route (Sherwood 1965, 116). Allen's account of Yukon River trading, transportation, and Indian relations gives a microcosmic view of pre-Gold Rush conditions as Euro-Americans and Natives adjusted to new realities. Many Natives still engaged in traditional fishing at river camps as the salmon arrived on scheduled runs. Others from the better trapping locales flocked to the trading stations where traders competed for their furs.

The designs of the Alaska Commercial Company to monopolize trade and close inefficient trading substations are resented by hold-over Russian Creoles, who, unemployed by these actions, tell the Natives of the exorbitant prices charged by AC Co. agents. Indian tyones or chiefs threaten to resist the closing of trading posts that would inconvenience them and consolidate the A.C. Co.'s prices and control (Brown 1988, 78).

Prospectors ranged the Yukon tributaries, laying the groundwork for later rushes that soon swept the country. Indians from the Tanana, Fort Yukon, and the Koyukuk gathered at the Tanana's mouth, the historic boundary between British and Russian spheres of influence in the Yukon fur trade. Trading, games, dances, feasting, and fishing combined function and pleasure for Natives and Euro-Americans alike, including patriotic salutes on July 4. Here, nascent but building, were all the patterns, complaints, and ventures that would rule the river for the next fifty years.

Allen astutely documented the changes he observed in Koyukon society, both in his narrative of encounters with Native people and in his summary reflections. He found that even the remote villagers on the Kanuti and the South Fork had suffered death or impairment from epidemics radiating from trading stations on the Yukon and the coast. He noted that there were few men to hunt for disproportionately large numbers of women and children and understood that in hunting and gathering societies this is a most distressing condition, particularly at a time of extreme game scarcity. He viewed the Indians' poverty-stricken and miserable lives with compassion, urging charity: "If the Government desires that this people should continue to exist, some provision for them should soon be made" (Allen 1887, 141–42).

Navy and Revenue Cutter Service Explorations

Exploration of the Kobuk River by the Revenue Marine Service and the navy began in 1883 as the offshoot of a special mission of appreciation to Siberian Natives. After delivering gifts to the Siberians for rendering aid to shipwrecked sailors, Naval Lt. George M. Stoney proceeded to Kotzebue Sound aboard Captain Healy's Revenue Cutter *Corwin*. While Healy continued his cruise up the coast, Stoney, with a boat, rations, and a crewmember from the cutter, spent two weeks examining Hotham Inlet and the delta and lower course of the Kobuk. From a local Native he learned of an interior river, the Colville, that flowed to an ocean filled with ice, and of another major river, the Noatak, emptying into Hotham Inlet. His informant also told of portages and passes between the rivers. Thus was the basic geography of the western Brooks Range revealed. This initial and somewhat accidental collaboration of the two services led to rival claims of discovery of the Kobuk River by Stoney. The upshot of competitive expeditions was the rapid mapping of major rivers and travel routes in northern Alaska, thus integrating cartographic knowledge of coasts, rivers, and mountains (Sherwood 1965).[1]

Upon Stoney's return from the lower Kobuk reconnaissance in 1883, he requested authority from the navy to further explore the river the next year, for he believed it to be "an excellent highway into the heart of Arctic Alaska." His request was granted and in April 1884 he sailed north from San Francisco commanding the schooner *Ounalaska* (Stoney 1974, 535–36).

Meanwhile, Captain Healy organized his 1884 summer cruise aboard the *Corwin* for full-scale exploration of the Kobuk by the Revenue Marine Service. Captain Healy's long career in Alaskan waters, though marred by bouts of intemperance, brought him praise from Congress, the whaling industry, and missionary groups that he performed his difficult and dangerous duties efficiently and zealously. As the *Corwin's* commander, Healy directed the 1884–1885 explorations of his officers Lt. John C. Cantwell and Engr. S. B. McLenegan on the Kobuk and Noatak rivers.

Upon *Corwin's* arrival at Kotzebue Sound, Third Lt. J. C. Cantwell took command of a steam launch and boat's crew and on July 8, 1884, began ascent of the Kobuk. His orders from Healy required survey of the river and description of its inhabitants and "in general, everything of interest to science and commerce" (Healy 1889, 49).

Stoney entered the Kobuk's mouth in a steam cutter eight days later. Both parties proceeded upriver more than 300 miles, mapping the river and gathering valuable experience for the next year's effort. Cantwell turned back first, being short of rations and plagued by the troublesome steam launch. The expeditions passed each other in the neighborhood of Jade Mountain, Stoney still on the ascent. Neither party reached the headwaters in 1884, but Stoney proceeded a few miles beyond Cantwell's farthest point. Informed by an Eskimo that the river headed in a series of large lakes, Stoney took off across country to discover and name one of them, Selby Lake. Upon his return downriver to the schooner, Stoney assigned Ens. J. L. Purcell to a week-long survey of Selawik Lake near the Kobuk delta.

Cantwell had also left the main river on a reconnaissance to Jade Mountain, where he gathered mineral specimens. Cantwell's relations with the Natives, whom he viewed as energetic if not attentive to personal hygiene, were mainly good. His ethnological notes of the 1884 expedition provide a valuable record of late-traditional, early-contact times on the upper Kobuk (Stoney 1974).

For both explorers, the 1884 expeditions had been valuable shakedown cruises. The difficulties encountered led to improved outfits for the coming year. In Stoney's case, planning and logistics revolved around an overwinter expedition that could take full advantage of both riverine and overland travel. Both Cantwell and Healy wanted to reach the Kobuk headwaters and prove by their own travels the geography and travel routes described by Native informants, particularly connections between the Kobuk, Koyukuk, Noatak, and Colville rivers. Both recognized the importance of a land link across the mountains to the Arctic Ocean to allow succor or rescue of ice-bound whalers. They wanted to fill in the blank spaces and contact new Native groups in the mountains and north of them. Cantwell would seek more data on valuable minerals, whose signs he had noted along the upper Kobuk (Healy 1889).

The next year, the Revenue Marine expedition of 1885 aimed for the Kobuk River headwaters. Cantwell quickly reached the head of navigation for the improved steam launch, getting a few miles past Stoney's highest point of the year before. As they worked up the river, Cantwell noted the abundance of game, particularly young geese not fully fledged, which they easily caught. The low banks of the river supported dense willow thickets, which made finding campsites difficult. Heavy timber clung to ridges and mountainsides. Many streams heading in small lakes flowed into the river. The topography indicated that they were approaching the watershed between the Kobuk and the Koyukuk rivers (Healy 1889).

It is really marvelous what judgment and skill are shown by them in handling the skin boat . . . in this peculiar style of navigation (J. C. Cantwell in Healy 1889, 33).

On July 16, Cantwell and his Native crew passed the Ung-ee-let-ar-geeak (Reed) River and began the final push toward Big Fish Lake, now shown on maps as Walker Lake. Big Fish Lake was the largest of the Kobuk's feeder lakes and symbolized for Cantwell the primary source of the great river. The struggle up the last forty river-miles is best told by Cantwell himself:

Rapids at the outlet of Walker
Lake. W.C. Mendenhall photo
227 of 1901, USGS Historical
Photo Library, Denver.

The weather continued fair and intensely hot. The mosquitoes were simply terrific, and our lives were a burden to us altogether until we emerged from the low country and reached
a portion of the river enclosed by high bluff banks. At 6:30
the Indians stopped as if at a signal, and Tah-tah-rok called
my attention to a low rumbling noise ahead. I thought at first
it was thunder, but its steady sound, and the fact that thunder
is seldom heard in these latitudes, convinced me that it was
falling water. We pushed ahead, and my feelings can scarcely
be imagined when, at eight o'clock, we rounded a high, rocky
bluff and came suddenly in sight of a seething mass of white
water bursting its way through a gorge composed of perpendicular masses of slaty rock two hundred to three hundred
feet high, surmounted by a forest of spruce and birch. The
channel was completely choked with sharp-pointed rocks,
past which the water flew with frightful velocity, breaking
itself into mimic cascades of foam and spray. The Indians, as
if sharing in my pleasure, set up a wild chant, which echoed
along the steep banks, and caused hundreds of gulls nesting
in the crevices of the rocks to leave their perches and with
loud discordant cries to circle round our heads (in Healy
1889, 34–40).

Shortly, they left the Kobuk's true headwater channel and tracked up
Walker Lake's outlet stream. The shallows finally forced them to beach
the boat and make camp. From this point they hiked to a hill from which
they could see the lake:

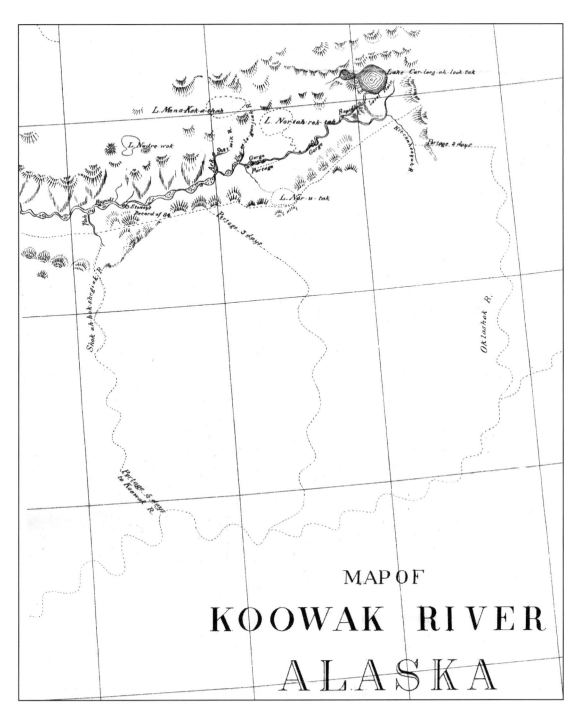

MAP OF

KOOWAK RIVER

ALASKA

Four or five miles away, and almost completely surrounded by mountains from twenty-five hundred to three thousand feet high, the blue sparkling waters of the long-sought lake burst upon my view. The sensations of pleasure and triumph which took possession of me as I gazed upon its waters, now for the first time seen by a white man, amply repaid me for the long, tedious journey. As the last rays of the setting sun gilded the rugged peaks and the shadows of approaching night crept silently upward, we turned back toward our boat, and the Indians set up a wild chanting "Hung-hi-hung-ay" of joy.

Detail of map of the upper Kobuk River in Lt. J. C. Cantwell's narrative report, from Healy (1889).

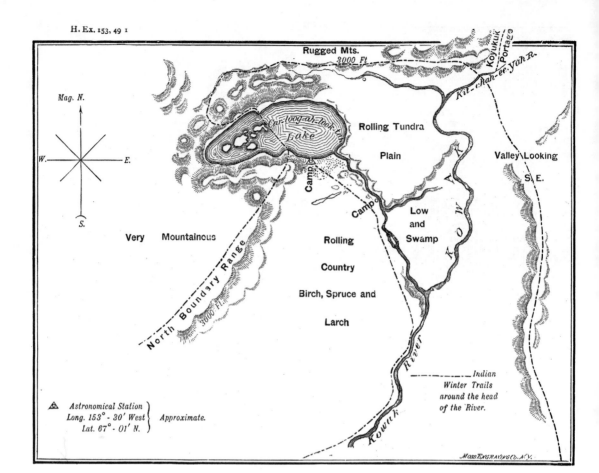

Detail of the Walker Lake area in Lt. J. C. Cantwell's narrative report, from Healy (1889).

With Tah-tah-rok and one other Indian I ascended the mountains which bordered the southern side, and from this point obtained a magnificent view of the entire lake and country in every direction. All the northern conifers spread the deep green of their branches on the mountain slopes, and the larch, the birch, and willow were massed in clusters of deep foliage, through which the waters of the lake sparkled like a jewel (J. C. Cantwell in Healy 1887, 37).

. . .

Having completed the reconnaissance of the lake, we returned to our boat, and next morning set out for the smaller branch of the river by means of a shallow stream which leads from the lake outlet almost across the low swampy land which lies between this river and the Kowak [Kobuk]. We made a short portage and reached the Kowak, up which we began to shove the boat. The river here was not over fifty yards wide and scarcely more than one foot deep anywhere. All day we pushed the boat up the shoal stream past the mouth of a small stream called the Kit-chah-ee-yak, and did not rest until the lightened boat, drawing five inches, would no longer float.

The Kit-chah-ee-yak River, which flows into the Kowak near the foot of Lake Car-loog-ah-look-tah, drains a valley in the southeast which lies at right angles to the Kowak Valley, and it is the most noticeable, in fact the only, break in the mountain-bounded horizon. The natives informed me that by crossing the ridge which forms the northern boundary of the Kit-chah-ee-yak one day's journey in winter brings them to the Ah-lash-ok [Alatna] River, which is a tributary of the Koyukuk. This is the route taken by the Kowak Indians

when they wish to meet those of the Koyukuk in order to trade (Healy 1889, 34–40).

Cantwell's downstream journey through the Kobuk canyons was nearly foiled by the patched and battered skin boat. Protecting it with a false keel made of a spruce tree and basketwork bumpers made of woven willows, the crew lined and portaged through the narrow passages, finally reaching deep water and the launch.

While Cantwell steamed and boated up the Kobuk, another of *Corwin's* officers, Asst. Engr. S. B. McLenegan, and Seaman Nelson struggled up the Noatak River in a twenty-seven-foot bidarka. Theirs was an arduous journey through barren, rainy wilds with hardly any respite from hardship and suffering. During the month's ascent to a point more than 300 miles above the river mouth, they spent endless hours waist deep in the freezing current harnessed to the tracking line. Short rations, constant cold and wet, and grueling labor mark this heroic exploration (Sherwood 1965; Healy 1889).

McLenegan characterized the river as "known only from native accounts, for there is no record of it ever having been visited by white men" (Healy 1889, 58). Even the Yukon traders knew nothing of this river, noting "how utterly blank was that vast region even to those best informed" (ibid.). McLenegan traced the river through alternating mountains and lowlands, ending in its upper midcourse "lying on the tablelands of the interior . . . an elevated plateau, rolling occasionally into hills and then stretching away into vast tracts of moorland" (ibid.).

In 1885, as in 1884, the Revenue Marine's Cantwell, on his return down the Kobuk, passed Stoney on the way up. But the more deliberate Stoney had compensated by organizing and equipping for a new kind of interior

Our point of observation was about half way down the lake on the south side. Here the cliffs were almost perpendicular masses of granite, broken into many peculiar forms by frost. Upon one of these cliffs I carved my name and the date of the arrival of the party at this point (J. C. Cantwell in Healy 1887, 38).

arctic exploration. Not satisfied with the limitations of summer recon-naissance, he had provisioned for a twenty-month overwintering expe-dition manned by a large contingent of officers and men. His well-laid plans included two river steamers, one a flat-bottomed boat for low-water travel, and a portable steam-driven sawmill. This he used to build a winter camp, Fort Cosmos, some 250 miles up the Kobuk. From this base, near the location of the modern village of Shungnak, he could send out expe-ditions in all directions—using dogs for extensive winter travel through the mountains and toward the Yukon. He assigned his officers specific scientific and expeditionary responsibilities, maintaining discipline and a strict military schedule (Sherwood 1965; Stoney 1974). An impressive list of accomplishments resulted from this regime, summarized here by Morgan Sherwood:

> Once settled in at Fort Cosmos, Stoney organized a number
> of winter trips. Surgeon F. S. Nash was sent inland to collect
> ethnographic information. On December 26, Engineer A. V.
> Zane crossed over to the Koyukuk and descended it to the
> Yukon and St. Michael, returning in February of 1886. Stoney
> himself explored Selawik Lake and River, began observations

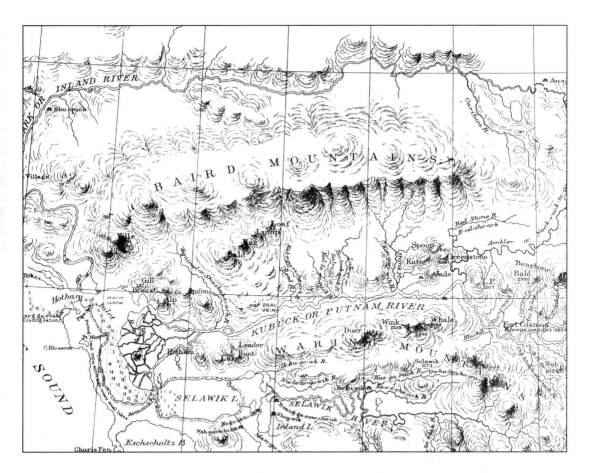

for a base line to triangulate the Kobuk Valley, and examined the headwaters of the Noatak and the Alatna. He reached Chandler Lake and a tributary of the Colville, where he was told by natives about a route to Point Barrow. By the end of the summer of 1886, Stoney had completed an instrumental survey of the Kobuk Valley, prospected the famous jade mountain, and sent a party to complete a survey of the Noatak.

The most original exploration of the Stoney Expedition was undertaken in April by Ensign W. L. Howard. With two white men and two natives, Howard struck due north across the Noatak and portaged to a native village visited by Stoney earlier in the year. Howard then descended to the Colville and followed it a few miles before crossing to the Ikpikpuk, which took him to the Arctic Ocean near Point Barrow (Sherwood 1965, 130).

Stoney's full report with finished maps was never published, nor were the individual scientific reports of his officers. Stoney asserted that both the Secretary of the Navy and the Congress had approved report publication, but "in some way the papers have mysteriously disappeared" (Stoney 1974, 533). Historians attribute the loss to various causes: interservice rivalry, personal rivalry between Stoney and Healy, or the fears of Navy brass that Congress would charge them with wasteful duplication

Section of Lt. George M. Stoney's map of exploration on the Kobuk River, published originally in the U.S. Naval Institute Proceedings in 1899. Note Fort Cosmos, winter quarters in 1885–86, near the lower right of the map.

The stream again pursued a very tortuous course, winding in and around the mountains, through deep canyons and gorges, where, in spite of the wretched weather, we could not fail to admire the grandeur of the scenery. In the mean time the fresh breeze of morning had increased into a gale which fairly whistled through the chasms, and hoisting our sail, we were driven rapidly forward, notwithstanding the opposing current in the river. The work now became exciting in the extreme... Imbued with a spirit of boldness bordering on recklessness, the canoe was driven before the gale (J. C. Cantwell in Healy 1887, 66).

Late in the afternoon we found on the left bank what appeared to be a grave, and, prompted by curiosity, I determined to halt and examine it. Upon gaining the spot we discovered that it was a well-disguised cache, containing a large quantity of skins, native clothing, boots, and a general assortment of native possessions, together with a sledging outfit. The significance of these caches now became evident; the extreme difficulty attending the navigation above this point made it clear that the natives, on returning from the coast, abandoned the river here and completed their journey on sledges (J. C. Cantwell in Healy 1887, 69).

of effort on the Kobuk River (Sherwood 1965; Caswell 1956). Alfred Hulse Brooks of the U.S. Geological Survey greatly admired Stoney's accomplishments and lamented that only Stoney's later abbreviated account, the expedition log, and the manuscript maps survived the suspected purge of records (Brooks 1953).[2] That abbreviated account, first published in the Proceedings of the U.S. Naval Institute in 1899, remains the principal source for Lieutenant Stoney's 1885–1886 Northern Alaska Naval Exploring Expedition.

From both Stoney's account and the log book of the U.S.S. *Explorer* (the shallow-draft sternwheeler that served as expedition workhorse on the Kobuk) emerges a picture of detailed planning, logistics, and camp operations. Stoney knew the value of Native clothing; he traded tobacco and other goods for Native boots, pants, parkies, mitts, and skins as the charter schooner *Viking* conveyed the party up the coast to Kotzebue Sound. He used Native labor extensively in relaying his elaborate inventory of supplies up the Kobuk, using cache camps at intervals up the river, for his boats could not haul all the goods at once.

Once established at Fort Cosmos, the race against winter commenced in earnest. The prime necessities—shelter, wood, meat, and fish—provided heat and food for both man and dog. Natives and whites alike were employed in many tasks according to Stoney's division of labor into specialized work gangs—fishermen, woodcutters, carpenters, and sawmillers. Native women dried salmon for winter use. Refined modes of water supply, heating, sanitation, and exercise, along with careful diet and food preparation, assured a healthy camp. Established routines, amusements, and technical instruction eased the psychological burdens of camp life. By late September the boats were laid out for the winter, beyond the reach of crushing winter ice. Supplies were cached, the men had moved into the large winter house, and serious exploration could begin.

From the central location of Fort Cosmos, well up the Kobuk River, "we were able to strike across the several divides into the adjoining river-valleys by comparatively short routes" (Stoney 1974, 561). As soon as ice and snow conditions allowed, beginning December 1, individual exploring parties fanned out to the Noatak headwaters and across the Arctic Divide, to the Koyukuk and St. Michael, to the Reed River hot springs, and to Selawik Lake. Later Stoney set up a base line for triangulation of the Kobuk Valley; still later he proceeded from its head to the Alatna headwaters and over the Arctic Divide to Chandler Lake, named by Stoney for the secretary of the Navy. On his trips across the divide where the streams flowed north into the Colville River, Stoney contacted mountain Eskimos. They refused to guide him to the Arctic Coast in winter because they would starve for lack of game, but they agreed to do so in the spring. This set up Howard's trip to Barrow.

On June 15, 1886, Fort Cosmos was abandoned and the boats started downriver. In the general movement toward the coast, and later from Camp Purcell on Hotham Inlet, side expeditions to the lower Noatak,

Jade Mountain, and Selawik Lake completed Stoney's survey goals. On the night of August 25 the entire party came together on the Revenue Cutter *Bear*, which had earlier retrieved Howard at Barrow, and sailed next morning for San Francisco, courtesy of Captain Healy (Stoney 1974).

The following excerpts from Stoney's "Explorations" (including Howard's formal report of the Barrow trip) convey the discoverers' views of a new country. They also give a last view of interior Eskimo life at the break point between traditional ways and the new ways brought by traders, whalers, and other white men whom the Eskimos met each summer at the coast. By 1886, most of the Eskimo groups had been severely affected by the combination of caribou decline and the diseases and trade goods of the white man—particularly introduction of the rifle, which largely eliminated communal hunting patterns. Starvation, death from disease, and a desperate kind of mobility as people fought for survival and access to addictive trade goods had already disrupted normal seasonal rounds and wreaked social havoc. "Howard (and Stoney) traveled through an impoverished Eskimo world, shorn of many of its participants and contaminated by introduced traits, a world that would soon cease to exist" (Hall 1977, 81–87).

Lieutenant Stoney's account comprises summary reflections on conditions and techniques of travel, shelter, and the like, punctuated with interludes of direct experience and observation. He was a bluff, no-nonsense man, seemingly impervious to doubt or introspection. This sampler, including trips to the Noatak headwaters and up the Alatna River past the Arrigetch Peaks, which Stoney recorded for the first time, shows a leader of exploration at work:

> On December 1st, 1885, I left Fort Cosmos, with Ensign Howard and four natives, to explore the headwaters of the Notoark (Noatak) or Inland River, and to decide on the practicability of sledging to the northward to Point Barrow. My outfit consisted of three sleds, twenty dogs, rations for twenty-five days, and complete traveling equipment.
>
> . . .
>
> To cross the thin ice over running water, the natives make a bridge by laying saplings, two and three feet apart, over the crust and covering them with brush, which makes a slippery surface for the sleds. A long line is made fast to the end of the drag-rope and the other end is manned by natives on the other side of the bridge, who haul the dogs on to the bridge; once on, they quickly get over to the strong ice. By these bridges I crossed, with a sled weighing several hundred pounds, over ice so thin that it could not bear the weight of a single dog.
>
> On December 9th, I reached Nimyuk (Cotton-wood), the highest settlement on the Notoark River. The village consisted of four huts and thirty inhabitants, subsisting almost exclu-

After two o'clock we entered the "home stretch" of the river and eagerly strained our eyes to catch the first glimpse of the sea. In the distance, on the opposite shore of the inlet, the clear-cut headlands stood out in bold relief against the evening sky. The feelings of joy and relief which rose within us found no room for expression, and the prospect of a speedy termination of our journey, after the many hardships of the summer, was indeed cheering (Healy 1887, 74).

During the whole period there was not an accident or a case of illness of any kind, though the life was one of unusual hardship and unceasing exposure, often in a temperature seventy degrees below zero. Each officer and man entered into the spirit and purpose of the work with cheerfulness and determination, and each and every one did his duty well, and in a manner worthy of the highest commendation, and I take this opportunity of again thanking them. Nor should the natives be forgotten. They were honest, willing and obedient, and of incalculable service to the expedition (Stoney 1974, 846–47).

sively on deer-meat of which they had at least two thousand pounds on hand. The day of my arrival they killed thirteen deer: and in some of the caches were as many as thirty.

. . .

From Nimyuk I stood to the northward and eastward, following one of the branches of the Notoark to its source in the mountains, then over the dividing ridge where I struck the headwaters of the Colville River, down which I traveled several miles, coming to Issheyuk, a village of fifteen huts, situated near the northern limit of the mountain range. Approaching the settlement, I was stopped by some natives who demanded tribute; my natives becoming terrified, advised compliance. Suspecting foul play, I told them I would consider their request when the village was reached, and so proceeded on, and soon learned that my supposed ignorance of their ways had induced some scamps to attempt to impose on me. Their failure was laughed at by the body of natives at the village, where several hundred of them were gathered from all parts of the Notoark and surrounding country to have a big dance. This large body of natives surrounded us, the men beating tom-toms and the women singing, and for a time we felt anxious; but, their ceremonies over, they gave the hand of friendship and extended the freedom of their village. I remained one day at Issheyuk and learned that some of the natives went to Point Barrow every summer. . . . I offered every inducement to be taken to Point Barrow, but without success, for they declared that to go at such a time would result in starvation. However, they offered to take me next spring. Not having enough provisions to last until then, I decided to return to Fort Cosmos and to try more to the eastward. Before leaving I made arrangements with the most influential man, Owpuk, to send a party with him to Point Barrow in the spring in case I could find no better route to the eastward. So on December 12th, I left for home, following the same route, and arrived at Fort Cosmos, December 19th (Stoney 1974, 563–77).

Stoney's trip to the Alatna River, providing the first recorded description of the Arrigetch Peaks, occurred in March 1886:

Ten miles up the Al-lash-ook (Alatna) to the northward and westward, the A-koo-loo-ik River enters the left bank. Still higher up at the bend in the river, the Ping-ing-a-look River comes in on the left bank. At this point the valley narrows to less than two miles and is well wooded: the mountains are nearly bare and steep, with numerous waterfalls running down to the swift and tortuous river here only thirty yards wide. About five miles beyond, the Koo-to-ark [Kutuk] River comes in from the northward and eastward. The configuration of the surrounding heights [Arrigetch Peaks] at this junction is worthy of note. They appear in every conceivable way and shape; there are rugged, weather-scarred peaks, lofty minarets, cathedral spires, high towers and rounded domes, with circular knobs, flat tops, sharp edges, serrated ridges and smooth backbones. These fantastic shapes form the summits of bare, perpendicular mountains.

The Al-lash-ook followed to a fork near its head and then the Koo-to-ark, a small branch on the left bank, was taken, and followed to its headwaters. The Koo-to-ark River at its junction with the Al-lash-ook is thirty yards wide. It flows from the northward in a tolerably straight course. Coming close down to the water are dome-shaped mountains 3000 feet high, for the most part bare, with here and there little patches of soil with a scant growth. Twenty miles up the Koo-to-ark even this growth practically ceases, excepting at long intervals, when a few poor cottonwoods and willows are found. At one of these spots near the headwaters is the small village of Nimyuk [cottonwood], well up in the mountains. It is a stopping place for deer-hunters and traveling parties.

After thirty-five miles on the Koo-to-ark, I crossed the mountains to northward and eastward over a pass 1070 feet higher than the Koo-to-ark, and came to the village of My-og-arg-a-look. Twelve miles beyond to the northeast, we came to O-co-mon-e-look after crossing a pass 1000 feet higher than the previous one. The road then lay in the gorges over small streams filled with boulders and snow. When ten miles northeast from O-co-mon-e-look, I crossed another pass, unmistakably the work of a glacier, and reached a chain of lakes and the limit of the mountains.

The largest lake, which I named Lake Chandler, after the Hon. Secretary of the Navy, lies between two regular mountain chains, which rise 1050 feet above its level. The shape is regular, running ten miles in length, N.N.E. 1/4 E., and from one mile to 1000 yards in width, and it is so deep that no bottom can be seen. The lake was frozen with ice five feet three inches thick. There is no growth about the shores nor on the mountains. The lakes undoubtedly are supplied with water from springs; the numerous air-holes and cracks indicated this, as well as the bubbling appearance of the water. I was told that this lake rarely froze over completely, ordinarily a strip of water six feet wide remained open all winter. This part of the journey was still harder because of the scarcity of fuel and consequent sameness of food, frozen deer-meat.

. . .

When at the head of the last lake I felt the actual need of some warm food and drink. No fuel could be procured and my alcohol being out, I purchased a sledge for fuel so that some meat could be cooked and tea made. When the former owner of the sledge saw the labor of so many days' hard work being burnt, aroused by his superstitious fears, he became very much incensed. I was afraid for awhile I would have very serious trouble, which indeed, was only prevented by being very positive with the native, saying it was my sledge, and that I could do as I pleased with it (Stoney 1974, 575).

I reached the lake on March 18, and learned that there were no natives beyond this point until the coast was reached. I again endeavored to get the natives here to go with me to the Point Barrow coast, but they refused, saying, however, that later, when the rivers that flowed to the northward broke, they would take me. Seeing the impracticability of going any further at this time, I decided on returning as quickly as possible, in order to send an officer with these people some of whom went to the Arctic Ocean every spring. So arrangements were made with them for taking a party later on (Stoney 1974, 575).

Ensign Howard, in contrast to Stoney, had to overcome the normal human foibles of fear and uncertainty in strange places. With perseverance and growing confidence throughout his journey, he did overcome, brilliantly. A keen and respectful observer, he was willing to live off the country and follow the lead of the Natives, whose knowledge he admired. In short order, they incorporated him into their lifeways and seasonal rounds in a manner that transcended formal hospitality. On April 12, 1886, Howard left Fort Cosmos with Crewman F. J. Price and three Eskimos, en route to Barrow. As on the earlier trip with Stoney, the party ascended the Ambler River and crossed the divide into the Noatak basin in search of Owpuk, the Eskimo leader who in December had pledged to Stoney his guide services for the trip to Barrow. Howard's participation in and description of the traditional mountain Eskimo spring gathering and trade journey to the coast is one of a kind. There is no other first-hand record of this event (Hall 1977).

April 15, made Koolooguck and learned that Owpuk, the native with whom I intended traveling to the coast, was still at Issheyuk. The deer hunters returned, bringing five deer. April 16, left the village and reached Aneyuk on the Notoark river, distant about ten miles N.W. Found the guide of my former trip, Ashewanuk, who said Owpuk was not at Issheyuk and that the village was deserted. Hired this guide to help me find him. April 17, left Aneyuk and arrived at Shotcoaluk twenty miles distant N.E. where I remained until the 20th on account of a heavy wind storm that filled the air with fine snow obscuring the nearest objects. Here I received one hundred pounds flour that had been sent ahead. April 20, left Shotcoaluk for the mountains. The snow drifted so the leading dogs could not be seen, and everybody suffered from the piercing cold. Connected all the dogs and sleds in line ahead and made for the nearest valley, clinging to the sleds to avoid getting lost. Finally went into camp in a shelter cut out of a large snow drift. April 21, left this camp; made about 12 miles north and reached the Etivluk River, whose headwaters are at Issheyuk and which helps form the Colville River. The village, twenty miles west of Issheyuk, contained one family, and I was informed that all the natives had gone down this river and were encamped below. April 22, started down the Etivluk came to a deserted village and was disappointed in not finding Owpuk. Continued on and reached the village of Tooloouk where I found him. The natives seemed glad to see me and sent dogs to help as soon as we were sighted. There were ten houses in this village and seventy natives; but this number varied as people were constantly coming and going. After a long talk with the natives, Owpuk consented to take me to "salt water." In the meantime a special hut had been built for myself and party, out of poles stuck in the snow with their upper ends bowed and lashed together and over this frame was put a cover of sewed deer skins. At this place I discharged my new guide and sent back the two natives brought from Fort Cosmos, with a large sled and eight dogs, and a written report of my trip up to date.

We spent a week at this village situated in a deep valley just off the Etivluk River. May 1, twelve sleds, including mine, left Tooloouk. Each sled averaged four natives and four dogs. Some were bound down the Colville River and some down the Ikpikpuk. . . .

May 2, under way; making frequent stops to allow the old people to catch up. All hands traveled on snowshoes, the sleds being too heavily loaded for any to ride. . .

[On May 5 the travelers made camp] at the limit of the mountains; on all sides and ahead was undulating land. May 6, under way, making frequent stops; made about six miles N. by W. During the day an addition was made to the party in the form of a baby boy. A place was hollowed out of a snowdrift and a couple of deer skins put in. The caravan then continued on leaving the woman behind alone. Towards evening the mother with her infant came into the camp, having walked a distance of three miles.

May 7, under way. Made about twelve miles N. by W. when reached the village of Etivoli-par. This is situated at the point where the Etivluk River flows into the Kungyanook, or Colville River. At this place those who go down the Colville River leave their boats in the fall and wait for snow to sledge to the mountains. Most of the natives with whom I was traveling remained here waiting for the ice on the Colville to break up.

. . .

May 8 to 12, remained at the village, during which time it was either snowing or raining. The natives opened their caches made last fall, and deer meat and fish were taken out frozen solid and in perfect condition. On May 11, the first goose of the season flew over, the natives were very jubilant

These natives had immense bundles of skins to trade on the coast for seal oil, rifles, etc., the natives on the coast depending on them for their skin clothing. The skins are dried and kept in bundles outside the houses, except wolf skins which are hung from poles at some distance from the village, as a charm against disease. Whenever the sleds stopped the wolf skins were first taken off and hung away as above (Stoney 1974, 813).

The woman with the baby had hard work to keep up; upon my offering her a ride the other interfered, saying she must go on foot; she also had to make her own fire, cook her own food and use her own special utensils; according to their superstitions to do otherwise would result in misfortune to the child (Stoney 1974, 815).

and by imitating the goose's call kept it circling overhead several minutes.

. . .

May 12, eight sleds, including my own, started for the Chipp or Ikpikpuk River, going on down the Colville. ...May 23, under way. Made the rendezvous village of Kigalik, consisting of thirty tents and one hundred and fifty natives. . . . As we neared the village our party was met and assisted with extra dogs and escorted to the lower end of the camp which had been reserved for us. In the center of the village a large dance house had been made by sticking poles into the ground and hanging skins over them. . . . In this house the men worked at new boat frames during the day and all hands danced at night, their food being carried there by the women. The latter spent their time in tanning skins and making clothing. The wood for the boats came from the rivers to the southward, passing through many native hands. The boats are lashed with strips of whalebone: the oomiaks are covered with sealskin and the kyaks with deerskins.

May 24 to 30. In camp at Kigalik Made a sledging trip to the headwaters of the Ikpikpuk River.

. . .

June 2 to 8. In camp at village. The ice began breaking and the river rising. . . . The river rose six feet by June 6, and then commenced falling. Boats were got ready and all stuff not needed for the journey was cached.

June 8 left Kigalik, five oomiaks starting, and made about fifty miles down the river. Just before camping passed a small creek coming in on the left which was stated to be very long. . . . Stopped often to get mashoo root for food, and killed three deer at the last stop. Upon reaching camp the boats were discharged and turned up to dry. This rule was always followed, and occasionally they were well rubbed with oil. . . . Their principal food now was the seal meat and oil which had been brought up the previous fall and cached. . . . Sighted a few deer, all hands started after them, some going barefooted over the snow and ice tundra, but none were killed. . . . The surrounding country was now changed to a level waste of tundra with an occasional mound-shaped sandhill from 50 to 100 feet high. The river banks were low and of sand, on top of this was a network of roots. Low brush grew in scattered places. From this point no rocks were met with, hence all the boats carried stones to crack bones upon.

June 15 to 19. In camp; detained by bad weather.

. . .

June 20, under way and made about twelve miles.

June 21 to 23, in camp, detained by sick people. The natives could not shoot game on this account and I was asked to do it. Only wooden bowls could be used in dipping water from the river as to use metal pots would cause the fish to leave. The fish caught here were dried and kept for future use, as they became less plentiful lower down.

June 24, under way and made about thirty-five miles. Banks of river so low as to be scarcely perceptible. Passed through two lakes made by the river widening over the tundra...While crossing the second lake we sighted two tents of Point Barrow natives which caused the wildest excitement, the natives paddling their hardest, and shouting with all their might, although the tents were several miles away. I came to the conclusion from later observations that these people are afraid of the Point Barrow natives, though they have never harmed each other. The paddling and shouting were kept up until we reached the tents. These Point Barrow natives were filthy in appearance and condition, their clothing being covered with grease and oil. As soon as we landed they brought us whale and walrus blubber to eat which even the dogs refused, though the natives ate it with apparent relish. . . . These natives had left Point Barrow a week before and were at this place to hunt deer and fish. . . . They communicate and trade with the Hudson Bay natives, the latter sometimes visit Point Barrow, and some of them visited us at this camp.

. . .

June 25 to July 12. Remained at this camp waiting for the ice to break off from the coast. I offered every inducement to natives to take me to Point Barrow, but without success. . . . Considerable trading was done here, the interior natives exchanging all kinds of skins for rifles, cartridges, caps, lead and tobacco, which the coast natives had in abundance.

July 12. Ten oomiaks started for Point Barrow. We followed, the edge of the ice being out of sight of land about an hour. Camped on beach. July 13, in camp, detained by ice.

July 14. Underway, pushing through the ice. Dense fog set in part of the time and we were out of sight of land. The navigating of these people was wonderful. We made our way through leads, heading in every direction, and towards evening made the beach along which we tracked until 4 AM the next day, only six boats reaching this camp, the others being delayed by the ice and difficult navigation.

July 15, tracked along the coast, and at 9:30 P.M. made Point Barrow six miles above the old headquarters of the U.S. Signal Station, under Lieutenant (P.H.) Ray, U.S. Army. I made my way overland, and at 2 A.M., July 16, reached the house, ninety-six days from Fort Cosmos (Stoney 1974, 821).

Aftermath of Military Exploration

As a result of the military explorations of 1883–1886, the geographic framework of the central mountains and upper rivers became available to experts on the Arctic and to the prospectors who now began to filter into the region. Given its remote location hundreds of miles up difficult and fluctuating rivers, this fringe land above the Arctic Circle offered little to white men. Even the Natives were few in number and scattered across vast distances. Gold mining in these early years centered on the upper Yukon, hundreds of miles away. Trading posts found no profit where only occasional prospectors roamed, where Native trappers and fur-bearing animals were spread thin. The explorers' search for a transmountain rescue trail from Kobuk or Koyukuk to the Arctic Coast had died in the mountain topography and seasonally closed expanses of northern Alaska. Evidence of precious metals brought back by the explorers and the prospectors who followed them would bring miners in some numbers to the region, especially in the false rush of 1898–1899, but never near the scale of the Yukon and Nome rushes. Remoteness and difficult access would hold the region essentially in trust until the airplane and the recent discovery of giant oil fields broke the barriers of distance and economic limbo. Thus, geographic discovery did not trigger an ordered progress of settlement and civilization in this region. Instead, excepting occasional short-lived gold-mining flurries, the country would remain largely a refuge for people who liked being on the edge of nowhere, Native and white person alike. Lacking the necessary critical mass of economic incentives and numbers of people, progress passed the region by.

In this perspective, the history that ensued after 1886 is a story of minor booms and long busts, of tiny communities not quite getting there, struggling to keep alive such symbols of civilization as a post office or a school, or folding entirely—with the deserted sites then salvaged by the hard core of Natives and whites who dwelt in the distant camps of a marginal place. It is this concept of the margin, of the borderland, and of the kinds of people who by heritage or choice lived there that dominates the history.

The people who lived in and visited this remote part of the world, and their relationships to each other and to the harsh environment, form the central theme of this history. People were few, institutions practically nil. So this is personal history—biographical and anecdotal. Great movements and faceless masses did not surge this far north. Everyone who stayed more than a season hardened up and became a part of the country.

The code of time and place allowed plenty of room for idiosyncrasy; it required self-reliance. But individualism was tempered by the notion that nobody would let down a neighbor when the chips were down. The selection process, a fine screen of demanding natural and social conditions, worked along these lines.

Miners panning on Myrtle Creek in the Wiseman District, 1899. Note cleavage and attitude of gold-bearing schist. F. C. Schrader photo 402, USGS Historical Photo Library, Denver.

Chapter Three

Early Mining and Klondike Overflow

Even as the first explorers reported their findings, prospectors extended their quest toward the central Brooks Range. In fact, an old miner named Miller went up the Kobuk with Lieutenant Stoney in 1884, hired to chop wood for the steam launch. Wherever they stopped, Miller washed the sand of the stream bars looking for "color," the specks of fine gold that might lead to riches. He "invariably found traces of precious metal" and begged Stoney to stake his further search, which Stoney could not do (Stoney 1974, 824). Lieutenant Allen associated with prospectors along the Yukon, rating them the most qualified men of the country for any wilderness enterprise. He had traveled with prospectors Bremner and Johnson from Copper River to the Yukon. These two would follow Allen's tracks to the Koyukuk in 1887. Over the next few years a pattern emerged of single prospectors and scattered mining partners testing the streams and bars of the main Koyukuk and its South and Middle forks. A few small strikes were made, enough to keep a cadre of twenty or thirty men looking further (Cole 1983; Sherwood 1965).

These men and the traders who staked and supplied them operated initially from Yukon River stations and, as best the record indicates, held mainly to the Koyukuk drainage, leaving the other rivers of the region to later waves of prospectors. Blessed with river transport to bring tools and supplies, a tight community of knowledgeable men thus came together on the far margin of the Yukon gold fields. They were mainly old hands, veterans of the Sierras and Rockies. Some had pioneered the early placers on the upper Yukon, beginning in the 1870s. These were the rugged scouts in ceaseless search of gold. They prowled the far creeks and in time found paystreaks that spurred inexperienced hopefuls to actual and rumored fields of gold (Berton 1974).

Typical of these hardy men was James Bender, who died in 1932 in Fairbanks. Sourdough historian Joseph Ulmer sketched Bender's life for the Pioneers of Alaska: Bender's family, originally from Germany, followed a hundred-year course westward from Pennsylvania to Minnesota, where James joined the Union Pacific Railroad construction as a wagon boss. He then hauled supplies to gold camps in Montana, became a deputy marshal, and later joined the rush to the Little Rockies in Montana. In 1887 he and thirteen others crossed Chilkoot Pass and went down the Yukon to the Fortymile River, where he hooked up with Al Mayo and floated down to Nuklukayet. There he met John Bremner and Pete Johnson, Lieutenant Allen's former partners. In the fall of 1887 the three of them went overland to the mouth of the John River on the Koyukuk. Next spring they whipsawed lumber for a boat and ascended the John, working the bars that summer and taking out fair pay. Bender and Johnson returned to Mayo's Landing (Tanana) while Bremner continued prospecting along the Koyukuk. On his way out, an Indian killed him. A messenger from Nulato brought the news to the miners, who were waiting for the last boat upriver. A miners' meeting was called and Gordon Bettles was chosen as judge, Jim Bender as marshal. Numbering more than twenty men, they commandeered a river steamer and proceeded up the Koyukuk to apprehend the murderer, who after being tried by a jury was executed by hanging. Later, trader Jack McQuesten outfitted Bender and he mined for a number of years in the Circle District, finally settling in Fairbanks. Ulmer concludes: "He was an outstanding figure of that type of real frontiersmen" (Ulmer "Historical Sketch of James Bender" n.d.)[1]

Nulato on the Yukon River in 1909 from bow of steamer Sarah, looking across the barge being pushed. A. G. Maddren photo 14, USGS Historical Photo Library, Denver.

Capt. Billie Moore, son of Capt. William Moore of Skagway and White Pass fame, was another Koyukuk pioneer. He had come down the Yukon from Fortymile to Nuklukayet at the same time Jim Bender did. With Bender and Bettles, he joined the avenging posse, serving as engineer of the commandeered steamer *Explorer* on the cruise up the Koyukuk to find John Bremner's killer. After the hanging, he went to St. Michael and sailed for Juneau, where he helped his father build a 20-ton schooner. Then, in the summer of 1889, he came back to the Yukon via Chilkoot Pass. After mining for three years in the Fortymile and Seventymile country, near the Canadian border, Moore and a partner gave it up, because the bar didn't pan out as well as they had expected.

Capt. Billie Moore's early mining career on the Koyukuk ended in disappointment. But that did not stop him. He went on to spend many more years as master and pilot of Yukon River steamers, as well as a miner,

Steamer on the Yukon River at Weare (Tanana), 1898. A. H. Brooks photo 148, USGS Historical Photo Library, Denver.

fisherman, and trader. In old age he finally consented to the pleadings of his friends and left St. Michael for the Pioneers' Home in Sitka. His work as Gordon Bettles's partner on the Koyukuk was part of the slow creep up that river. Their little 35-foot, open-hold steamer *Cora* and the building of Arctic City some 400 river-miles up the Koyukuk provided an advanced base for miners, who built their own cabins there so they could overwinter. Indians from nearby villages began trading furs, forcing Moore and Bettles to give them the same prices as prevailed on the Yukon. Thus Arctic City became the prototype of the typical upriver post, with a trader, miners, Indian trappers and hunters, and a small river steamer to keep them all supplied. The 150-mile leap upriver from Arctic City to Tramway Bar on the Middle Fork had been strongly aided by the *Cora's* supplies in 1892–1893. All this set the stage for further advances by trader Gordon Bettles. As more miners heard the news of upper Koyukuk strikes, a perceptible momentum—well short of a rush,

The town of Bettles on the Koyukuk River in 1899; slope of Mt. Lookout rises to left. F. C. Schrader photo 808, USGS Historical Photo Library, Denver.

Weare (Tanana) Trading Post on Yukon River in 1898. A. H. Brooks photo 145, USGS Historical Photo Library, Denver.

but promising—began to gather. Bettles read the signs and put his chips on the Koyukuk, shifting his trading operations ever farther upstream (Bettles 1941; Case 1947).

Depending on which generation of oldtimers was talking or writing, Gordon Bettles was the father or grandfather of the Koyukuk mining district. Nor, with good reason, was he loath to accept this tribute. As a trader with mining interests in a remote, underpopulated region, he became a skilled promoter of the region's prospects. In 1893, with George T. Howard, former printer of the *St. James Mission* (Tanana) press, Bettles set up the *Yukon Press* at Fort Adams, six miles down the Yukon from present Tanana. With its first issue of January 1, 1894, it began the printed call that echoed ceaselessly down the decades for better transportation and communication with the States, including mail to the interior stations at least once each winter—as a government responsibility, not dependent on the good graces of the Alaska Commercial Company. Bettles was well suited to his varied work, having trained as typesetter and newspaperman in Ontario and Detroit and having mined throughout the west, British Columbia, and Juneau before coming to the Yukon (*Seattle Sun-Times* 11 July 1937; *Yukon Press* 1 January 1894).

The *Yukon Press* provided a running commentary on the development of the Yukon corridor, together with reflections on the larger prospects and problems of the country. In the first issue, Bettles, who wrote most of the copy, traced the miners' progress up the Koyukuk through 1893, including the Tramway Bar strike. He stated that twenty-two miners were on the Koyukuk and six more were wintering at Tanana Station. He concluded with the caution that the Koyukuk looked promising, but it was not a place of easy riches and miners should be prepared to overwinter.

In the January 1, 1896, issue, Bettles editorialized on the "Downfall of the Indians and Eskimos." He spoke of the evils of liquor, supplied to the Natives by whalers and traders. He castigated the salmon canneries established at river mouths, which destroyed Native food supplies. He criticized the introduction of reindeer as a flawed plan to relieve the starvation problem. And he advocated supplying the Natives with breech-loading rifles through legitimizing firearms trade. All in all, it was an enlightened plea, based on his day-to-day contact with the Alaska Natives, for them to receive the same justice and protection afforded to those in the states.

In that same January 1, 1896, issue it was reported that recent gold excitements at Birch and Munook (Minook) Creeks, up the Yukon, were drawing miners away from the Koyukuk, partly because of easier steamboat access at these near-Yukon sites. Bettles was not discouraged, citing in the June 1896 issue a number of facts showing that the area was experiencing growth and prosperity.

The next two issues of the *Yukon Press* record the initial effects of the Klondike discovery in Canada's Yukon. Klondike fever would first drain the mid-Yukon and Koyukuk country, then create a back-surge of disappointed miners seeking claims in Alaskan gold fields. By the fall of 1897 the rush of miners already in the country, plus the early waves of

Native fish-drying camp near mouth of Alatna River, 1899. F. C. Schrader photo 447, USGS Historical Photo Library, Denver.

St. Michael and the harbor, with barge near shore, 1898. A. H. Brooks photo 157, USGS Historical Photo Library, Denver.

stampeders from the outside world, had already glutted the Klondike with thousands more claimants than there were claims available. An estimated 6,000 prospective miners now centered on the upper Yukon—at Dawson and the Klondike itself, or marooned at river stations such as Circle and Fort Yukon. The riverboat transportation system, beset by the short open-water season and the business-as-usual distribution of food supplies to competing trading stations, proved unable to match people and food. Chaos threatened. Adding to the clamor was the imposition of restrictive Canadian law relating both to mining claims and royalties and to the stern enforcement of law and order by the Mounties (Bearss 1970; Berton 1974; Schneider 1984; *Yukon Press* April 1897 and March 1898).

By the late winter of 1898, the migration of stampeders from Canada's Klondike to Alaska was already underway. Army Capt. Patrick Henry Ray, exiting the upper Yukon after a reconnaissance to check conditions in the gold fields, met "fully 300 people going down the river (from Dawson), and the general answers to my questions were, they were going to Alaska to stay" (Ray 1900, 502). By this time, transfer of foodstuffs to areas of need had averted the immediate threat of starvation. But the deluge of stampeders poised on the upper river and lakes, and at Skagway and Dyea just below the passes, disturbed him greatly. He estimated that nearly 18,000 people would flood the Yukon country as soon as the river broke. They would be reasonably well supplied because the Canadians required them to haul a year's supply of food across the passes. But what would happen when they got to the Klondike and found nothing for them there? They would flood on down the river into Alaska, which was "without any semblance of law, civil or military" (Ray 1900, 502). To avert anarchy, Captain Ray urged that military posts be established at the mouth of Mission Creek (where overflow miners were already building Eagle City), at the mouth of the Tanana, and at St. Michael (Ray 1900).

Already, in the fall of 1897, armed parties of miners had commandeered food from river steamers. By December, dogs for winter travel had become rare and valuable commodities. Inflationary prices for food, climbing rapidly with demand, would keep climbing as the flood of people gained volume. Scurvy, the product of a beans, bacon, and flour diet, had struck down miners in the Klondike. The prospect loomed of a horde of unemployed stampeders—armed, dangerous, and desperate—roaming the country in predatory packs gleaning the last scraps of food, ultimately dying of starvation, scurvy, and cold (Ray 1900; Wells 1900).

Captain Ray and his Canadian counterparts in the Mounted Police agreed that speculators and transportation companies had conspired to broadcast to the world an endless bonanza in the Klondike. Thus lured, the unwary and inexperienced came in droves to buy worthless claims. True, the operating mines at Minook Creek, Birch Creek, and Fortymile, and the promising prospects along the Tanana and Koyukuk showed that gold was available in Alaska—but only in limited amounts, far from supply points, where the cost of food would allow only a few miners to survive, much less make a living. Only deliberate development of the country, based on roads and trails to the remote gold fields, could assure orderly progress in Alaska. To this end, Ray proposed roads to the Interior from Seward, one of them north to the Koyukuk (Ray 1900, 503).

This was the atmosphere as spring turned to summer in 1898. The waves of people bound for the Klondike crested at this time. Those camped on the lakes at the head of the Yukon rafted and boated down the river to Dawson as soon as breakup allowed. More and more gold seekers

Below: Riverboats on ways at St. Michael, 1916. J. B. Mertie photo 488, USGS Historical Photo Library, Denver.

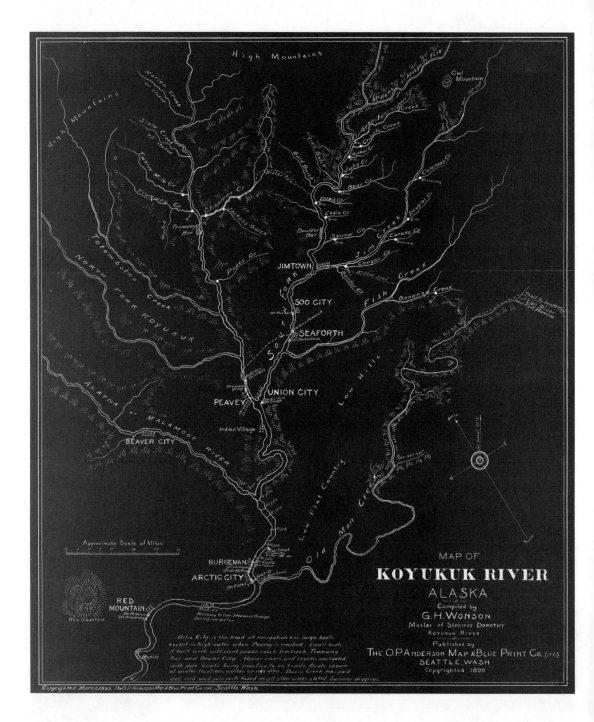

MAP OF
KOYUKUK RIVER
ALASKA
Compiled by
G. H. WONSON
Master of Steamer DOROTHY
KOYUKUK RIVER
Published by
THE O. P. ANDERSON MAP & BLUE PRINT CO. (INC)
SEATTLE, WASH
Copyrighted 1899

An inaccurate guide map of 1899. Map 12025 of the Alaska Historical Maps Collection, Library of Congress.

landed at Skagway and Dyea, then funneled through the passes. All were too late for good claims. Other parties came by ocean steamer to St. Michael, and took passage on the scores of river steamers now plying the Yukon. Some of these took heed of rumors and of direct word from disappointed Klondikers floating down the river: the Klondike was filled up. As the word spread, some adventurers—not to be denied their adventure—looked to other fields, for they meant to strike it rich even if it took all summer. Both Koyukuk and Kobuk figured in the search for alternatives.

Thus did the Klondike overflow evolve. In part it was made up of people who had physically got to Dawson and experienced the welter of crowded frustration there; in part it recruited newcomers en route to the Klondike who branched off to the Koyukuk and other fields from the Yukon River, or reset their objectives while still at sea. Some of these latter would go directly to Kotzebue Sound to test the rumored wealth of the Kobuk.

In the main, these stampeders knew almost nothing of the country or of prospecting and mining. They were hopeful innocents, recruited from every occupation and walk of life in the States and many other countries. For economic or family reasons, prodded by intangible yearnings, they had taken the leap to adventure promised by the Gold Rush. With few exceptions they were ill-equipped physically and mentally for wilderness life. Too numerous for the slim pickings of the upper rivers, and unprepared for the winter rigors of arctic Alaska, they nevertheless entered the country with high spirits (Berton 1974; Cole 1983; Marshall 1991; Richardson 1900).

The camps or "cities" on the Alatna and the Middle and South forks ". . . were mostly clearings in the woods along the riverbanks, with a few shacks, a sawmill, and a steamboat. Almost all of them were abandoned in less than a year" (Cole 1983, 31).

Bergman on the Koyukuk River, 1899. F. C. Schrader photo 453, USGS Historical Photo Library, Denver.

Gordon Bettles, meanwhile, kept track of events through association with traders and steamboat men along the Yukon. The progress of prospecting on the Koyukuk boded well for that district, just as the Klondike overflow picked up stride. In 1898, with discovery of gold in paying quantities at Bergman—a few miles up the Koyukuk from Arctic City—Bettles established another trading post or "beanshop" at that location. When that one got flooded out, he established yet another beanshop farther upstream and called it "Bettles." Later that year a sudden freeze stranded

Building steamboats along river-front at Whitehorse, Yukon Territory, 1901. W. C. Mendenhall photo 137, USGS Historical Photo Library, Denver.

some sixty-eight steamers on the Koyukuk for the rest of the winter. According to Bettles,

> There were nine hundred persons on these sixty-eight steamers, and when these adventurers realized that they would have to remain a whole year in this desolate part of Alaska, five hundred and fifty of them took emergency rations and mushed out to the Yukon. A good many went downstream to St. Michael, vowing never again to visit such an inhospitable country.
>
> Those who stayed in and around Bettles numbered three hundred fifty stampeders, and I assure you we had quite an interesting winter with such a varied assortment of men in camp. However, most of them were broke. But with the supplies they had on the sixty-eight ships and the two hundred fifty tons of provisions we had, none went hungry that winter. Before spring I had to carry the camp on my books to the extent of just about an even $100,000 (Bettles 1941, 5, 20).

The stories of these overwintering stampeders and the camps they built survive in the diaries and letters of the participants. For most of them, people and camps alike, it was a one-winter stand. Probably 90 percent of the people departed in the spring without once looking back at the scenes of their suffering.

Despite hardships and, for most, failure—as measured by bags of gold—the Koyukuk stampeders speak in their diaries and letters of other, rarer values found in the far north of darkness and perpetually frozen ground. Hamlin Garland, a "Ninety-Eighter" himself, touched on the force that moved so many:

> I believed that I was about to see and take part in a most picturesque and impressive movement across the wilderness. I believed it to be the last great march of the kind which could ever come in America, so rapidly were the wild places being settled up. I wished, therefore, to take part in the tramp of the goldseekers, to be one of them, to record their deeds (Gruening 1966, 165).

Typical of this breed of gold seekers were the members of the Iowa Company, who would prospect and mine for small returns on a midcourse tributary of the Koyukuk during the 1898–1899 rush. This large company hauled tons of machinery and supplies over White Pass. On the shores of Tagish Lake they built two boats, the 60-foot sternwheeler *Iowa* and the smaller, screw-driven *Little Jim*. At breakup in June, they, with thousands of others, descended through the Yukon's canyons and rapids to Dawson. After visiting the mines of Bonanza and Eldorado Creeks, where he saw a fortune in nuggets and fine gold, E. G. Abbott of the Iowa Company declared: "This district is all taken and no chance to locate anything within sixty miles." With rumors of fraud and fakery abounding, he yet could say, "We hear nothing but good reports from the Koyukuk country [where we will go] to try and find the elephant ourselves" (Hunt 1973, 6).

You never saw so many heartbroken, discontented people as there are here. No work at any price and no money nor anyway of earning it. Wages are $10 per day, but you can't get a day's work at any price. It costs nearly $10 a day to live. It is a shame for people to rush in here the way they are. Men here are doing everything they can to get out. You ought to hear their tales of woe; it is heart rending. I am glad we have some other place in view. We still think we will find the Eldorado. Everyone we see who has been on the Koyukuk river says it is good and we are sure to hit it (T. T. Barbour 1898, in Hunt 1973, 7).

Below: Interior of trading post at Bergman on the Koyukuk River in 1899. F. C. Schrader photo 845, USGS Historical Photo Library, Denver.

Steamer Luella on the Koyukuk River above Bergman, 1899. F. C. Schrader photo 449, USGS Historical Photo Library, Denver.

This optimism was ill-founded. The Koyukuk enterprise of the Iowa Company ended up "a dead failure," stuck on a fine-gold creek that could not pay with the crude mining techniques of that day.

By far, the majority of Koyukuk stampeders came by ocean transport to St. Michael, thence by steamboat up the Yukon, and then, overland or by a variety of river craft, up the Koyukuk. St. Michael became a caldron of activity, full of rumors, competing shippers, mountains of freight and miners' outfits, and thousands of gold seekers, off-loaded from ocean ships, clamoring for riverboat passage up the Yukon. Thousands more of the disappointed from Dawson, most of them broke and desperate, fought for passage home on the returning steamers. The presence of this fleeing army, and the stories they told of dispossession and despair in the Klondike, steered many newcomers to the Koyukuk.

In most ways, the 1898–99 Koyukuk rush (and its contemporary on the Kobuk) was a repeat of a phenomenon patterned in earlier mining camps. The same varieties of characters assembled: the strong, the weak, the knowing, and the innocent. By far, most of them were decent people, though villainy was not entirely absent. Most of them came away with nothing, and in the Arctic gold fields the incidence of success was slimmer than usual.

Differences between this rush and others hinged partly on remoteness and climate. For all but the experienced and well equipped there was no way out once winter closed. Moreover, the economic geology was marginal. To this day, placer mining in these districts above the Arctic Circle is a small-scale affair. In that day, with frozen-ground mining methods yet to be perfected and prospecting in these fields in its infancy, it was possible to find color, but rare to find a real paystreak and nearly impossible to develop and exploit it. Few of the stampeders came equipped for the years of patient labor that later miners lavished for occasional big pay, but usually modest returns. Remoteness and difficulty of access prohibited re-supply and a second start for most novices—who had already liquidated all they once owned to get there in the first place. As get-rich-quick dreams flickered and died with the disappearing sun, the dark, sub-zero winter demoralized all but a few. These factors in combination turned the rush around in a hurry; it became a nearly complete evacuation as soon as energy or breakup allowed. Many people went out during fall and early winter, at least as far as the Yukon. By June, with rivers clear of ice and in flood, most of the rest flooded out, too, riding the high water.

This ephemeral quest produced different kinds of heroes. Some just hung on tight, then left as soon as they could. Others, weak and homesick at first, hardened up and kept trying. Many, who did no mining (most of the novices gave up after an empty prospect hole or two), kept busy with camp chores or saw the country while hunting and ice-fishing, throwing occasional holiday parties to brighten their spirits. Sprinkled thinly through the few hundreds who got to the upper rivers and creeks were some tough, competent cases who went about their prospecting and mining with high energy and optimism, taking the cold and darkness and difficulty in stride. All of these varied folks, including a number who wandered off and froze to death and others who hunkered down in far cabins and watched the black-leg scurvy rot their bodies away, were, if not individually heroic, at least participants in a heroic venture.

The settlement of Beaver on the Yukon River, entrepot to the Chandalar District. A. G. Maddren photo 149 of 1910. USGS Historical Photo Library, Denver.

Chapter Four

Far North Camps and Communities, 1900–1930

I n autumn 1899 the Revenue Steamer *Nunivak* took station on the Yukon River. After wintering at the mouth of the Dall River a thousand miles up the Yukon, the steamboat's commander, First Lt. J. C. Cantwell of Kobuk fame, began the Revenue Marine Yukon River patrols that marked a growing governmental presence in Interior Alaska caused by the gold rush.

Prospectors with horses on raft approaching Dall River junction on the Yukon in 1901. W. C. Mendenhall photo 178, USGS Historical Photo Library, Denver.

During the summer of 1900 the lingering momentum of the Klondike rush helped swell the rush to Nome, which now became a torrent. Down the Yukon came hundreds of boats, scows, and rafts loaded with people, equipment, horses, and beef cattle, "bound for that distant land of promise and prospective wealth" (Cantwell 1902, 60).

Lieutenant Cantwell made constant stops to help travelers, mend boats and equipment, and resolve disputes. He noted that some boats had been cut in half and the new ends then patched, so that erstwhile partners could sail separately after altercations (Cantwell 1902).

At Fort Hamlin, an Alaska Commercial Company post above Rampart, he inspected steamboats for proper marine documents and compliance with customs laws. Three steamers, the Canadian *Florence S* and the Alaska Commercial Company's *Victoria* and *Leah,* carried parties of miners and provisions from Dawson bound for the Koyukuk mining camps,

Steamer pushing barges upriver on the Yukon, 1916. J. B. Mertie photo 475, USGS Historical Photo Library, Denver.

which reportedly were in distress. To discover the facts, Cantwell sent 2d Lt. B. H. Camden up the Koyukuk on the *Leah* in early June 1900 (Cantwell 1902).

Camden found Arctic City deserted, "its departed and prosperous days" attested only by fourteen abandoned cabins. At Bergman, metropolis of the Koyukuk, a fluctuating population of some fifteen whites and one hundred Indians patronized the Pickarts and Bettles store. Near the South Fork junction, Union City stood silent, its sawmill rusting. Peavy, fifty miles above Bergman, hosted only Mr. Rose, the land commissioner; otherwise its fifteen or twenty cabins were empty.

The Teddy H. approaching Bettles with freight barges. Robert Marshall photo. Courtesy of the Bancroft Library, University of California, Berkeley.

Twenty-eight miles above Peavy was the *Leah's* objective, the new station of Bettles. Here the latest Pickarts and Bettles store supplied the upper Koyukuk camps, which were yet another 50 or 75 miles up Koyukuk forks and tributaries. Small, shallow-draft steamers could get as far as Bettles during times of high water. But the *Leah*, drawing five feet, and even the 20-inch-draft *Victoria* sent ahead as a scout, grounded a few miles above Peavy when the water abruptly dropped on June 13.

Captain Young of the *Leah* unloaded his 160-ton cargo and 110 passengers and waited for a surge of water to carry him back down the river.

Meanwhile, Gordon Bettles confirmed that the Bettles post and the camps were critically short of supplies, which he asserted would lead to an exodus within two weeks lacking re-supply. He requested and received special permission from Lieutenant Camden to activate the abandoned, light-draft steamer *Dorothy* so he could relay the *Leah's* off-loaded cargo to Bettles, where pole boats could get supplies to the scattered camps (Cantwell 1902).

Horse-drawn freight scow on Middle Fork, Koyukuk River, at Coldfoot enroute from Bettles to Wiseman-Nolan mining camps in 1909. A. G. Maddren photo 19, USGS Historical Photo Library, Denver.

Town of Peavy on Koyukuk River below Bettles, 1899; note small, shallow-draft steamboat used on upper river. F. C. Schrader photo 437, USGS Historical Photo Library, Denver.

This grounding of steamboats short of objectives, followed by piecemeal relaying and hauling of supplies up ever shallower and swifter streams, was repeated each year on the fluctuating Koyukuk. At Bettles, some 400 river-miles from the Koyukuk's mouth, the costs of goods and transport began to overtake the gains from mining. Every mile of additional haulage by pole boat, dog team, and later horse-drawn scows and freight

Hughes City on Koyukuk River, 1911. P. S. Smith photo 750, USGS Historical Photo Library, Denver.

BEN HUR OF NOME.

Gin-pole and self-dumping bucket at Big Creek mining operation, Chandalar District, 1924. J. B. Mertie photo 948, USGS Historical Photo Library, Denver.

sledges further whittled away the net value of gold extracted. Thus did this and neighboring far-north mining districts become a separate province of Alaska mining, hovering always on the margin. Compared to their peers in more southerly districts along the major rivers, far-north miners led spartan lives, developed simplified versions of mining equipment and technology, depended less on store-bought goods, and salvaged for reuse everything that could possibly be adapted to future utility.

Camden summarized his impressions of the Koyukuk with an essay on the enormous costs and distances that had to be overcome if this district were ever to rank with the more fortunate gold fields of Alaska. Surprisingly, he estimated that as many as 360 miners might be scattered through the fan-shaped district north of Bergman, bounded by the Arctic Divide and the Alatna and South Fork (Koyukuk) Rivers. Most of them centered on the Middle Fork at the Myrtle and Slate Creek diggings, where a cluster of cabins called Slate Creek was about to become Coldfoot, in ironic tribute to green stampeders who got cold feet and left the country. Still more miners were on the way, traveling overland from Fort Yukon via the Chandalar route (Cantwell 1902; Marshall 1991). Residual overflow from the Klondike still lapped against the northern mountains, but with smaller waves composed mainly of experienced men.

Sluicing gold placers on Myrtle Creek near Coldfoot, 1899. F. C. Schrader photo 407, USGS Historical Photo Library, Denver.

Camden estimated that 300 Indians occupied the Koyukuk drainage that June of 1900. This number dropped in late summer as epidemics of measles and influenza compounded by pneumonia swept up the Yukon and its tributaries, laying waste whole villages. Cantwell's *Nunivak*, the Army at St. Michael, and missionaries, traders, and agents at Yukon River stations rendered aid and supplies to the sick and starving Natives. But disease was on a rampage, with sick, dying, and dead everywhere. *Nunivak*'s surgeon, Dr. J. T. White, lamented that "though we went everywhere, distributing food and medicine and doing the best we could, [the Natives] . . . lay about waiting for death to relieve them" (Cantwell 1902, 245; Stein 1981).

Surgeon White found relief from the tragedy during a visit to Fort Gibbon, the new Army post at Tanana. Freshly assigned West Pointers hosted the Revenue Marine officers to drinks and dinner, dress uniforms and all. Cantwell remarked that Fort Gibbon had "an air of civilization somewhat out of keeping with its wild surroundings" (1902, 62). Its well-made frame structures overlooked graded streets, and the hum of machinery echoed from bordering woods (Stein 1981).

Geologist at work with planetable on Koyukuk near Alatna, 1899. F. C. Schrader photo 463, USGS Historical Photo Library, Denver.

Fort Gibbon was the largest of the recently established Army posts serving the Yukon, including Fort St. Michael, Fort Egbert at Eagle, and temporary camps at Rampart, Circle, and other points. What a change from 1897–1898, when Captain Ray and Lieutenant Richardson provided the only United States authority along the entire Yukon frontier. In the summer of 1899, Patrick Henry Ray, now a major and commander of the Military District of North Alaska, had the satisfaction of distributing whole companies and battalions of troops at the posts he had recommended in 1898 to regulate and assist the miners flooding the country (U.S. Army 1969).

In addition to the Revenue Marine and the Army, the U.S. Geological Survey began the series of expeditions that would probe the range soon to bear the name of the survey's chief Alaska trailblazer, Alfred Hulse Brooks (Sherwood 1965). The U.S. Congress had provided authority and wherewithal for all these initiatives. More important, as the century turned, it passed a body of laws that gave remote Alaska improved civil government and a smattering of administrative and judicial functionaries to carry it out, even to the fringes of the arctic mountains. These developments and others resulted from the phenomenon called "Klondicitis." The gold rush first, then glimmerings of copper, coal, and oil suddenly changed the territory's accustomed slow pace to full speed ahead. Business interests around the nation smelled wealth in the natural resources of Alaska and in the trade that would be generated by their extraction. Congress was responding to these interests and to the plight of both un-

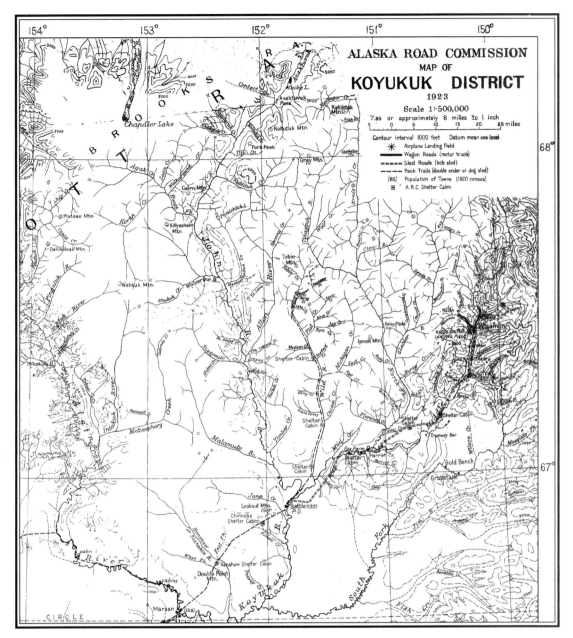

ALASKA ROAD COMMISSION
MAP OF
KOYUKUK DISTRICT
1923
Scale 1:500,000
7.89 or approximately 8 miles to 1 inch
5   0   5   10   15   20   25 miles
Contour interval 1000 feet   Datum mean sea level
✳ Airplane Landing Field
━━━ Wagon Roads (motor truck)
━═━═ Sled Roads (bob sled)
━─━─ Pack Trails (double ender or dog sled)
(85) Population of Towns (1920 census)
⊠ A.R.C. Shelter Cabin

prepared newcomers and a Native population reeling from the negative effects of Klondicitis (Nichols 1963).

For Alaskans, it had been a long time coming, this congressional shift from disdain and neglect of the worthless possession, Seward's Icebox. Alaska was the first noncontiguous territory administered by the United States. In his essay on its early governance, Alfred Hulse Brooks dwelt on the nation's seeming unfitness to cope with problems of colonial administration. For seventeen years, he demonstrated, Alaska had had no civil government at all. Passage of the 1884 Organic Act finally provided a semblance of civil government. Alaska became a civil and judicial district, but was governed under the laws of Oregon. This expedient relieved Congress of the task of drawing up a new code, but saddled the northern stepchild with laws only marginally

This full-size section of the Alaska Road Commission's Koyukuk District map of 1923 shows the pack trails (single dash) and sledge trails (double dash) in the Bettles to Wiseman and Wild Lake areas. Note the many ARC-built shelter cabins, the tram and ferry connections across Middle Fork, and the importance of Wiseman, with its post office, wireless station, and landing field. The two spur wagon roads out of Wiseman serve the Nolan and Hammond River mining camps. RG 126, Map 21, National Archives.

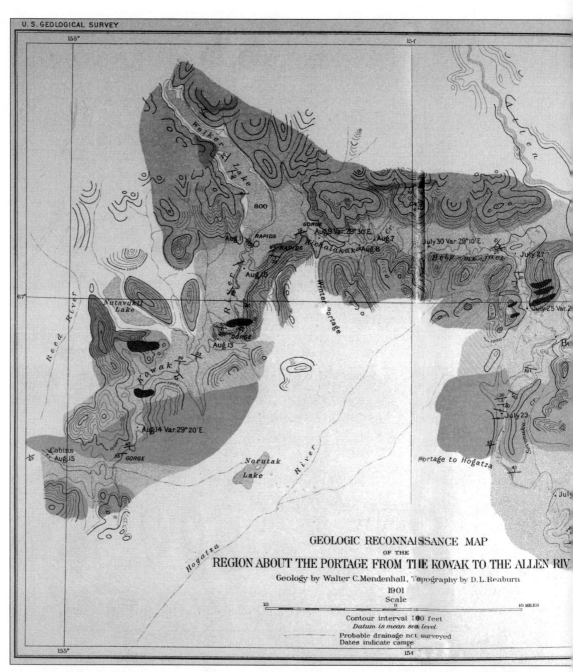

U. S. GEOLOGICAL SURVEY

GEOLOGIC RECONNAISSANCE MAP
OF THE
REGION ABOUT THE PORTAGE FROM THE KOWAK TO THE ALLEN RIV
Geology by Walter C. Mendenhall, Topography by D.L. Reaburn
1901
Scale
Contour interval 100 feet
Datum is mean sea level
Probable drainage not surveyed
Dates indicate camps

Geologic Reconnaissance Map: Region about the Portage from the Kowak to the Allen River. Mendenhall (1902).

applicable to Alaskan conditions. A governor and various judicial and administrative officials appointed by the president were based in the southeastern Panhandle and for a time at the Aleutian port of Unalaska, leaving mainland Alaska void of any authority. Provision was made for representative government. Although general land laws were excluded, thus disallowing homesteading, the mining laws of the United States came into effect. The rights of citizenship now followed the flag to Alaska, and a criminal code allowed selective law enforcement where there had been virtual anarchy. In remote areas, however—and that meant all of Alaska north of Pacific waters—the code meant little; judicial officers had no travel budgets, nor were there established travel routes into the unmapped Interior. The only sign of district government in all inland Alaska was

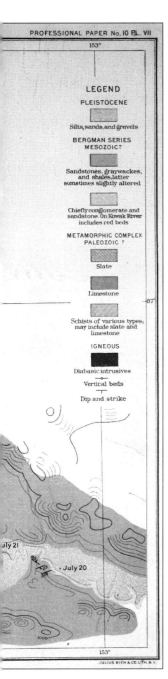

a roving revenue officer on the prowl for intoxicating liquors, prohibited by the act (Brooks 1953; Gruening 1954).

Ernest Gruening judged that the most significant benefits of the 1884 act were extension to Alaska of the mining laws, thereby making mining possible, and of the principle of public education through a small appropriation for that purpose. The governor, largely a figurehead, did have a voice to the nation through his annual report to the secretary of the interior. But for four successive administrations, the governors' recommendations and pleas for Alaska "were in varying degrees crying in the wilderness" (Gruening 1954, 53).

In the far reaches of this district that was not yet a territory, the small communities and placer camps forged ahead anyway. They rigged their own governments, most of them under the Miners' Code clause of the mining statutes. They adopted mining claim regulations and enforced their own decrees. Lacking any other authority, the codes comprehended all essential elements of community life, with a majority vote in the miners' meetings the mode of policy and judgment. In criminal cases, imprisonment being impractical, three punishments sufficed: hanging, banishment, or a fine. An elected recorder was the only permanent official. For a set fee he recorded claims, minutes of meetings, and the disposition of civil and criminal cases. He also filed homemade certificates of marriage, signed by principals and witnesses, after the simple "I do's" that consummated betrothal in a mainly preacherless realm (Brooks 1953).

In the far north, the flurry of Congressional enactments between 1898 and 1900—the response to Klondicitis—changed only slightly the tenor of life established during the previous decade. Extension of the homestead laws in 1898 meant little to miners living in unsurveyed, mostly unmapped regions. Mining claims occupied their interests, and these they filed under mining statutes already in effect. The Criminal Code Act of 1899 provided for impaneling of legal juries in Alaska, heretofore impossible because the patched-on Oregon law required jurors to be local taxpayers, and until 1899 Alaskans paid no local taxes—one of many paradoxes in the Organic Act. In practice the miners' meeting had served the same purpose as juries. In fact, in the smaller settlements typical of the far north, the advent of the jury system caused problems during litigious periods, which matched the rhythm of seasonal discontents. If several cases were on the docket, the mix of judicial and law enforcement officers, lawyers, jurors, plaintiffs, defendants, and witnesses exhausted and overlapped the population.

The 1899 act recognized the futility of prohibition enforcement; liquor became legal, including homemade hooch, and the taxing of liquor licenses, along with other occupational taxes, was used to fund the district government.

All of these provisions awaited the Civil Government Act of June 1900, which provided the administrative machinery to implement them. For the northern hinterlands, the most important parts of this act were those extending and enhancing the administration of justice. Now a judge sat at Eagle, and he could circuit-ride his vast Interior judicial division. The judge in turn appointed commissioners in local precincts. These officers, assisted by marshals and deputies, performed the functions of justices of the peace, recorders, probate judges, and coroners. Except for the most serious cases, which were reserved to the division judge, the commissioners exercised magisterial power, combining judicial, administrative, and enforcement authorities. Given this latitude and the fact that commissioners served without salary, "living off the land" by fees collected, the commissioner system was subject to abuse and generally came under heavy attack. But in remote parts like the upper Koyukuk, the commissioner was usually appointed from the community and subject to its constraining pressures. In its better guise, where temptations were few—as in the Koyukuk precinct—the commissioner system had the advantages of immediacy and proper scale for frontier conditions (Gruening 1954; Nichols 1963).

• • •

The theme of the nation's neglect of Alaska has been pervasive through its history, as has its opposing theme: the tyrannical meddling of the federal government in affairs that only Alaskans can comprehend. Because much that follows in this narrative is illuminated by these arguments and the documentation they produced, an interlude of discussion is useful for perspective. Always there have been those who, for economic reasons, opposed Alaska's evolution beyond colonial status. Often representing moneyed interests from "Outside"—Seattle, New York, London—they sought freedom to harvest or extract wealth from this natural storehouse without interference from strong regional or local governments, which would tax and regulate their enterprises and conserve resources for public purposes. At the same time, these interests wanted what is today called infrastructure assistance from government—ports, roads, and the like. And they knew how to match their interests with those of local boomers, who also wanted that kind of assistance and little interference. Others, local to the land, wanted freedom from all these forces, governmental and economic. And finally, settlers, missionaries, and community builders simply wanted Alaska to progress from wilderness to civilization along the same path followed in the western territories and states.

Compounding and complementing these strands were others of climate, geography, and extremes of seasonal and cyclic economy. These factors hindered development of stable populations and foiled unitary solutions applicable across the many Alaskas.

Alfred Hulse Brooks and Ernest Gruening, among many others, spoke eloquently to the neglect thesis. Jeannette Paddock Nichols, who watched much history happen as secretary to Judge (and later Delegate to Congress) James Wickersham, recounted the "complexity and perplexity" of the natural and human combinations during Alaska's first half-century under United States rule.

With a bow to all of these, a later historian, Ted C. Hinckley, qualified the neglect thesis by asserting that Congress was probably as well informed and generous respecting Alaska as it had been with the western territories, particularly given the accelerating pace of the nation's domestic and international affairs as the nineteenth century became the twentieth. He concludes that until 1940, Alaska, with its remote and tiny population, was simply irrelevant to the nation's central concerns.

Even the Klondike and subsequent Alaskan gold rushes proved ephemeral in real terms, however enduring as romance. Because Alaska lacks the holding power of agricultural and commercial alternatives to mining, as in California and Colorado, the gold excitement could not remedy the population deficiency. Because of this deficiency, everything else suffered. And because Alaskans could not solve this problem, they blamed their government. Nor could pioneer or boomer have expected to subdue Alaska in short order. Even the trans-Mississippi West, with its overland trails and later railroads, its advancing frontiers of settlement, and the attractions of the West Coast and the Pacific trade, had taken generations to transform. The weekly steamship to an Alaska hardly populated except for a cluster of towns in the southeast Panhandle could not compare.

Hinckley (1968) credits military invasion and the application of technological might to military strategy and natural resources for Alaska's arrival in the national consciousness. He suggests that Alaska could not be prematurely unlocked by a few pioneers and symbolic gestures from government. Larger combinations were needed. In the big business combinations of the early twentieth century—the Alaska Commercial Company trading monopoly, the Morgan-Guggenheim copper and transportation syndicate—he glimpses the future that would happen, when ready, whatever the intervening rhetoric or Congressional mood. The combination of modern technology, militant geopolitics, and big oil became that future—overcoming distance, terrain, climate, and all. These things, not tracts and speeches, finally wrenched the door off Seward's Icebox.

If Hinckley is right in terms of structuring forces and trends, then Alaska in its entirety must be viewed as a fringe area until the threat and actuality of Japanese invasion moved it to at least the wings of the national stage. Only then did a critical mass of population, investment, and political concern, extended by post-World War II strategies and oil, begin to counter the dominance of empty distance and high latitude.

Ernest Gruening noted the population problem in his history of neglect. As the number of Alaskans declined after the 1900-era gold rushes, the populations of western states and territories continued to increase. The northern giant was slipping back into dormancy. He attributed this to a national policy designed to thwart Alaska's evolution into the family of states. Neglect of Alaska's constitutional and political aspirations for representative government, locking up of the coal lands, withdrawal of virtually all timbered areas into national forests, and failure to extend to Alaska railroad subsidies of the sort that opened up the West were critical elements of that thwarting policy. In Gruening's view, neither the 1906 law that recognized Alaska as a territory and authorized a nonvoting delegate to Congress, nor the Home Rule Act of 1912, providing limited self-government by a territorial legislature, could counter that national policy.

Hinckley sees less a designed policy in all this and more a back-burner reality based on geography, demographics, and the economics of resource development. Resource development in Alaska still requires exceptional richness, gigantism, or strategic necessity to warrant the costs of high-latitude exploitation. In this view, national policy, such as it was, did not cause Alaska's condition but merely reflected it.

This thesis, applied with the aid of a microscope, illuminates the history of the far north camps and communities within our study area. Remote, isolated by lack of roads and fluctuating rivers, marginally productive of gold—until recently its only commercially attractive resource—this was an area that could not evolve beyond its frontier beginnings. It was a holdout until just yesterday of the 1900-era Alaska that once raised such howls of national neglect and is now nostalgically yearned for (Brooks 1953; Gruening 1954; Hinckley 1968).

• • •

In the summer of 1903 a subcommittee of the Senate Committee on Territories visited Alaska to assess conditions there and take testimony from its citizens. Of greatest import to the far-north miners were the interrelated problems of attenuated transportation and the high cost of supplies. The next most perplexing matter was the unrestricted use of power-of-attorney in locating mining claims. This provision of mining law allowed fast-stepping speculators, "pencil miners," to grab up whole groups of claims, crowding out real miners on the ground. As a side effect of this practice, the thin-spread judicial system staggered under a mounting press of mining litigation (Nichols 1963).

Partly as a result of the subcommittee's visit, which highlighted transportation problems, a limited system of winter pack trails and wagon roads would be developed, beginning in 1905, by the Army-run Alaska Road Commission. But not until 1912 did Congress finally impose restrictions on the number of claims a person could stake on one creek (Gruening 1954).

For many years, Koyukuk and other far-north miners benefited little from the roads and trails program, whose limited funding in a vast territory lacking "a single public wagon road over which vehicles can be drawn summer or winter" (U.S. Congress 1904, 9) naturally gravitated to richer, more populous mining districts south of the Yukon and around Nome. In time a rudimentary system of winter pack trails and shelter cabins would reach north of the Yukon to the upper Koyukuk and Chandalar districts, and east from Kotzebue Sound. Still later, a short, isolated road system would serve the Koyukuk's Middle Fork communities and camps. But throughout the historic mining period from the late 1890s to the 1930s, and indeed until the 1970s, no road suitable for all-weather transport of bulk goods and heavy equipment connected the far-north districts with the outer world. Small-scale steamboating and scows on rivers intermittently navigable, with limited overland transport on winter trails, as reported in the 1903 testimony, remained a fair description of far-north logistics until North Slope oil development began. The airplane would ameliorate personal isolation after 1925. But not until World War II and

Stone cabin on Big Creek headwaters, Chandalar District, 1924. J. B. Mertie photo 947, USGS Historical Photo Library, Denver.

Creecy's open-cut operation on Big Squaw Creek, Chandalar District, showing flume and miners, 1924. J. B. Mertie photo 949, USGS Historical Photo Library, Denver.

its aftermath would significant air freighting begin. And when it did, it largely overflew the far-north mining districts en route to North Slope defense installations and oil-exploration camps.

This situation shaped the history of the region. Thus did the upper rivers and central mountains form a sort of island deep within the mainland. Small in population and lacking any but marginal economic attractions, the region could not swing the political weight to achieve a transportation breakthrough. In due course, after the sequence of localized gold strikes ended about 1916, the region became a sociocultural island as well, its population slowly eroding as old timers emigrated and died to be replaced only in part by new recruits.

Of all the government enterprises flowing from the gold rush, the one most apparent and of greatest interest to the folk of the upper country was the work of the U.S. Geological Survey. Beginning with its first formal expedition to Alaska in 1895, and emphatically from 1898 on, in response to the gold rush, the survey adopted the role of the nation's trailblazer in Alaska. It stressed practical information on geography, routes and conditions of travel, and the realities rather than the hopes and false lures of economic geology. The objectives of this service-oriented mission were two: to help the serious prospectors and miners who were opening up the country and to caution and guide inexperienced stampeders. Alfred Hulse Brooks first came to Alaska in 1898 with these objectives already paramount. Shortly thereafter, appointed head of the survey's Alaska work, he assembled and supervised a corps of volunteer geologists, topographers, and other scientists that conducted mapping and geological investigations throughout the known and unknown regions of Alaska. Brooks was himself a field scientist of the first order, always encouraging his men to combine practical geology with "researches which advance the knowledge of basic principles" (Smith 1926).

The reports of the survey men comprise the best early documentation for the upper country. Details of the country abound even in the published USGS Bulletins; the original field notebooks are richer still. Here, among sketch maps and marginal notes, with the occasional pressed remains of a pesky mosquito dead nearly a century, are the names, places, and exploits of those early days.

The survey people got on well with the prospectors and miners. Like everyone else before the airplane, they traveled light and tough with dog teams, pack horses, and canoes—often for months, through the whole round of seasons. They all shared information with one another. The prospector knew the local country; the geologist added science to the miner's practical knowledge. The fellowship of far places shines in these notebooks, along with some of the oddities. Usually, prospectors had been there, wherever it was, first. But prospectors did not make maps and geological assessments for other people. The survey did, producing in aggregate a splendid system of public and scientific knowledge about Alaska's geography and geology (Brooks 1953; Sherwood 1965; Smith and Mertie 1930).[1]

In a special publication, the USGS (1899) summarized existing knowledge of travel routes and mining prospects in Alaska. By providing authentic data and maps, the USGS aimed to counter a burgeoning Gold Rush literature, more often than not inaccurate and promotional, that was luring stampeders to disappointment and disaster.

The section on the Koyukuk River derived from Lt. Henry Allen's 1885 exploration and subsequent scraps of information from prospectors. It warned that above the 67th degree of latitude "no surveys have been made," a reference to Allen's northernmost attainment on the John River. Beyond that point, the sketchy map could not be compared in accuracy "to the results of even the roughest surveys which have been made elsewhere in the Territory" (USGS 1899, 88). The Kowak or Kobuk River description cited Lt. J. C. Cantwell's explorations and, again, fragmentary data from prospectors and miners. Despite hints of gold throughout the Kobuk drainage, no well-authenticated finds of gold had been reported. Brief mention of the Noatak River relied on S. B. McLenegan's 1885

As to claims and their regulation, the Koyukuk precinct had made local laws under the Miners' Code clause. Claims were 1,320 feet long, following the creek, and 660 feet wide. The Koyukukers allowed only one claim per man per creek or bar.

Filing the claim entailed going to the recorder, i.e., the commissioner, within 90 days of locating and staking the claim to file the notice of location. This notice described the claim by metes and bounds, and gave the owner's name and the date of location. The first claim on a creek was designated discovery claim, with subsequent claims numbered 1, 2, 3, etc., above and below discovery. McKenzie estimated that $225,000 in gold came out of the Koyukuk in 1902, but that had been a dry year with little water for sluicing. He forecast three or four times that return in 1903 (U.S. Congress 1904, 103).

Ruby Creek Mine in Cosmos Hills near Shungnak of Kobuk River, 1910. P. S. Smith photo 522, USGS Historical Photo Library, Denver.

exploration and noted that in 1898 a party of prospectors had ascended the river 250 miles in rowboats but found no gold. As the 1899 season began, this pittance was the state of public knowledge about the upper country; the only solid information dated from the original explorations of the 1880s (USGS 1899).

Members of the Mendenhall party pulling a canoe through riffles on the way to the Kobuk River in 1901. W. C. Mendenhall photo 182, USGS Historical Photo Library, Denver.

Even as the USGS guide was being assembled for printing, the first of the USGS far-north expeditions got underway. In the period 1899–1911, six major USGS reconnaissances traversed the upper country, mapping its topography and general geology, and defining the patterns of economic geology so important to prospectors and miners.

These pioneering expeditions, mostly during the "open season" up swift rivers and across endless stretches of soft, wet country, hauling bulky survey and photographic gear, must be viewed with greatest respect. The survey network now extended from the Yukon to the Arctic Ocean, from the Chandalar to Kotzebue Sound. In human terms, a tradition of indomitable wilderness endeavor and self-reliance had been established. The esprit of the survey men was legendary. In the amazing heat of arctic summer, alternating with chilling rains and freezing nighttime temperatures, besieged by mosquitoes and fatigued by constant setting up and breaking of camp, climbing rugged mountains to investigate exposed formations, they yet produced exquisite maps and finely wrought drawings of geological sections. Sweat and human blood from sated insects blur the old notebooks, but the gathering of data went on unabated.

USGS party lining boat up Alatna
River, approaching Alatna-
Noatak portage, 1911. P. S. Smith
photo 753, USGS Historical Photo
Library, Denver.

As the miners discovered, and as the USGS geologists explained, gold
mining in the southern foothills of the central Arctic Mountains[2] traces
a belt of gold-bearing schist that forms an arc from the upper Chandalar
across the Koyukuk forks and then cuts southwesterly across the Wild,
John, and Alatna rivers. The schist is bounded on the north by a massive
shield of limestone that covers the gold-bearing rocks and cuts off mining. Spotted through this schist belt are domes and mountain masses containing lode gold in quartz lenses and veins. Fractured and glaciated in the
past, these mountains are eroded and drained by streams that transport
fragments of gold released from the mother quartz down valley, where
they are deposited in the rock and gravel of the high gulches and in the
sands and silts of the lower valleys. In the higher creeks coarse gold is
found; farther downstream the gold gets progressively finer.

USGS pack train on tributary of
upper Kobuk River, 1910. H. M.
Eakin photo 116, USGS Historical
Photo Library, Denver.

Mendenhall party dragging canoes through shallows of Helpmejack Creek, near Alatna Portage, 1901. W. C. Mendenhall photo 215, USGS Historical Photo Library, Denver.

Sluice boxes and gin-pole at Vern Watts' claims on Hammond River. Robert Marshall photo. Courtesy of the Bancroft Library, University of California, Berkeley.

Chapter Five

The Civilization of the North

As early as 1912, gold mining on the upper rivers had largely settled into a subsistence and modest-strike pattern that would not change significantly until World War II and its aftermath of gathering technological momentum. Perturbations and promotions—such as the Hammond River boom of 1911–15, the partial exodus for outside wages during World War I, and the attempt to mechanize mining on the Hammond in the Twenties—only temporarily modified this pattern. The hard facts of economic geology and logistical isolation determined this decline in active mine development.

Shoveling in at Vern Watts' claims on Hammond River. Robert Marshall photo. Courtesy of the Bancroft Library, University of California, Berkeley.

For the remainder of the historic period, the center of mining activity would be the upper Koyukuk, especially the Middle Fork and its tributary creeks from the Coldfoot vicinity north to the Hammond River–Gold Creek diggings. Wiseman, strategically located between these points as well as a gateway to the Nolan Creek and scattered North Fork mines, emerged as a supply and social center for the extended camp. Trails also connected Wiseman to outpost mines on Wild Lake and Bettles River.

Eastward, the Chandalar district struggled on: the Sulzer operation glimmering fainter and a few placer miners probing the creeks east of Chandalar Lake. Bettles continued as a relay point for Wiseman and directly supplied small operations on South Fork and on Wild and John rivers.

Identified as the Detroit Mining Company site on Hammond River by Harry Leonard. Robert Marshall photo. Courtesy of the Bancroft Library, University of California, Berkeley.

Upper Kobuk mining stayed pretty much as Lewis Loyd described it in 1909: quiet and limited to streams draining the Cosmos Hills. Stories of lost mines invited occasional prospectors to the upper reaches of Alatna and Noatak, where colors, but not pay, kept the legends alive.

Increasingly as the years passed by, gold mining became a kind of medium for a way of life. It shifted from being the end of human endeavor to becoming a means, joined with others like hunting and trapping. An occasional modest fortune taken from some deep-hole pocket on Nolan or Hammond kept gold in force as the ostensible reason for it all. But the community of people meant more to most of those people than the driblets of gold that allowed them to stay on as members of the community. That this evolution was happening already before World War I has

The Nolan Camp in its heyday in 1909, showing boiler cabins, gin-poles, and dumps in operation. A. G. Maddren photo 37, USGS Historical Photo Library, Denver.

A complete drift placer plant in operation at Nolan, showing miners' tents and cabins, left, gin-pole and dump, center, boiler cabin and stacked wood fuel, right, with water flume in background. A. G. Maddren photo 40 of 1909. USGS Historical Photo Library, Denver.

been documented ("I seem to leave my heart here when I go out"). That it gained strength after the war, on through the Thirties, was documented powerfully by Robert Marshall—by the friends he made, whose lives and words told him and us why they stayed.

In this historical perspective, gold is transmuted, as by some powerful alchemy, into something more valuable than gold. The theme of this history changes accordingly. The mining story continues as a core foundation for economics and stated motivations. But building upon this foundation,

Nolan Creek drift mining plant, with Smith Creek Dome in background. Robert Marshall photo. Courtesy of the Bancroft Library, University of California, Berkeley.

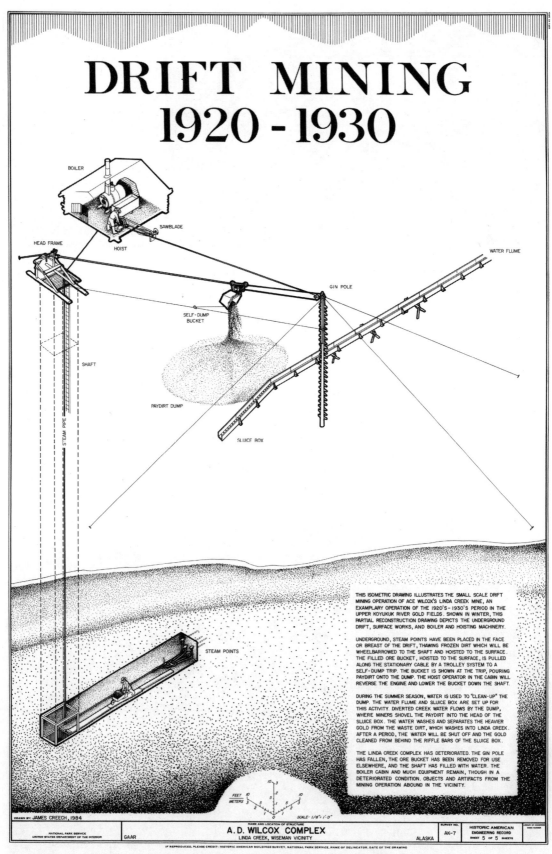

DRIFT MINING
1920 - 1930

BOILER

SAWBLADE

HEAD FRAME

HOIST

WATER FLUME

SELF-DUMP BUCKET

GIN POLE

SHAFT

STEAM PIPE

PAYDIRT DUMP

SLUICE BOX

STEAM POINTS

THIS ISOMETRIC DRAWING ILLUSTRATES THE SMALL SCALE DRIFT MINING OPERATION OF ACE WILCOX'S LINDA CREEK MINE, AN EXAMPLARY OPERATION OF THE 1920'S-1930'S PERIOD IN THE UPPER KOYUKUK RIVER GOLD FIELDS. SHOWN IN WINTER, THIS PARTIAL RECONSTRUCTION DRAWING DEPICTS THE UNDERGROUND DRIFT, SURFACE WORKS, AND BOILER AND HOISTING MACHINERY.

UNDERGROUND, STEAM POINTS HAVE BEEN PLACED IN THE FACE OR BREAST OF THE DRIFT, THAWING FROZEN DIRT WHICH WILL BE WHEELBARROWED TO THE SHAFT AND HOISTED TO THE SURFACE. THE FILLED ORE BUCKET, HOISTED TO THE SURFACE, IS PULLED ALONG THE STATIONARY CABLE BY A TROLLEY SYSTEM TO A SELF-DUMP TRIP. THE BUCKET IS SHOWN AT THE TRIP, POURING PAYDIRT ONTO THE DUMP. THE HOIST OPERATOR IN THE CABIN WILL REVERSE THE ENGINE AND LOWER THE BUCKET DOWN THE SHAFT.

DURING THE SUMMER SEASON, WATER IS USED TO "CLEAN-UP" THE DUMP. THE WATER FLUME AND SLUICE BOX ARE SET UP FOR THIS ACTIVITY. DIVERTED CREEK WATER FLOWS BY THE DUMP, WHERE MINERS SHOVEL THE PAYDIRT INTO THE HEAD OF THE SLUICE BOX. THE WATER WASHES AND SEPARATES THE HEAVIER GOLD FROM THE WASTE DIRT, WHICH WASHES INTO LINDA CREEK. AFTER A PERIOD, THE WATER WILL BE SHUT OFF AND THE GOLD CLEANED FROM BEHIND THE RIFFLE BARS OF THE SLUICE BOX.

THE LINDA CREEK COMPLEX HAS DETERIORATED. THE GIN POLE HAS FALLEN, THE ORE BUCKET HAS BEEN REMOVED FOR USE ELSEWHERE, AND THE SHAFT HAS FILLED WITH WATER. THE BOILER CABIN AND MUCH EQUIPMENT REMAIN, THOUGH IN A DETERIORATED CONDITION. OBJECTS AND ARTIFACTS FROM THE MINING OPERATION ABOUND IN THE VICINITY.

FEET
METERS

SCALE: 1/8" 1'-0"

DRAWN BY: JAMES CREECH, 1984

NATIONAL PARK SERVICE
UNITED STATES DEPARTMENT OF THE INTERIOR

GAAR

NAME AND LOCATION OF STRUCTURE
A. D. WILCOX COMPLEX
LINDA CREEK, WISEMAN VICINITY

ALASKA

SURVEY NO.
AK-7

HISTORIC AMERICAN
ENGINEERING RECORD
SHEET 5 OF 5 SHEETS

IF REPRODUCED, PLEASE CREDIT: HISTORIC AMERICAN BUILDINGS SURVEY, NATIONAL PARK SERVICE, NAME OF DELINEATOR, DATE OF THE DRAWING

Drift Mining 1920–1930, by James Creech, 1984. A. D. Wilcox Drift Mine, Historic American Engineering Record illustration.

Bettles about 1930. Robert Marshall photo. Courtesy of the Bancroft Library, University of California, Berkeley.

even requiring its extension, rises an edifice of many components. Its elaborations are social, intercultural, scientific, and aesthetic. People—Native and non-Native, resident and visitor—enrich a society of a few hundred folks profoundly integrated with landscapes that produce pay not only of the gold kind, but also of human mettle and appreciation.

Wiseman

Wiseman's heyday lasted about five years, from 1911 to 1915. It was fueled by continuing production from Nolan Creek Valley and the $1 million taken from deep placers on Hammond River, starting with Vern Watts' discovery in 1911. Wilderness preservationist Bob Marshall's history of Wiseman during this period is heavily loaded with whiskey and prostitutes. Of 400 tons of freight brought to Wiseman in the peak year of 1915, fully 60 tons was booze—400 pounds (including kegs, bottles, and packing) for each of the 300 whites and 75 Natives living in the area. That year fourteen prostitutes plied their trade.

One miner, John Bowman, reputedly blew $11,000 on a prostitute in a two-week period. A reformer gave $2,500 to a "soiled dove" to improve herself with an education, but skeptics urged that "she knew too much for him already" (Marshall 1991, 43).

This flurry of high pay and high living ended quickly. Exhausted bonanzas, World War I wages in the States, and Prohibition hustled the boomers outside and quenched the appetites of those permanents who had strayed. Population and economy declined precipitately to low levels: less than 100 whites, with gold production less than $100,000 annually (much less than that some years) for the entire district (Marshall 1991).[1]

Wiseman from across the Middle Fork, Koyukuk. Robert Marshall photo. Courtesy of the Bancroft Library, University of California, Berkeley.

Those who were left tightened up a notch or two and turned to the business at hand: keeping their community alive and functioning. One of the old-timers, Albert Ness, put it this way to Marshall:

> Always, after any stampede, it's not the successes who build up the country. They go home with the stakes they made. It's the failures who stay on, decade after decade, and establish homes (Marshall 1991, 47).

In 1911, Wiseman boasted two stores, the N.C. Co. and Plummer's General Merchandise, as well as a number of roadhouses. Cabins and other business houses had been disassembled and moved from Coldfoot to Wiseman. The Alaska Road Commission trail was extended from Caro to the Middle Fork via the South Fork and Slate Creek. The main trail from Tanana closely paralleled Henry Allen's route to the Kanuti,

The old roadhouse at Wiseman, with the 1929 'Cat hauling logs. Robert Marshall photo. Courtesy of the Bancroft Library, University of California, Berkeley.

then ran upriver via Allakaket, Bettles, and Coldfoot to Wiseman—a distance of 273 miles. These trails were strictly winter dog-team trails for many years.

Martin Slisco's Roadhouse, Wiseman. From the Alaska Sportsman Collection, Archives, University of Alaska, Fairbanks.

In 1912, a Nolan Creek miner put in a telephone system that eventually connected Wiseman with Nolan Creek and Hammond River. This was a great convenience, for these next-door neighbors were still a hard day's round-trip apart. Now the far-spread camp could set a date for a dance, alert its members of arrival of important mail or supplies, or mobilize for emergency (Marshall 1991; U.S. Bureau of Outdoor Recreation 1977).

Caro on the Chandalar River at Flat Creek. J. B. Mertie photo 930 of 1924. USGS Historical Photo Library, Denver.

In 1918, the people of Wiseman petitioned Territorial Governor Thomas Riggs Jr. for a wireless station. They based their request on Wiseman's position as the largest and most centrally located town "in the heart of the present mining industry being carried on and developed throughout a vast section of country lying north of the Arctic Circle." Citing the deficiencies of a mail service monthly in its intervals, they prayed further: "The great retarding factor in the present and future development and advancement of this great North Region is the lack of adequate and speedy communication with the outside world" (letters and petition for Wiseman wireless station, Alaska State Archives, Juneau; Marshall 1991).

The School Board met . . . and decided to have a chopping bee at Coldfoot to cut the wood and pile it for the school-house, on Oct. 8. Fifteen men turned out and we cut ten cords of wood and in the evening had a very good dance. . . . We decided to hold a raffle . . . to raise money to have the wood delivered to the school-house and worked up for the stove. The articles donated for the raffle are one Morris chair, one caribou and one crate of potatoes (Daniel Webster Oct. 21, 1921, from Wiseman School District letters, Alaska State Archives, Juneau).

The governor recommended the Wiseman wireless station in his annual report for 1918, and followed up with both the Army Signal Corps and Congressman Sulzer. As it turned out, the wireless station came to Wiseman in 1925, the same year as arrival of the first airplane (Marshall 1991).

On August 13, 1917, Daniel Webster of Wiseman forwarded a petition for a school district to the clerk of the district court in Fairbanks. The clerk, one J. E. Clark, responded testily to Mr. Webster's communication, citing that there were not enough school-age white children. Territorial statutes required a minimum of ten white children for establishment of a school district. The proposed Wiseman district had only eight, plus four children of mixed Japanese and Eskimo descent. Clark returned the petition (Clark to Webster Sept. 17, 1917, in Wiseman School District letter file, Alaska State Archives, Juneau).

Webster—a man of means and reputation in the Koyukuk district, viewed locally as a reincarnation of his famous namesake and ancestor—took the matter up directly with the governor, who took quick action. By letter of February 25, 1918, he counseled the clerk at court:

There are certain equities in the Wiseman case, which have moved me to waive to some extent the strict legal technicality of the law as to "white" children. I cannot bring myself to think that it would be an act of justice . . . to deny a school to eight white children in a community as remote as is Wiseman, when there are sufficient other children of school age . . . to make up the requisite ten (Wiseman School District letter file, Alaska State Archives, Juneau).

In due course, despite further delays brought about by the Alaska attorney general's review of the case, the Wiseman school district was authorized and a school was built in Coldfoot, which was more centrally located, in time for the fall 1919 term. Over the course of the next ten years, the school district faced such challenges as getting a school building erected, trying to get and keep qualified teachers, temporary closures due to reduced enrollment, and lack of funding. Their ally during this time was Lester D. Henderson, Commissioner of Education in Juneau.

For the decade of his tenure, Henderson filled the funding gaps caused by communication lags. He personally attended to emergency supply requests, sending wires to suppliers in the States, arranging steamboat and dog-team relays of supplies thus obtained. He mediated altercations between teachers and parents with letters full of wisdom and the counsels of patience. In return, the people of Wiseman—whose school was a central, perhaps the central, institution attesting their civilized attainments in the wilderness—reciprocated with earnest endeavor and honest employment of Henderson's largesse. Wiseman's decline as a mining camp seems to have unleashed enlightened energies that focused on the school. In truth, beyond personal matters and social affairs, such energies had few other targets.

Relations Between Whites and Natives

The presence of Eskimo children in the Wiseman school is part of a larger acculturation story that evolved parallel with the mining booms and their aftermath. Relationships between Natives and whites in the upper country varied from place to place—partly because some Native groups were more receptive than others to Euro-American ideas and technology, and partly because the geographic spread of the region isolated and insulated some groups more than others. The core of the region was far beyond the easy transportation and dominant white populations that enhance the influence of missionaries, teachers, and government agents. Thus, their ability to impose ideas and dictate cultural change was inhibited at the center, greater at the periphery along the Yukon and the Arctic Coast. Many Natives did respond positively to the jobs and technology brought by miners and traders, and to the ideas of missionaries and educators. But in the upper country the Natives exercised a large element of choice in these responses.

Archdeacon Hudson Stuck understood the need for accommodation between Euro-American and Native values. To his missionaries at St. John's he conveyed the philosophy that "The wise teacher, the wise missionary, will not seek to keep boys at school who should be out in the woods serving their apprenticeship."

In 1917 he preached to the assembled people of Alatna and Allakaket:

Reading and writing are good things, and the other things the school teaches are good things, and that is why we put the school here to teach them, but knowing how to make a living on the river or in the woods, winter and summer, is a very much better thing, a very much more important thing, and something that the school cannot teach and the fathers must. Let us have both if we can, but whatever happens don't let your boys grow up without learning to take care of themselves and of their wives and children by and by.

It is recorded that old Chief Moses came up to him and thanked him, saying that "he was always trying to tell his people the same thing" (Stuck 1920, 38).

Natives of Noatak Village on Noatak River. W. R. Smith photo 199 of 1925. USGS Historical Photo Library, Denver.

As previously noted, the general lifestyle in the far north camps and communities allowed little distinction between Natives and whites based on wealth or hierarchies of work; particularly after 1915, most people lived pretty much alike, combining cash and subsistence economies to make ends meet. Moreover, the upper Koyukuk mining area lacked the wealth of furs that, in richer places, segregated Natives into a fur trapping-subsistence economy. Sparse population and marginal resources drew Natives and whites together in a mutually supportive blend of lifestyle and labor. Isolation buffered change, slowing and diluting the directed change of outside agents—giving Native people the chance to pick and choose, to balance change with ongoing elements of traditional life. And since most of the whites in the upper country concentrated on their mining and commercial enterprises, only incidentally harvesting wildlife, there was minimal competition on the land between them and traditionally oriented Native people. This allowed Natives to be opportunistic: they could take jobs with the whites, they could hunt and fish, or they could do both.

What emerged was an upper country society in which social distinctions between Natives and whites were not absent, but were muted because of continuing interdependence, including frequent intermarriage. Many Natives became proficient workers, and some became partners with whites in mining, transportation, and mercantile enterprises. At the same time, because these "imported" activities occurred seasonally or at marginal levels and could not sustain families year-round, traditional hunting and fishing expeditions kept families close to the land. Children, accompanying their parents, learned traditional ways of travel, harvest, and survival. Thus recruited, they carried on those traditions.

In 1927, George Huey, a community pillar, proclaimed: "We have the best little camp in the North today. . . . There is not a lawyer, a preacher or a doctor in the camp, and we don't need 'em" (quoted in *Alaska Weekly*, Nov. 4, 1927, 5).

The upshot of these combinations on the south flank of the divide was a more comfortably blended Native-white society than that found in most parts of Alaska. Out of this functional context evolved Native people competent in both modern and traditional ways.

The Nunamiut people, north of the divide, had a different history. Gold mining played only a minor role in their home territory. Because of the attractions of coastal trading and the decline of caribou after the turn of the century, the Nunamiut began to leave the mountains, a few going to the Kobuk and to Wiseman, but most of them relocating along the Arctic Coast. When some families began returning to the high Brooks Range in the mid-1930s, they came back to an area and a pattern of life that would remain isolated from steady white influences until about 1950.

Thus, whether in the societal combinations of the upper Kobuk and Koyukuk rivers, or in the high mountain valleys of Nunamiut country, the buffering effects of isolation would help perpetuate strong traditional components in both Eskimo and Indian societies. These were certainly not pre-1850 people. All of them, including the Nunamiut during their coastal interlude, had absorbed large doses of Euro-American disruption, culture, and technology. But relative to more accessible regions, Native people of the upper country had more time to adapt under less intense acculturative pressure.

Eskimo dog team and sled near Noatak Village. W. R. Smith photo 202 of 1925. USGS Historical Photo Library, Denver.

Among the whites who shared the upper country with the Natives during this period, there was more of a live-and-let-live attitude than usual. Most of these whites were not over-socialized themselves, and were, like many of the Natives, far removed from steady institutional pressures to become so. As a result, the usual progressive attitudes of the day respecting material and spiritual uplift applied only marginally to most resident whites, some of whom had rejected any rigorous adherence to them. Missionary impulses at Allakaket (Episcopal), Shungnak and Noatak (Friends), and among the Nunamiut (Presbyterian) spread thinly across a vast area, competing with, rather than utterly dominating and erasing, traditional views and values. As with so many other Euro-American approaches to

this marginal country, religion had to settle for half a loaf, in a kind of partnership with place and people.

Eskimo children at the mission swing, Shungnak on the Kobuk River, 1917. H. M. Eakin photo, USGS Historical Photo Library, Denver.

• • •

Biographies of Arctic Coast and upper Kobuk Eskimos describe the early migrations of members of these societies into the upper Koyukuk mining area. Long-established trade patterns and travel routes between these people and the Koyukon Indians had set the scene for these movements. The Koyukon, having withdrawn southward toward river trading posts, had effectively vacated the country north of Bettles. In this unexploited territory, game abounded relative to the Kobuk, where caribou populations were crashing. Arctic coast Eskimos were drawn and pushed toward Koyukuk game and mining camps by ties to Japanese traders and the weakening whaling industry on the coast. Opportunities on the Koyukuk included market hunting for the miners and wage jobs in mining and freighting (Will 1982).

Subsistence activities had to coincide with seasonal availability of wild resources. And so it remains today: In the mixed cash-subsistence economy of village Alaska, wage jobs often conflict with wild-harvest seasons. One cannot be two places at once, so a division of labor allows some people to hunt and fish, others to work at a wage job. After the season is over, wild

Village of Alatna on Koyukuk River. J. B. Mertie photo 1061 of March 1924. USGS Historical Photo Library, Denver.

In a late-life interview, Frank Tobuk commented on the difficulty white people had pronouncing Eskimo names. His father's name, Duvak, became Tobuk. Frank's own Eskimo name, Dalakaduk, became Aklanuk, but with customary politeness he acquiesced, "That's close enough, I guess" (Madison and Yarber 1980, 24).

harvest and store-bought goods are shared. Often these roles rotate so everyone in the family gets time on the land.

There are numerous stories that illustrate how Native life has changed over the years. Take Frank Tobuk, born in 1900 on Hunt Fork of the John River while his family was out hunting. Frank's father worked for the steamboats for a while at Bettles, mostly longshoring in the summer. In winter and spring the family followed traditional hunting and fishing rounds. Then the family moved to a Kobuk Eskimo camp called Alatna, at the mouth of that river, for better fishing. After the Episcopal Church established a mission across the river from Alatna, and the Tobuk children began attending school there, the old patterns changed. Frank recalled that once the mission came, "our family didn't travel out to winter camp or spring camp much any more. Mostly all we ate was fish and rabbits."

The mission of Allakaket. Robert Marshall photo. Courtesy of the Bancroft Library, University of California, Berkeley.

The missionaries at Allakaket. Robert Marshall photo. Courtesy of the Bancroft Library, University of California, Berkeley.

One of Tishu Ulen's earliest memories was a trip to fish camp at Kotzebue with her mother and uncle. At that time the town was just an assortment of drab cabins. The place to be was down on the beach, where tent camps of Eskimos from Kivalina, Noatak, Kobuk, and Seward Peninsula villages—even some from Siberia—lined the beach for miles, each group in its own established camping place. (Even today these distinct fish camps still line the beach south of Kotzebue.) Tishu's mother, a woman noted for assertive character, even irascibility, would not stand for the missionaries' attempts to stop Native dancing. She, in Tishu's words, "jumped the hired Eskimo police" who tried to enforce religious restrictions and curfews, and the dances went on (English 1983, 98).

Kaypuk, Nakuk, and Mary English (Tishu Ulen's mother). Robert Marshall photo. Courtesy of the Bancroft Library, University of California, Berkeley.

No big game in Alatna then. Dinook (his mother) and Tobuk wanted us to be in school so we were tied up. Can't go nowhere" (Madison and Yarber 1980, 24).

Scientific Studies

Since the early explorations, only the geologists of the USGS had viewed the central Brooks Range through scientific eyes. Even for them, pure science remained subordinate to basic mining geology and reconnaissance mapping. Alaska's more accessible regions had attracted biologists, paleontologists, vulcanologists, glaciologists, and ethnologists, but the upper country remained, in most contexts, a neglected region.

Broader scientific investigations in this mountain fastness awaited some functional stimulus. The mixing of imported reindeer with the native caribou of Alaska provided a small nudge in that direction. Modern biological studies began in the central Brooks Range with the arrival of the Murie brothers, Olaus and Adolph, during the winter of 1922–1923. Olaus had been hired by Dr. Edward W. Nelson, chief of the U.S. Biological Survey and an old Alaska hand himself, to study the relationship between wild caribou and domestic reindeer.

At the brink of the mountains, Olaus looked back on December 21, 1922, at the barrens they had just crossed:

... wide, almost level stretches of tundra and gently sloping plains. These opens somehow impressed me profoundly. I wanted to linger and assimilate the full beauty of them. I do not know in what it consists, the charm of it all. Perhaps the dog teams trotting along, threading a ribbon trail across it, belonged in the picture. I thought of herds of caribou dotting such a scene. Certainly the wildness of it and the expanse of it seemed to require some wide-ranging animals and perhaps therein lay its charm for me. I seemed to want to roam over these plains myself, like the caribou, and feed on lichens, face the winds, and travel on and on (O. Murie 1973, 131–32).

Reindeer had been introduced to Alaska from Siberia by Presbyterian missionary Sheldon Jackson in 1892 to provide a stable food supply for Native people. Spreading from the Nome region, reindeer herds became an important staple or supplement of village food supplies, with one herd proximate to the upper country of this study based at Shungnak from 1907 to the early 1940s. Reindeer, a smaller and less robust animal than the native caribou, tended to join caribou as they passed by on migration. Dr. Nelson feared the effects on caribou of cross-breeding with the inferior domestic deer. He wanted scientific data on caribou ranges and migration patterns so reindeer-industry regulations could be designed to keep the two varieties of deer apart (Foote 1966; A. Murie 1961; O. Murie 1935, 1973; Stern 1980). In his summary report, Olaus described the Alaska-Yukon caribou as primarily a mountain animal, despite its seasonal resort to lowlands. He showed that areas of caribou concentration "practically outline the main divides between river systems" (O. Murie 1935, 50). The mingling of the Yukon-Tanana plateau herd and the Brooks Range herd, which at that time migrated south along the Koyukuk-Chandalar divide, "takes place by means of the only mountainous routes available—near Rampart, where more or less rugged topography reaches the Yukon from both sides" (O. Murie 1935, 50). His recording of Eskimo and Indian information on caribou population and range fluctuations, and responsive Native hunting patterns through the years, was a significant contribution to knowledge of long-term caribou cycles.

Aside from scientific contributions, this trip and one taken two years later by Olaus and his wife, Margaret, provided valuable perspectives, both social and esthetic, about the upper country. Preservationist Bob Marshall read Olaus Murie's writings and later consulted with him and Margaret.

This association helped to lure Marshall to the central Brooks Range. In time it led to a team effort by Marshall and the Muries that resulted in joint development of a wilderness philosophy and eventually, formation of the Wilderness Society in the 1930s.

The Muries' travels took them up the Alatna and Kutuk rivers, to Bettles, then on to Wiseman, where their caribou study actually began. They lived with and learned from Natives they met along the way.

The 1920s and 1930s

Gold mining was a dwindling endeavor that seldom yielded much return for the amount of work involved. Throughout the drainages of the upper Koyukuk were the evidence of mining busts.

Remains of automatic boomer dams and long walls of piled rock begin to hint at the incredible hand-labor required to remove overburden and get to pay gravel and bedrock in these high creeks and gullies. Pockets of gold did exist, and a few ventures paid well. But time after time a season's work on dams, rock piles, and shafts produced $100 or less (Reed 1938).

In the larger view, the Alaska of the 1920s was on the skids and going backward. Ernest Gruening called the period "The Twilit Twenties." He summarized Alaska's problems with a quotation from Isaiah Bowman: "Civilization needs continuity of effort in place" (Gruening 1954, 269). Such was not the condition in most of the territory. The exodus of population caused by exhaustion of easy placers and the high wages of World War I industries was not followed by a new wave of immigrants after the war. Rather, the lusty and expansive economy in the States during the 1920s kept people there. They were not prodded by hardship to seek fulfillment of desperate dreams in the distant territory.

Except for completion of the Alaska Railroad from Seward to Fairbanks, federal programs and initiatives atrophied. Alaska Road Commission appropriations plummeted, and what limited funds did come through had to be used mainly for maintenance. This meant few new Alaska Road Commission roads and trails even in the economically active regions. The upper country remained isolated by lack of any but winter-trail overland connections to the outside world. An internal road-and-trail system completed in the 1920s connected Bettles to Wiseman by winter sled road and Wiseman to the Nolan and Hammond diggings by wagon road. Beginning in the mid-1920s, a significant part of territorial (and local) transportation funding supported construction of airfields under Alaska Road Commission supervision (Alaska Road Commission annual reports 1922–33).[2]

The upper country's rudimentary transportation and communication system, completed by about 1930, would remain essentially unaltered until after World War II. It comprised small steamboats, barges, and scows on the rivers; isolated, internal road-and-trail systems, with tenuous winter

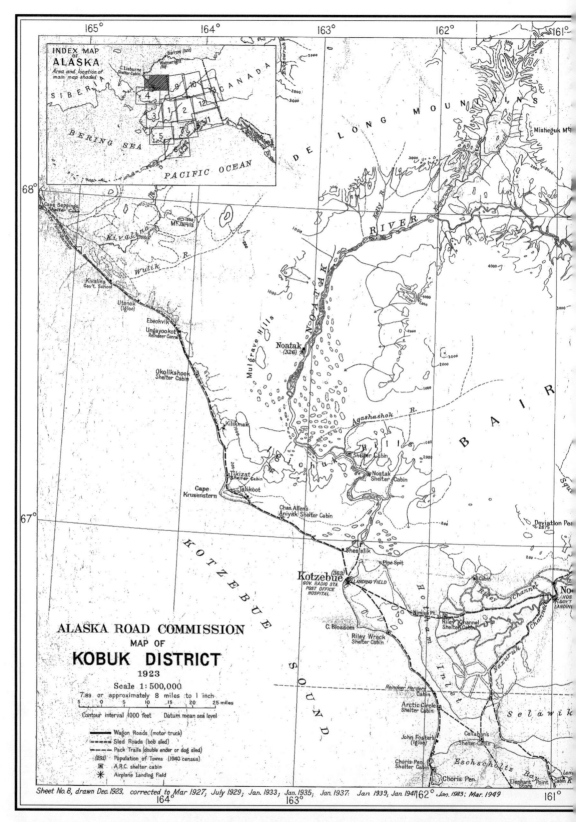

This segment of the Alaska Road Commission's Kobuk District map of 1923 shows the development of transportation and government activities in that district, including a landing field on Dahl Creek to serve the Cosmos Hills miners, post offices at Kobuk and Shungnak villages, and a government school and a wireless station at Shungnak. RG126, Map 20, National Archives.

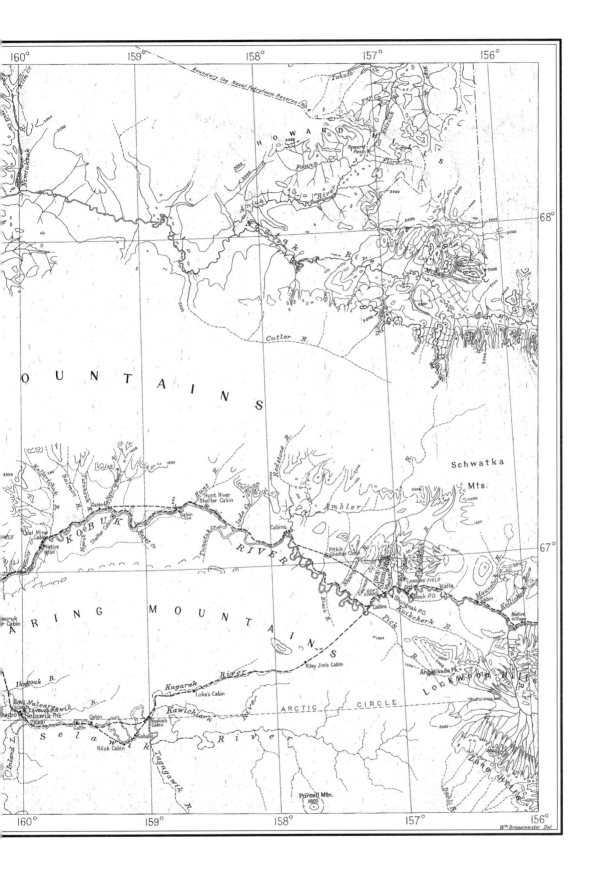

trails marked by occasional shelter cabins extending to the Yukon River and to Kotzebue Sound; and scattered wireless stations and airfields. The winter-trail extensions to the periphery became marginal as the airplane became more prevalent.

Another modification occurred in the Wiseman area when in 1929 Sam Dubin bought a Caterpillar tractor and brought it to Wiseman. Hauling freight on sledges from Bettles to Wiseman and the camps, bringing in wood, and performing all manner of hired jobs for miners, this one machine would in time put Jack White's horse scows out of business and generally replace dogs and manpower for the heavy work of the community.

The Cat made life easier in the way of labor. But in an economy as marginal as the upper Koyukuk's, its economic impact was profound. Teamsters, dog-sled freighters, wood haulers, and mine laborers lost their jobs to the machine. And most of the money grossed by the Cat went outside for imported fuel. So the net result was fewer jobs and less money in the community (interview with Walter Johnson, June 12, 1984; Naske 1986).

Other examples show that machines fitted uneasily into Alaska's frontier conditions and economy. Airplanes put dog-sled mail carriers out of business; and, in contrast to the all-weather mushers, pilots waited when the weather closed down. As the mail carriers faded from the scene, the Alaska Road Commission reduced its maintenance of mail routes and shelter cabins. Trails deteriorated, inhibiting trail travel. Roadhouses that served travelers went out of business. Many people in remote camps were effectively stranded by the neglected trails and the cost of air travel.

Both airplanes and the railroad worked to destroy river commerce and the culture that had grown up around it. Steamboat freighting and riverway trading began to decay. Woodcutters and the scores of camps and roadhouses along the steamboat routes withered on the vine. The sense of community that linked the riverine camps and villages ended when people flew directly to Fairbanks, missing the leisurely visits with friends and trading partners along the steamboat routes. People paid for progress as they embraced it (Goddard 1934; see Webb 1985 for a survey of transportation in the Yukon Basin).

The amazing effects of the Alaska Railroad on Yukon steamboating stemmed in part from a natural phenomenon. Because of the breakup sequence on the Yukon, the lower river stays closed a month longer in the spring than the middle and upper reaches. For this reason, as soon as the railroad was completed to Nenana on the Tanana River, the Koyukuk trading firm of English, Feger, and Dubin shifted from the St. Michael upriver supply route to the Tanana-Yukon downriver route. Others in the Interior, short-seasoned by its fleeting summers, followed this example. In a flash, Nenana on the Tanana became the freighting entrepot for the Interior. Now the mouth of the Yukon could open when it liked.

St. Michael and rows of dry-docked steamboats were soon rotting on the beach (*Alaska Weekly* Mar. 23, 1923; Webb 1985).

The Great Depression brought a flurry of New Deal programs to Alaska, but they hardly touched the upper country. It was out of sight and out of mind, even in Alaska. Moreover, economic depression had been its condition long before 1929, so nothing much had changed.

By executive order in 1933, the price of gold rose from $20.67 to $35 an ounce. This stimulus helped the big mining companies with major dredge operations in the Nome and Fairbanks districts, but could not propel the marginal mines of the upper country out of the doldrums. Its rich paydirt apparently exhausted, its logistics prohibitive for any outside-capital development that might discover new riches, the region continued through the 1930s with the small-scale mining and subsistence pattern set during World War I. World War II produced another exodus for war-industry wages, and gold mining was declared nonessential to the war effort, killing what little remained of the mining economy. But the postwar years did not bring recovery. By 1952, for example, only 21 people lived in Wiseman and the surrounding area (Gruening 1954; Naske 1986).

A general pattern of low-level stability prevailed on the upper Kobuk during the interwar period. Small-scale mining continued in the Cosmos Hills. Commercial, governmental, and missionary activity serving the upper-river Native villages—freighting, trading, health services, and schools—produced a more diversified economy and more stable communities than on the Koyukuk. With improved health services after World War I, a steadily increasing Native population allowed miner-entrepreneurs like the Ferguson family to gradually expand their transportation and trading businesses in the Kobuk-Shungnak area.

A dearth of wage jobs forced most Kobuk Eskimos to depend heavily on fur trapping for cash to buy coveted store goods. When fur prices crashed in the early 1930s, buying of store goods declined. But fur trapping and trading, however paltry the profits, continued anyway, for furs were the sole source of cash for most Native families.

With the coming of hard times, Native people reverted to greater dependence on traditional fishing and hunting, as observed by anthropologist J. Louis Giddings in 1940. Lack of caribou in the Kobuk Valley had earlier forced some Kobukmiut eastward to Koyukuk-Chandalar country. Those who stayed on in the Kobuk villages responded to the lack of big game by taking long hunting trips into the upper Noatak country—an unpopulated area during this period, because the Noatagmiut of the high mountains had gone downriver to Noatak village and most of the other Nunamiut had evacuated to the Arctic coast. Caribou and sheep met meat and clothing needs, and a sideline of wolf, wolverine, and fox trapping brought in a little cash.

The relative diversity of resources on the upper Kobuk and in easily adjacent drainages—minerals, timber, fish, wildlife, and fertile gardening soil—gave the Kobukmiut enough alternatives to weather hard times and make a reasonable living (Foote 1966).

The flexibility and mobility of the Kobuk people during this period exemplifies an ancient pattern. Survival over the centuries in a sparse environment required a constant readiness to shift from one combination of resources to another, wherever those resources might be found. It took a huge geography in the Arctic to find new combinations when starving times hit the home territory. This need for access to alternatives is a living part of the Native heritage today, especially in those traditional villages where subsistence livelihood remains strong. It is a culturally ingrained form of insurance. After all, the modern world has its cycles, too, just like the caribou. Tomorrow may bring hard times. Then the people may have to range widely—over the mountains, down to Selawik, across the portage. Lines on maps do not change this reality.

USGS Surveys

In 1923, the USGS began the last and most ambitious of its old-style explorations in northern Alaska. During his 1901 traverse to the Arctic Ocean, geologist Frank Schrader had found the North Slope to be a great sedimentary basin. Coal deposits and oil seeps and pools had been reported by many others. In 1914, Ernest de Koven Leffingwell, a private scientist who volunteered his findings to the USGS, obtained a sample of petroleum residue from the Smith Bay–Cape Simpson area. Tests of this and other samples from various North Slope locations indicated that the asphalt-based residues came from rocks hard enough to show well-defined structures. Based on these clues, it seemed likely that deep reservoirs of oil might be found. In February 1923, President Warren G. Harding issued an executive order establishing the Naval Petroleum Reserve No. 4

USGS party back-packing and dog-packing in Arctic Alaska. J. B. Mertie photo 1401 of 1926. USGS Historical Photo Library, Denver.

in arctic Alaska. The Navy Department called upon the USGS to provide geographic and geologic information about the new reserve that would allow its proper administration. Immediately, Alfred Hulse Brooks, director of the survey, wrote a paper summarizing the current state of knowledge about the tract and pointing the way for field studies and laboratory research. His charge to the leaders of the multiyear exploration was to provide a regional-framework geology based on extant data and original information gathered in the field. Because so much of the immense tract was unknown, basic

"Camp of Gens de Large Indians near head of Robert Creek on the portage to Koyukuk River." Natives from this camp helped Schrader and his USGS party over the portage. F. C. Schrader photo 335 of 1899. USGS Historical Photo Library, Denver.

Geologist and horse mosquito-proofed in northern Alaska. J. B. Mertie photo 1575 of 1930. USGS Historical Photo Library, Denver.

Smith-Mertie party with eight sleds on way to Killik River winter camp; note nested boats on last sledge. J. B. Mertie photo 1078 of March 1924. USGS Historical Photo Library, Denver.

topographical and geographical studies were an essential part of the project (Brooks 1923; Leffingwell 1919; Reed 1958).

In the 1920s, the laborious overland-and-overwintering expedition style was still the only way to conduct geological reconnaissance and mapping in the Brooks Range and upper Colville area. Not until development of World War II-era fixed-wing aircraft logistics, coupled with the later arrival of the helicopter, could modern transportation match the effectiveness of foot-slogging geology.

All of the experience gained in three decades of survey work in Alaska came to focus during this great exploration from 1923 through 1926. Of the many expeditions that ranged along the Arctic Coast and followed the rivers of the Arctic Slope, the most important for this history was the one led through the Brooks Range passes to the upper Colville drainage by Philip S. Smith and his co-leader J. B. Mertie Jr., because of its scope and scale and because it laid the groundwork for major oil discoveries.

Facing page (top): Aerial view of Killik River Pass through Brooks Range. The Smith-Mertie USGS party of 1924 winter-camped in the area shown and floated down the Killik in the spring. R. M. Chapman photo 368 of 1947. USGS Historical Photo Library, Denver.

Facing page, (bottom): Uncrating canoes in preparation for Colville River survey of Smith-Mertie party. J. B. Mertie photo 1129 of May 1924. USGS Historical Photo Library, Denver.

The Smith-Mertie expedition winter-camped in 1924 at timberline on an upper Alatna tributary, the Unakserak River. During February, members of the party had transported winter and summer supplies and four crated Peterborough freight canoes by sleds and dog teams from Tanana. This wintering strategy gave them a jump on the short summer season; a summer-only traverse to the remote Colville headwaters would have left little time for exploration. In April the party moved over the Arctic Divide to the Killik River, setting up camp at the mouth of April Creek.

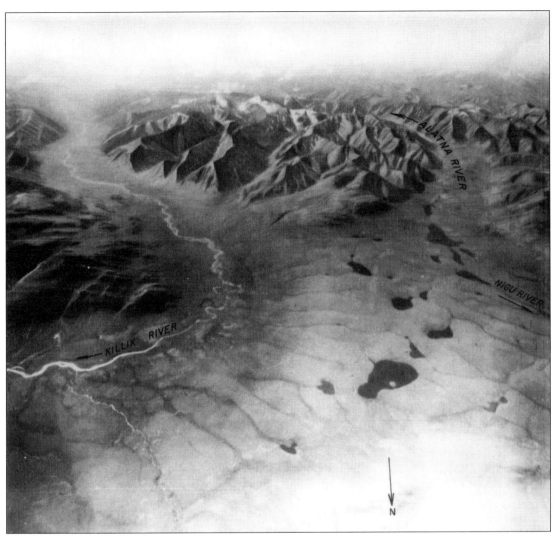

Topographer R. K. Lynt returning from a sheep hunt to USGS winter camp in Brooks Range, March 28, 1924. J. B. Mertie photo 1099, USGS Historical Photo Library, Denver.

From both camps, geologists and topographers surveyed several thousand square miles of hitherto unmapped and undescribed country.

At breakup in late May, the party broke out the canoes and loaded them for travel. Smith and topographer R. K. Lynt quickly floated down the Killik to the Colville, then turned westward upstream and investigated a large part of the upper Colville basin, including about twenty miles of the

Geologist J. B. Mertie taking the first bath of the spring at the USGS winter camp site in the Brooks Range, May 28, 1924. P. S. Smith photo 1596, USGS Historical Photo Library, Denver.

Etivluk River. Later they turned eastward down the Colville, portaged into the Ikpikpuk drainage and floated north to the Arctic Ocean.

Meanwhile, Mertie and topographer Gerald Fitzgerald slowly descended and surveyed the Killik, ascended some miles back into the range on the Okokmilaga River, mistakenly thought to lead to Chandler Lake, then descended the Colville to a point that gave access to a portage route near present Umiat. Both parties came together on the Ikpikpuk, then split again, with Mertie's group descending the Chipp River to the coast, whence they all proceeded to Barrow (Reed 1958; Smith and Mertie 1930).

Above: Two Smith-Mertie Party geologists in Peterboro canoe on Colville River. J. B. Mertie photo 1185 of July 1924. USGS Historical Photo Library, Denver.

Below: A moment of rest while hauling a canoe over arctic portage. W. R. Smith photo 278 of 1925. USGS Historical Photo Library, Denver.

Another USGS expedition in 1924, the W. T. Foran party, dragging a canoe up narrow Meridian Creek on the approaches to the Arctic Divide. The Foran party traveled the Utukok River, reaching its headwaters in late August. They nearly starved on the return trip over the Brooks Range in early winter and back down the Noatak River. W. T. Foran photo 59 of 1924. USGS Historical Photo Library, Denver.

The 1924–1926 USGS exploration of the Naval Petroleum Reserve succeeded in providing "a reasonably adequate but still very generalized picture of the major geologic features of the Reserve" (Reed 1958, 19). Both the geology and the geography of the reserve were mapped to reconnaissance scales. Though Smith and Mertie had very little stratigraphic information, the widespread occurrence of oil shales and indicators of favorable structural features led them to express conditional optimism about retention of petroleum in pools at a depth within reach of drilling. Not until World War II would their recommendations begin to be carried out for further geologic field studies and drilling for stratigraphic and structural information. But they had alerted the nation to a

potential that would lead in forty years to one of the more significant oil finds of all time, one that would change Alaska forever (Mangus 1980; Smith and Mertie 1930).

• • •

The 1920s drew to a close quietly in the upper country. Its bonanzas, such as they had been, were over. Improvements in mining technology and capitalization in other parts of Alaska had been unable to penetrate this remote region. In the larger perspective, its social and economic development had plateaued earlier and in the 1920s became eroded and entrenched. Those people who chose to remain persevered in their own ways at their own pace, largely untouched by the actions of national or territorial government and insulated from progressive trends to the south. The future was put on hold.

But events of local interest kept happening. Mercifully, the people did not accept the notion that their world was moribund. In time, some of them believed, they would get a road; a new strike would revive mining; a new round of excitement would ensue. Others, deprived of modern economic opportunities, fell back on traditional ways, adaptively reviving the seasonal rounds of hunting and gathering. In a melded sort of way they all adapted and adjusted to a lifeway low on cash and modern institutions, substantial in dependence on each other and the wild resources of the country.

Into this arrested region came a forester to study the advance of spruce trees toward the Arctic Divide. Quickly that scientific inquiry became an excuse for an affair of the heart, the human and geographical exploration

A geologist holds a mammoth tusk on Colville River near junction of Etivuluk River. P. S. Smith photo 1681 of 1924. USGS Historical Photo Library, Denver.

of the central Brooks Range. In the mix of few people and large country, the integration of environment and attitude, Bob Marshall divined a set of values that would enlarge the meaning of wilderness.

He came from a man-built world that he and a growing number of others viewed as a dynamo accelerating toward destruction, dragging a diminished humanity along with it. In the landscapes and people of the Brooks Range, he found an alternative to the careening madness of the artificial world outside. For him and for his followers, wilderness became a sanctuary where people could revive their connections to the real world that had mothered them.

Given the development trends of the modern world, he and others like the Muries sought preservation of wilderness landscapes so there would be some places left where the connection between people and the wild-lands that had first nourished them could always occur. This was far from an exclusivist, elitist mission. Wilderness was not to be preserved *from* people but *for* them.

Pioneers of the Koyukuk identified by Marshall, left to right: Billy Burke, Ace Wilcox, Jess Allen, Martin Slisco, Smithy Wanamaker, Carl Frank, George Huey, Pete Davey, Jack Hood, Earl Workman. Robert Marshall photo. Courtesy of the Bancroft Library, University of California, Berkeley.

Chapter Six

Robert Marshall's Koyukuk

What impresses one about Robert Marshall is the breadth of his interests and the energy with which he pursued them. A ramble through his many publications and the letters, research notes, and field journals in the Marshall Collection at the University of California's Bancroft Library reveals a man of liberal instincts striving for a world enlightened and equitable. He believed that decency and fairness should extend not only to people but also to a natural world besieged by misdirected political, industrial, and technological forces. As a man of substance and reputation, Marshall corresponded with scientists, academics, and men of power across the United States and around the world. During his short life, he fought with equal vigor the destructive commercial forestry practices that were desecrating America's timbered country, the rise of fascism in Europe, and a host of other evils and derelictions that caught his roving attention.

In the northern Alaska wilderness he found a place and a people that represented the antithesis of the many things going wrong with the stressed world beyond. His fondness for the friends and haunts of Alaska could only be heightened by the ominous developments outside during the 1930s. Through his northland adventures and his writings about the Koyukuk country, he channeled part of his powerful energies toward a saner and more civilized world. It may seem ironic that in this wilderness and its outpost community of Wiseman, he found values that he believed could help remedy the problems of the larger world.

Though Bob Marshall had started out as a shy lad, he became a man who radiated charm and dragged people along with infectious enthusiasm. In the Koyukuk wildlands, in company with the competent people who found satisfaction there, he discovered personal growth as well as a wondrous geography. Born in New York City in 1901, his father was a prominent constitutional lawyer, leader in Jewish affairs, fighter for minority rights, humanitarian, and a conservationist. Marshall naturally became a professional man, but not in law or medicine. His boyhood treks and nature studies at the family's summer retreat in the Adirondacks led him to choose the study of forestry.

His academic career took him to the New York State College of Forestry, Harvard University, and Johns Hopkins, where he received his doctorate in 1930. During his advanced studies he worked with a U.S. Forest Service experimental station in Idaho and Montana, where he could combine the

Robert Marshall standing in front of his cabin at Wiseman. Courtesy of the Bancroft Library, University of California, Berkeley.

"mental adventure of science with the physical adventure of life in the woods" (Marshall 1970, xxv). With maturity and experience, he would become director of forestry for the Office of Indian Affairs in Washington, D.C., and later, chief of the Division of Recreation and Lands for the U.S. Forest Service, the position he held at his death in November 1939. Throughout his professional career he worked to improve the science and practice of forestry, the economy and opportunities of Indian people, and the preservation of virgin forest lands that would be accessible for the recreation of the people at large. His joy of living combined with moral courage to make him a potent force in the many causes he espoused. He needed both wilderness and people to fulfill his life. In Alaska he found an ideal mix of the two (Marshall 1970).

Marshall's affair with the upper Koyukuk country began with a search for uncharted places on the map. Turning his atlas pages to Alaska in the spring of 1929, he found a vast, blank zone in the central Brooks Range that lured him north for a summer in the Arctic.

> So I rationalized a scientific investigation as a reason for my expedition. As a forester and plant physiologist, it seemed eminently appropriate that I should make a study of tree growth at northern timberline.
>
> I cannot say that I learned very much either about tree growth or timberline. But I did come away with a vivid impression that

the few white and Eskimo people who were scattered through this remote region were on the whole the happiest folk I had ever encountered. It is so easy, however, to found an erroneous impression on the superficial contacts of a couple of months that I decided to return for at least a year in order to make a detailed study of this civilization of the North (Marshall 1991, 3).

Interior of Marshall's cabin at Wiseman. Robert Marshall photo. Courtesy of the Bancroft Library, University of California, Berkeley.

He would return to reside a year in Wiseman in 1930–1931 and for subsequent summer visits in 1938 and 1939. Thus, for the last decade of his life, the Koyukuk environment served as the touchstone for a maturing philosophy that celebrated the human values of wilderness.

In pursuit of his scientific investigation, Marshall established sample plots beyond the spruce timberline. Using white spruce seeds gathered locally and from the northern states, he sowed various plots to test his theory "that the only reason spruce is not far north of the present timberline is that there has not been enough time, since the last ice sheet receded, for seeds to blow north from the most northerly spruce trees left after the glacier" (Marshall 1939, 16). He calculated that the spruce forest advanced about a mile north every 250 years, each increment requiring maturation of trees for development of cones and scattering of seeds. One of his plots eight miles north of timberline on a North Fork creek "would be anticipating nature by 2,000 years" (Marshall 1939, 16). Revisits to two plots, nine years after initial sowing, showed no positive results. He pondered

The "School is Out" picnic at Wiseman. Tishu Ulen holding daughter Mary's hand at left. Robert Marshall photo. Courtesy of the Bancroft Library, University of California, Berkeley.

the reasons: environmental? faulty sowing technique? But from the beginning his other interests had overshadowed the mysteries of forest advance and the subtle combinations of plant succession. He shrugged off the disappointment of barren plots "as the clouds gradually disappeared from the mountains and the great peaks of the Arctic Divide jutted all around us into the sunlight" (Marshall 1970, 123).

More important than Marshall's botanical experiments were the geographic explorations and mapping that initially flowed from the timberline studies. Almost immediately these explorations—particularly the pioneering work on the North Fork—became the basic rationale for Marshall's upper country rambles. Using extant USGS maps; the services of local Eskimos, miners, and trappers; and his own rough surveys and triangulations, Marshall filled in the main physical features of an area long of interest to the USGS, but deferred because of other demands on the agency. Philip S. Smith, by now chief Alaskan geologist for the survey, encouraged Marshall and was instrumental in having his upper Koyukuk description and sketch map published as a USGS bulletin (Marshall 1934).

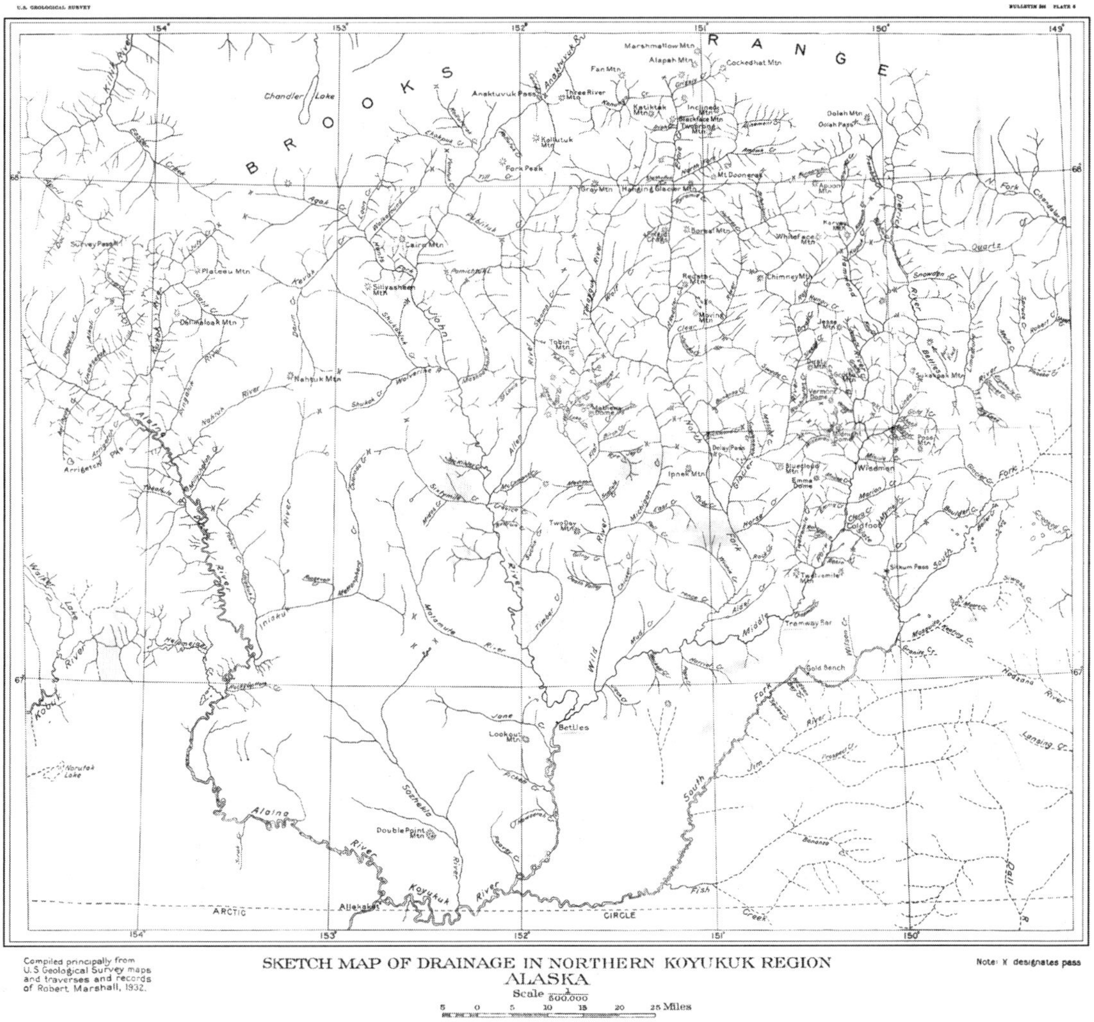

SKETCH MAP OF DRAINAGE IN NORTHERN KOYUKUK REGION
ALASKA

Compiled principally from
U.S. Geological Survey maps
and traverses and records
of Robert Marshall, 1932.

Note: K designates pass

In the bulletin's foreword, Smith stated that

> Mr. Marshall has prepared a sketch map showing all the prin-
> cipal streams of the region, has determined from local sources
> the names of many of the features, and has otherwise contrib-
> uted to the knowledge of the geography of the region. His re-
> cord . . . partly fills the need that has long been felt for more
> adequate and reliable information about . . . [the Koyukuk's]
> remote and less accessible parts (Marshall 1934, 247).

Even geographic discovery, a time- and culture-bound abstraction, faded
before the grand and tangible visions that Marshall met at every turn of
the Koyukuk's mountain drainage:

> It is doubtful whether any of the famous scenic areas in the
> United States contain more magnificent scenery than that at
> the head of the different Arctic tributaries of the Koyukuk
> River. To the writer the great U-shaped valleys at the head of
> Ernie Creek, the North Fork, and Clear River are not a whit

*Reconnaissance map of North
Fork of Koyukuk and Hammond
River drainages in Northern
Alaska. From USGS Bulletin 844-E,
Marshall 1934.*

less stupendous than those of the famous Yosemite, and the grandeur of the deep gorge of the Kenunga Valley is not excelled by any of the magnificent valleys of Glacier National Park. Grizzly Creek flows through a canyon two miles across at the top, with walls about 3,500 feet high on the north side and 2,500 feet on the south. Blackface Mountain, at the foot of the Valley of Precipices, has a sheer cliff of about 3,000 feet, resembling Gibraltar in appearance but more than twice as high. The Arrigetch Peaks of the Alatna River are a series of unscalable needle peaks such as probably cannot be duplicated anywhere else in the world. The Alatna and John Rivers flow for miles through high, rocky mountains which rise almost from the margins of streams. On Hunts Fork of the John River is Loon Lake, from the very shore of which a high, rocky mountain juts thousands of feet in the air, with a great waterfall plunging in several leaps for a drop of at least 2,000 feet.

All through this country in the clear days of winter the pure-white snow, the dark-green spruce trees, and the deep-blue sky mingle in an infinite variety of patterns. In summer the snow is gone, except on the north face of the higher mountains, but in its stead are the black and brown and gray and yellow rocks and the different colors of the varied vegetation, including the wild flowers, which blossom from early May until late August in gorgeous profusion (Marshall 1934, 248).

Spartan survivors of the survey's old Alaska Geology Branch had trouble swallowing such poetic flights in a USGS bulletin, nor could they happily accept his sketchy map—except there was no other. But they had to approve Marshall's alliance with local people who guided him and shared their knowledge of the country. Marshall credited Big Charlie Suckik, whose wide-ranging pursuit of game and furs provided the basis for mapping the Iniakuk River, large parts of the John River, and many other streams. Trapper Ernie Johnson led him through large parts of the North Fork, Allen River, and Wild River country. Wiseman miners Jesse Allen, Kenneth Harvey, and Albert Ness sketched in Middle Fork drainages and also served as guides, along with mining geologist and prospector Al Retzlaf of the Alaska A & M College at Fairbanks. According to Marshall, these men were "not only able field men but also companions with whom it was a great joy to live in the intimacy of the trail" (Marshall 1934, 249–50). Others whose landscape lore Marshall tapped included Selawik Sam, James Murphy, George Huey, Victor Neck, and Al West.

Always, Marshall's enthusiasm for the Koyukuk people and wildlands obtrudes from the lean pages of the USGS bulletin. Having paid his respects to those who knew the passes through the jagged and forbidding mountains, having applied local geographic names wherever possible and been smitten with the "innumerable mountains and streams in this unexplored country which, so far as could be learned, had never been named by either whites or Eskimos" (1934, 253), Marshall concluded his description of

the Koyukuk wilderness with a stunning statement on comparative population densities in the year 1930:

> The distribution of 127 people over an area of 15,000 square miles means that the region has an average population of only about 0.0085 per square mile. Compared with this figure, Alaska, as a whole, is about 12 times as densely populated, the United States proper 5,000 times, Belgium about 80,000 times, and Manhattan Island almost 10,000,000 times (Marshall 1934, 256).

Marshall's two major works on the Koyukuk country, *Alaska Wilderness* and *Arctic Village*, comprise a kind of stereopticon in which the Koyukuk landscape and the people living there dissolve into one another to form a single image. Yet the first is essentially a journal of exploration, the second a sociological study of Wiseman. The dominance of land and climate, and the response of a few isolated people to these dominant realities, fascinated Marshall.

Despite his chosen profession as forester and his extensive field work in the West, Marshall was essentially a displaced urban man, a highly educated man moved by ideas and the celestial visions manifest in the wilderness. It was this quality of everlasting youth, of unfailing faith in new glories to be discovered each dawn, that shaped his vision of the ultimate wilderness.

His adventuring soul, his zest for trekking, his zeal for doing more than his share of camp chores endeared him to those he met along the way. But most certainly, it was the minor discrepancy between him and those he traveled with—that shade of unconformity, of not being quite naturalized—that allowed him to see challenge and glory where Ernie Johnson, who also loved the country, saw a gradient too steep for pack horses.

Marshall's first trip in 1929 touched upon all the elements of his future studies and writing about the Koyukuk. He and Al Retzlaf flew from Fairbanks to Wiseman with Noel Wien to begin their summer adventure.

After two days in Wiseman getting supplies, renting horses, fixing pack saddles, and picking the brains of old timers about routes to the verge of the North Fork country they would explore, Marshall and Retzlaf set out. That first day of their twenty-five-day journey got them no farther than Ed Marsan's cabin on Nolan Creek, where his and his wife's hospitality could not be refused. Miners Charlie Irish and Jesse Allen dropped by and told them that in the memory of the locals only trapper Ernie Johnson had been farther north than the Clear River junction on North Fork. His line camp at the confluence of later-named Ernie Creek and North Fork was the last outpost. Beyond its environs, apparently, only Natives had traveled.

Ernie Johnson cooking at summer camp. Robert Marshall photo. Courtesy of the Bancroft Library, University of California, Berkeley.

Next day the packers traversed Pasco Pass and dropped into Glacier River valley, which they would follow to North Fork. On the way they rested

at Charlie Yale's cabin[1]—long abandoned by that early miner, but maintained by local people as a shelter on the Wiseman–North Fork–Wild Lake trail. Marshall marveled that for ten years the hermit miner's "lonely light [had] shone out on the snow with never a soul around to see it . . . for the sake of a fortune he never attained" (Marshall 1970, 8).

Beyond Yale's cabin the trail disappeared. Already sedge tussocks and mosquitoes were taking a toll. The mushroom-shaped clumps of cottongrass, with swampwater in between, made every step a pitching, lurching gamble both for the men and the heavy-laden horses. The insects descended in clouds, making headnets, gloves, and tucked-in pants essential.

Retzlaf's fishing skills provided grayling for lunch and dinner. A floored tent with tied-off tunnel entrance allowed respite and sleep despite the constant hum of mosquito hordes outside.

Finally they left Glacier River, cutting westward across Jack Delay Pass to the North Fork. Now they headed north, alternating between hillsides and brushy terraces on the one hand and gravel bars on the other, as dictated by the river's meanders. Whenever they stopped, Marshall made ecological observations: tree borings, plant types, exposure, slope, soil and air temperatures, and moisture.

Their daily progress settled into a routine of predictable tasks and sequences. Freed from petty decisions, they could absorb their surroundings and enjoy the country, despite the usual irritations of insects and tough terrain marked by snagging brush, slippery slopes, tussocks, and blocking canyons (Marshall 1970).

On July 31, after a rough climb above Clear River canyon—nearly losing the horses in the landslide steeps of what Marshall named Moving Mountain—they attained the peak some 2,500 feet above the water. Marshall's journal records the moment:

> The view from the top gave us an excellent idea of the jagged country toward which we were heading. The main Brooks Range divide was so high that it was entirely covered with snow. Close at hand, only about ten miles airline to the north, was the exceedingly precipitous east portal of the Gates to the Arctic, which I tentatively christened Boreal. The west portal I called the Frigid Crags (Marshall 1929, n.p.)

Next day they made good time. The higher reaches of the river were shallow enough to ford, so they crossed back and forth to the easily traveled gravel bars.

On August 3, after camping at the Ernie Creek–North Fork junction, they ascended Ernie Creek about six miles, where they stopped for rest and lunch. While Retzlaf fished, Marshall climbed to a summit about 3,500 feet above camp.

Fortunately this gorge was not in the continental United States, where its wild sublimity would almost certainly have been commercially exploited. We camped in the very center of the Gates, seventy-four miles from the closest human being and more than a thousand miles from the nearest automobile (Marshall 1970, 14).

In every direction rose mountains higher than mine. . . . To the southeast were three ragged giants with great glaciers near their summits. One of the three (Boreal) together with the ever cragged Frigid bounded the great Gates of the Arctic to the South. Westward, against a clouded sun six massive black needles projected into the sky, and there was also a great black basin at their base. Northward about 15 miles was the main Endicott Range, least jagged of the visible mountains, but higher than any and capped with snow. Through a notch I could see rocky mountains still farther beyond, on the Arctic side of the divide. They appeared utterly barren. In the same direction I could also look into the head of the . . . (Anaktuvuk) River, and could pick out the route we were to follow, though . . . (the) Pass itself was hidden by an immense nearby rock looking something like the pictures of Gibralter, but three times as high (Marshall 1929, n.p.).

Next day Marshall and Retzlaf pushed up Ernie Creek to camp near its head. After a tangle with grizzlies, with Marshall—on duty as camp guard—trying to hold the terrified horses and defend the camp at the same time, a climb out of Grizzly Creek toward the fog-shrouded divide, and days of rain that swelled the mountain streams, the men decided to return to Wiseman. High water forced them into difficult terrain, away from the easy crossings and gravel-bar travel of the ascent. Extremely rough ridges alternated with bog swales turned into quagmires by the constant rain.

The long haul back to Wiseman was cold, damp, and dreary. At Clear River, where they had camped twelve days before, they found their food cache intact, but it gave them only five days of slim rations for the 50-mile trek to Wiseman. The rains continued through the night, and even Clear River was not fordable. Rising waters surrounded their island camp.

At three in the morning they awoke to the sound of rushing water and found that the calm stream next to their camp had turned into a raging torrent. Within the next half hour the camp was in danger of being completely cut off from land, and Marshall and Retzlaf had to hastily carry everything across the swift, waist-deep water to safe shore beyond. There was no time to pack the horses, so many trips were made to carry the entire contents of the camp by hand, the horses being led across the treacherous waters last.

After more adventures with the raging rivers and a long hike on iron rations—ending up with only a few ounces of salt and tea—Marshall and Retzlaf made it back to Wiseman. Their reception was warm, made doubly so by fears that they had been lost.

As he left the northland that late summer of 1929, Marshall was already making plans for return the next year. Study of the "civilization of the North" would be his primary task, for he wanted to know if these people had truly achieved the balance and happiness he had observed and, if so, how. During his thirteen-month residence of 1930–1931, he would combine sociology with wilderness adventuring. As sidelines, he would make a bow in the direction of timberline studies and expand his preliminary mapping of the North Fork. And it was on this trip that he met Ernie Johnson, who would become his principal trail companion.

Johnson was held up among the pioneers of the region as the most competent woodsman of the lot. He lived most of his time alone on the upper reaches of the North Fork, spending all but two weeks a year away from the "cities" of Wiseman and Bettles. As a trapper and hunter he made about $2,500 a year. He could make much more as a carpenter, for his cabins were tight and dry and lasted for decades, "but I am staying out here because I like it among these ruggedy mountains better than anywhere else in the world" (Marshall 1970, 37–38).

On the spot, Marshall and Johnson agreed to an upper Alatna exploration together the next summer. Then they parted, Johnson floating south to his town base at Bettles, Marshall and his party heading for the Arctic Divide. For a moment the two camps had shared thousands of square miles of wilderness. A few days later Marshall and Al Retzlaf would camp near Johnson's cabin at the Ernie Creek-North Fork junction and use his cook stove.

Back at Wiseman after the September trip to the North Fork, Marshall began a series of long journal-based letters to his family and friends. These letters, with their anecdotes of travel and stories of friends made, form a large part of the *Alaska Wilderness* text. They also contain ruminations and summings up that show the progress of Marshall's thoughts as he discovered new places in the central Brooks Range.

As far as Bob Marshall knew or could know, this was a fresh world—unvisited, virgin. More recent discoveries indicate that the upper Koyukuk was a natural travel route and hunting area that had been used by Native Americans for millennia. Ernie Pass, between the headwaters of Ernie Creek and Anaktuvuk River, was a major access into the Koyukuk country for historic-period mountain Eskimos and for their prehistoric Indian and Eskimo predecessors, as was the pass between the North Fork and Itkillik rivers. Archaeological investigations in 1985 found scores of historic and prehistoric sites in these upper drainages. Their locations and artifactual remains indicate camping and hunting uses, including butchering stations. Scientific dating and artifact morphology give strong evidence of at least 6,000 years of human presence, probably several millennia more. Clustered sites at and within a few miles of the Ernie Creek–North Fork confluence show intensive use of a sporadic, seasonal sort from earliest times to the present. Camp sites and hunting lookouts have always been chosen for advantages of terrain, drainage, and visibility. These factors and their channeling influence over animal migration routes have changed little in the passage of recent geological time. Sheep are plentiful in the area today. Along with migrating caribou, they were probably major attractions in earlier times, as they still are (Kunz 1985).

Bob Marshall was not the first explorer to imagine himself the first human being in some remote place. Certainly his idols, Lewis and Clark, visited no place unknown to generations of vanished and living tribes. Since the early dispersions of humankind, geographic exploration has been a generational thing, a renewable resource in the world's wildlands where forgotten histories left few reminders. When Marshall spoke of preserving wilderness for its human values, this was part of what he meant. In wilderness, certain psychological processes could be revitalized—among them the sense of discovering an earth fresh and whole. That he had unwittingly partaken of his prescription for others—experienced the discoverer's exaltation where many had trod before—is fine irony and validation of his prescription.

That Bob Marshall and later pilgrims to the central Brooks Range could and can still have such experiences tells us much about traditional land use there. Anthropologist Richard Nelson draws this conclusion in a 1977 study of the subsistence way of life in what were then the proposed Alaska parklands:

> The areas proposed for new parks remain in an essentially pristine condition, with healthy populations of wildlife and virtually unaltered floral communities. Except for scattered cabins and threading trails, subsistence users have left the landscape practically free of visible human impact. Thus, several thousand years of continuous subsistence use has left us with environments worthy of preservation as the most wild and beautiful in our nation (1977, 13–14).

I thought of my friends on the Outside who were spending the night comfortably in steam-heated rooms in the heart of steam-heated cities. We spent that night scarcely less comfortably near the Arctic Divide, though the thermometer dropped to 40 below and we had only a thin canvas shelter. But ours was a single oasis of warmth and comfort in thousands of square miles of freezing wilderness (Marshall 1970, 59).

During the winter of 1930—1931, Marshall alternated his Wiseman studies with dog mushing trips. One ten-day circuit took him to the Dietrich River branch of Middle Fork, about sixty miles north of Wiseman. Jesse Allen and Kenneth Harvey invited him along to recover cached sheep from their fall hunt. Marshall discovered both the joy and dangers of winter travel—the rush of the dogs through starlit and twilit arctic landscapes; the menace of overflow on frozen rivers, where a breakthrough on crusted snow or thin ice can wet and freeze a foot in minutes.

At mid-passage of their journey Albert Ness showed up with a borrowed team to get Jesse, whose wife had fallen seriously ill. Jesse rushed back alone with an empty sled; Ness stayed on to haul the meat. It was an emergency "met by the community in a way typical for this frontier," considered by all involved as merely "normal neighborliness," no thanks or pay expected (Marshall 1970, 59–60).

In March 1931, Marshall joined Ernie Johnson on an expedition to the Clear River headwaters. No one locally knew whether it headed at the Arctic Divide or a south slope ridge. They would find out.

Following the usual route via Yale Cabin and Glacier River, the men and two teams aimed for Johnson's cabin at the Tinayguk–North Fork junction. After caching some food there, they mushed up Clear River toward the head of its lower canyon. There they set up a base camp in deep snow so dry that a person without snowshoes sank instantly to the waist. Camp routine started as Johnson stomped out a tent space with snowshoes and tied the tent ends and sides to spruce trees and brush. Marshall cut and spread spruce boughs for a floor and rolled out caribou hides and bags. Then they got the stove going. They melted snow for water in five-gallon tins, two for dogfood and one for themselves. The camp work—setting up, securing the dogs for the night, feeding themselves—kept them busy until late evening. But a warm tent and a pot of boiled meat capped the long day pleasantly.

They had books, for both of them were voracious readers. Good talk, however, was their basic fare once the work was done. Marshall caught Johnson's views and philosophy in another of those long letters to the folks. They had stimulating discussions about socialism and personal liberties and the freedom of bush living. Johnson was no socialist (as many Wiseman residents were), for he feared the anthill effect. But he was critical of the capitalistic order. "We've got to get some system . . . which will stop this amassing of fortunes, otherwise in a few years the whole world will be peonized to a handful of men." He admired the Natives for their lack of hypocrisy and their avoidance of false modesty. If he got $100,000 all at once he would not leave the country. He would get better equipment and go Outside for a wife, then come right back. "I wouldn't quit this life in the hills. . . . I know what the life outside is like and it don't appeal to me. I've lived this free life in here too long." His idea of working for someone else was summed up as "getting down on your knees and wearing out your pants legs." Johnson thought there might be a hereafter, but since neither he nor preachers knew what it was, he did not feel a need to attend church. He was contemptuous of the "modern, high-power publicity explorers" of the period: "Jesus Christ, do they call that exploring. Why, they had everything they could ask for except women. . . . They ought to get out in the hills here where they have to live on themselves, and can't radio for help every time they get in trouble." As Marshall confided, conversations with Johnson seldom ended in "tedious agreement" (letter of Apr. 10, 1931, Robert Marshall Collection, Bancroft Library).

Next morning they reconnoitered with light gear, leaving the constricted canyon and breaking out into a great, sunny amphitheatre about six miles long and three or four wide. At its upper end it appeared that Clear River issued from one of three gorges. But when they got there they found the river coming out of a long, hidden valley from the east. Great walls and domes rose 3,000 feet straight up. Pinnacles and jagged gorges embellished the scene. The serrated skyline at the head of the valley was built of summits towering nearly a mile above them, "and over everything the fresh snow, and the blue sky, and the clarity and sparkle of the midwinter atmosphere." As they proceeded up the valley, they found ten unique gorges, each, according to Marshall, worthy of National Monument designation, each a bit of perfection. "Taken all together with the main valley they formed a whole beyond even the characterization of 'perfect.'"

After other revelations of stunning beauty in this intricate and deeply gashed country, they tracked Clear River's head to a point that was later determined to be well south of the main divide (letter of Apr. 10, 1931, Robert Marshall Collection, Bancroft Library).

Nothing would ever top Marshall's first journey with Ernie Johnson up Clear River. It had become a series of transcendent days, each more amazing than the last. Finally, as the sated travelers started back, vistas that would have been great and memorable anyplace else became merely pleasant.

A break at Johnson's cabin gave them time to refit. Then the men broke trail up Tinayguk River and went over a pass to Flat Creek in the Wild River drainage. The climb over the last ridge to Wild River was the toughest mile of the trip. Breaking trail a hundred yards at a clip, Johnson would tramp the snow out once, then back to the sled and out again. Through the trough in the snow Marshall would pull the dogs with all his strength, but they still wallowed breast deep in the dry fluff, having to rest every 30 feet. The steep drop-off to the river required roughlocking the sled runners with wrapped chains and the men braking as hard as they could. When the chains caught on snow-covered snags Marshall chopped them out. Once he chopped into the runner itself, prevented from chopping through only by the steel at its center (letter of Apr. 10, 1931, Robert Marshall Collection, Bancroft Library).

At Spring Creek on Wild Lake, they were greeted by Ludie Hope, an immense Koyukon Indian woman who rushed out of her cabin and embraced Johnson and instantly made Marshall feel right at home. After sixteen days in the wilds he felt that he had stepped back into civilization. The Wild Lake camp took them in, with Johnson renewing old friendships and Marshall making new ones. After three days with this diverse, interesting, and pleasant company, Marshall and Johnson headed back to Wiseman via Bettles (letter of Apr. 10, 1931, Robert Marshall Collection, Bancroft Library).

In the last of his major journeys during the 1930–1931 residency, Marshall joined Johnson for their earlier planned summer circuit through the Alatna and John river drainages. Johnson rendezvoused with Marshall at Wiseman during the July 4 celebrations that attracted everyone from the distant creeks and camps for feasting, games, and endless dancing.

On July 5 the men traveled down the Koyukuk in a whipsawed boat that Johnson had made, powered by a 10-horsepower kicker. As they made

Like other roadhouses in Alaska . . . it combined the functions of hotel, restaurant, bar, banquet hall, dance floor, store, and major social center of Wiseman. Martin Slisco, the roadhouse proprietor . . . lent us shoes for the dance which they staged specially for us at the Pioneer Hall. . . . With the day still bright at midnight despite rain, with the long-yearned-for Arctic actually at hand, with the pleasant Eskimo girls as partners, . . . with friendly strangers smiling and welcoming, and with little Eskimo kids having hopping races with me— that evening seems today a dear, half-remembered dream (Marshall 1970, 5).

Dance at Pioneers Hall. Robert Marshall photo. Courtesy of the Bancroft Library, University of California, Berkeley.

their way up the Alatna, they mingled with Eskimos who had left Alatna village for their summer fish camps. Farther upriver, they encountered a team of prospectors.

From a base camp on Kutuk River, they hiked toward the Arctic Divide, past Arrigetch Peaks and on to the high country, to map the intricate drainages that fell away toward arctic seas and the Yukon.

On the way back down the Alatna, they found the old site of Rapid City. To Marshall the rotting cabins spoke of the horror that certainly gripped unprepared stampeders marooned by early freeze-up, their dreams of quick fortune dead, their isolation from family and accustomed comforts complete, perhaps permanent. And yet, he thought, those who finally made it back "to the desired safe and gregarious life of ordinary America" would surely in later years describe that lonesome winter as life's great adventure (Marshall 1970, 97).

The John River, swift and clear, with striking scenery, seems to have appealed more to Marshall than the muddy, meandering Alatna. The men and pack dogs ascended in Johnson's boat as far as Hunt Fork, whose headwaters they had glimpsed from the Alatna highlands. Switching to back- and dog-packs, they proceeded up the fork toward the passes across the divide.

Days more of exploration allowed them to tie together visually and on the map the mountain landmarks of previous experience in a great swath of the central Brooks Range from the North Fork to the Alatna. Then they returned to the Koyukuk and motored up its sunny valley toward Wiseman. At a point a few miles below the town, Johnson allowed as how they could easily make it all the way before dark. But they happily agreed that they should have one last camp—making an even fifty nights on the trail. Marshall knew that there was plenty of time to leave this wilderness, where good people lived the good life, for the outer world of growing misery and danger. They savored Johnson's lamb stew, then sat together in gathering darkness on a log by the fire.

> We didn't say very much sitting there. You don't when it is your last camp with a companion who had shared the most perfect summer of a lifetime. We just sat, with a feeling warmer than the crackling fire, exulting in the sharp-edged pattern which the mountain walls cut against the northern sky: listening to the peaceful turmoil of the arctic river with its infinite variation in rhythm and tone: smelling the luxurience of untainted arctic valleys: feeling the wholesome cleanliness of arctic breezes blowing on cheeks and hair (Marshall 1970, 109).

The later trips of 1938 and 1939 play again these many themes. Confined mainly to the Doonerak Mountain vicinity of North Fork—with sorties into the limestone canyons of the upper Anaktuvuk River and the headwater creeks of Hammond River—Marshall resolved many geographic questions raised by earlier explorations. As before, times of adventure and scrapes with death alternated with moments of ethereal beauty and quiet contemplation.

Like many philosophers before him, Bob Marshall found the wilderness a place of peace and purity, a pattern for the lost Eden of man's origins. He realized that only a minority of the world's teeming millions could or ever would find their happiness through direct experience with primeval nature. Yet he believed that perpetuation of the dream of Eden—"of freshness and remoteness and adventure beyond the paths of men"—benefited and could be shared by all people (Marshall 1970, 157).

Throughout his life Marshall associated and corresponded with people who shared his vision of preserved tracts of wilderness. As the destructive pace of the modern, mechanized world increased, he and those like-minded others focused their energies on founding the Wilderness Society to save representative fractions of virgin country from otherwise inexorable invasion and destruction. In time, with the aid of founders and supporters like Robert Sterling Yard, Aldo Leopold, Dorothy Jackson, and Olaus and Margaret Murie, the society would become a national force, engendering a movement that allied many conservation and other constituent groups, resulting eventually in passage of the Wilderness Act of 1964. Marshall's contribution to this movement was profound: as benefactor, as strategist and philosopher, as organizer and coordinating correspondent, and as propagator of the faith through his experience-based scholarly and popular writings. During the last decade of his life, the central Brooks Range vitalized his work, provided him the ideal of what wilderness should be and what it should mean to the nation. Gates of the Arctic National Park and Preserve, established by Congress in 1980 to perpetuate the country's wilderness character, bears the stamp of Marshall's ideal.[2]

With specific reference to Alaska, Bob Marshall became chief spokesman for the society. He believed that Alaska, as the last great frontier expanse of the nation, should be protected from the usual developmental intrusions and progressions that had wracked the rest of the country. In 1938, for example, the society opposed a proposal for a road through Canada to Fairbanks, declaring that easy international road access would upset both the fragile subsistence economy and the biological integrity of the Interior. Marshall argued that the wilderness and recreational values of an undeveloped Alaska were worth far more to the nation than agricultural settlement would be. The marginal environment and the distance to markets made proposals for agricultural development infeasible.[3]

In Marshall's view, the development of Alaska's resources should be retarded for social as well as economic and biological reasons—especially in northern Alaska, where both Native and pioneer people had evolved lifeways that would be lost in the modern hurly-burly. Promoters and speculators would destroy the last chance for a balanced, nationwide planning outlook, wherein Alaska's highest value would be realized through preservation.

When Alaska recreation is viewed from a national standpoint, it becomes at once obvious that its highest value lies in the pioneer conditions yet prevailing throughout most of the territory. . . . These pioneer values have been largely destroyed in the continental United States. In Alaska alone can the emotional values of the frontier be preserved (Marshall 1970, xxxiii–xxxiv).

The thirteen months that Marshall spent in and around Wiseman in 1930–1931 gave him an opportunity to check the impressions of northern civilization gained during his brief visit in 1929. As he had found joy exploring in the Koyukuk wilderness, so did he find joy in exploring the attitudes and behavior of Koyukuk people. From daily associations with his friends, painstakingly recorded in journals and on note cards, came a rich portrait of a unique community. He delved into the physical setting and history of the place, the people as individuals and as community, economy, sex, recreation, and philosophy. His study is rich in the anecdotes and perspectives of both Natives and whites and the communal blending that allowed them to live in basic harmony. It was a world that he captured, a panorama of humankind in exquisite and detailed miniature. In his own characterization, Wiseman exhibited "the independent, exciting, and friendly life of the Arctic frontier . . . 200 miles beyond the Twentieth Century" (Marshall 1970, 9).

Biner Wind, Bobbie Jones, Poss Postlethwaite, and Smithy Wanamaker (in shaft) on Nolan Creek. Robert Marshall photo. Courtesy of the Bancroft Library, University of California, Berkeley.

The prevalence of socialists in Wiseman astounded Marshall. Martin Slisco and Carl Frank thought the capitalists ought to be beaten or hanged. Militarism was another sore subject, as many immigrants had fled Europe to escape conscription. And religion came up often, usually resulting in spirited debates. From his first contact with Wiseman people, Marshall had been impressed with their sharp minds. He attributed this partly to voracious reading of magazines and books during the long winters, and partly to the selection process in a difficult environment where intelligence and foresight were essential to survival. His administration of Stanford-Binet intelligence tests to a cross-section of age and racial groups confirmed the early impressions. In every group, the tests registered a majority of above-average results. Children of Native and mixed parentage were all above normal in their attainments.

Carl Frank and Poss "came in 1898 and still active." Robert Marshall photo. Courtesy of the Bancroft Library, University of California, Berkeley.

Marshall delighted in copying verbatim the utterances of the old miners, "most of them cut off from the main stream of civilization for 30 or more years." For example, Vaughn Green's recipe of the best way to cook a porcupine was: "Place the porcupine and a rock in a kettle of water and boil. When the rock gets tender enough to stick a fork in it throw out the porcupine and eat the rock" (letter of Nov. 5, 1930. Robert Marshall Collection, Bancroft Library).

On election day, which was an excuse for holiday and hilarity, miners drifted in from the far camps to vote on who should be their territorial delegate to the U.S. Congress. Marshall stood by the Pioneer Hall voting booth and recorded the good-natured banter between proponents of Republican James Wickersham and Democrat George Grigsby. Nobody took the election too seriously, as these random remarks indicate:

It's a sure bet anyway that neither of them cares what happens to us.

Whatever way the vote goes, things will be just the same as ever on the Koyukuk when it's all over and the world will keep turning once in 24 hours.

Some of the old-timers at Wiseman, as identified by Tishu Ulen: (1) Ike Spinks, (2) Ekok, (3) Lucy Jones, (4) Albert Ness, (5) Martin Slisco, (6) Kitty Jonas, (7) Kenneth Harvey, (8) Vaughn Green, (9) Mamie Green, (10) Clara Carpenter, (11) Harry Snowden, (12) Vern Watts, (13) Victor Neck. Robert Marshall photograph 1930–31. Courtesy of Bancroft Library, University of California, Berkeley.

All these politicians have the same motto: follow me and you'll wear diamonds, otherwise I'll put you in jail.

Whichever one's elected, we know both of them ought to be in jail (letter of Nov. 5, 1930. Robert Marshall Collection, Bancroft Library).

Even today, in regard to government and its agents, one may hear similar sentiments expressed on the Koyukuk—and most other parts of bush Alaska.

In letters to his family, Marshall included vivid descriptions of the various residents with whom he spent those thirteen months in 1930–1931. They shared their lives and their stories with him, embracing him in a way that was truly remarkable. All this was reflected in his writings, in which he praised their fearlessness, independence, generosity, humor, and deliberate and practical approach to life in this inhospitable region.

Bob Marshall's *Arctic Village* narrative concludes with an excerpt from a letter he had received from Mrs. Pingel, who, with her husband, had left the northland for their farm in Iowa:

Mrs. Jonas and family in front of her sod house in Wiseman. Robert Marshall photo. Courtesy of the Bancroft Library, University of California, Berkeley.

People here [in Iowa] are so impatient with our love for Alaska as a land of scenic beauty when they hear you have to walk to see it. And mining is madness as long as you haven't made a lot of money, the pleasure of hunting treasures in the bosom of the earth is folly unless you know where to dig and where to pick up gold. The wild flowers by the roadside as we walk to town are not interesting to them if thereby you must walk.

Oh, these people here have everything a person could wish for—modern homes, electricity, radio, all the good things like eggs, milk, butter, fruit, berries, gardens. I wonder what they would wish more in heaven. Still they are only half awake—dull, routine slaves, tied down to follow each other.

When I picture the life in the North and here I say—my stomach is better off here but my mentality lives its best up there. The big open spaces are alluring, the lovely air, the near-by rainbow, the friendliness of the people. How interested we are up there in everyday occurrences and each other; helpful, ready to do all we can (Marshall 1991, 371–72).

The Pingels in front of their cabin on Nolan Creek. Robert Marshall photo, 1930-31. Courtesy of the Bancroft Library, University of California, Berkeley.

Marshall chose Mrs. Pingel's words as a kind of benediction that expressed the ultimate operating principles of the Wiseman community, overriding the petty conflicts of the moment. As well, these words reiterated his theme of blended landscape and people.

His own conclusions touched on the meaning of life, the bases of happiness. After his immersion in the civilization of the North, he stated his personal belief that "the average value of life rises higher above the dead level of oblivion to the people of the Koyukuk than it does to any of the other groups of American people whom I have known" (1991, 375).

To the attainment of this condition he attributed specific factors:

- Personal and economic independence, the ability to shape one's own destiny—meaning emancipation from the interplay of economic forces and the restraints imposed by other men.

- The fact that one can always make a living—from gold if fortune smiles, from living off the land if it does not.

- Interesting work requiring "skilled manipulation, continual planning, and genuine mental exertion." Routinized jobs do not exist; work is inspirited by the "lure of the unknown."

- Besides independence, there is almost unlimited liberty to do and say as one pleases, short only of hurtful crimes against others.

Because of the few people in the Koyukuk, each person "takes on a peculiar importance . . . is a vital element in the world . . . not merely one infinitesimal soul among millions." Relieved of the "neurotic strain of trying to be important" in the faceless mass, one is valued just because he is alive. Racial prejudice is eliminated because each person "fills an assured niche in his world" (Marshall 1991, 375).

Adventure, a daily experience in the wilderness, "adds tone, vitality, and color to the entire functioning of life," as does the Arctic climate, whose severe contrast between summer and winter provides variety—in effect, two distinct lifestyles each year.

Marshall's final meditation in his book *Arctic Village* (1991) ended with these words:

> It is impossible ever to evaluate just how much beauty adds to what is worth while in existence. I would hazard as my opinion that beautiful surroundings have a fundamental bearing on most people's enjoyment. Consequently, I believe

When Big Jim was still a young man in his native Sellawik country along Kotzebue sound, just north of the Bering Straits, he fell under the influence of the Missionaries. Their teachings became the dominant force in his life. All the complexities of nature, all the perplexity of how the infinitely varied world he knew came to be, all the fear provoking superstitions, were simply resolved in a perfect faith that a beneficient God, not so different in character than Jim himself only infinitely greater, had created the universe for the happiness of mankind. In a severe life in which young friends were continually being carried violently to death, in which beloved parents died and apparently rotted away, it was very consoling to learn that after death everybody would be reunited in an existence infinitely happier than that on earth. "We know nothing about all this, me no know how earth come, till me learn God business. Now me learn God business, everything fine" (letter of Jan. 27, 1931. Robert Marshall Collection, Bancroft Library).

Big Jim in front of Bob's cabin. Robert Marshall photo. Courtesy of the Bancroft Library, University of California, Berkeley.

John Mcphee's book, *Coming into the Country*, caused similar perturbations on the upper Yukon more than forty years later. Yet, he received a similar welcome when he returned to visit the people of the Eagle-Circle region whom he had written about, and for the same reason. People protested: "I wish he hadn't said that about me, even if it is true." Even today there seems to be a generous tolerance for the truth, warts and all, among bush Alaskans.

that the happiness of the Koyukuker is greatly enhanced and his entire life is made richer by the overpowering loveliness of the Arctic wilderness.

Most important of all, happiness in the Koyukuk is stimulated by the prevalent philosophy of enjoying life as it passes along. The absence of constant worry about the future and remorse about the past destroys much that tends to make men miserable. The fact that happiness is frankly recognized as a legitimate objective removes at once much futile pursuit of false ideals, and makes it possible for men to live openly as well as subconsciously for what they primarily desire.

Of course there are also factors which tend to make the Outside a happier place than the Koyukuk. The variety of goods which one may purchase, the every day conveniences unknown in the northern region, the diversified possibilities of entertainment, and the wider opportunities for personal acquaintanceship are clearly advantages for the outside world. Especially, the family life for which most of mankind seems to yearn has very little possibility of fruition among the white men of the Koyukuk.

Nevertheless, the inhabitants of the Koyukuk would rather eat beans with liberty, burn candles with independence, and mush dogs with adventure than to have the luxury and the restrictions of the outside world. A person misses many things by living in the isolation of the Koyukuk, but he gains a life filled with an amount of freedom, tolerance, beauty, and contentment such as few human beings are ever fortunate enough to achieve (376–79).

Despite this loving finale, *Arctic Village* caused some consternation in the Koyukuk after its initial publication in 1933. Marshall sent copies to his friends and they quickly went the rounds. Some of his frank judgments and descriptions of people cut deep. Yet, on his return to Wiseman in 1938, he received warm welcome.

Ominous speculations by others and his own qualms proved unfounded. As a gesture for all the help he had received, he had divided his book royalties fifty-fifty between himself and the 100 people of the Koyukuk camp (Marshall to Jesse Allen, Apr. 4, 1934; Robert Marshall Collection, Bancroft Library). This helped the reception somewhat. But the key to his welcome back was expressed by Kenneth Harvey in a later letter to Marshall's brother, George: "I like Bob's books as he printed the truth in them" (Marshall 1970, 167).

Despite the handshakes and jokes and wisecracks when he returned to Wiseman (including pointed questions about whether he was going to write another Wiseman book), Marshall's nostalgic reunion was marred. Wiseman had changed. Constant air traffic (two or three times a week), tourists, radios, even automobiles had made their appearance. Wiseman, to a degree unthinkable just a few years before, had become part of the world. Most important was the change in the people. In 1931, more than 80 percent of them had been old-timers of the Gold Rush era, freighted with "the distinctive mores developed in the romantic stampedes." By 1938 half of the people were newcomers, "who lacked much of the tradition of the old gold rush." Moreover, many of his friends—the splendid companions of an unforgettable year—had died. Marshall faced that common problem of not really being able to go home again (Marshall 1970, 113–14).

Indeed, Wiseman and the larger Koyukuk camp had changed. Mining was in decline. Fur prices crashed during the Great Depression. The school closed in May 1941. Population barely held its own, around seventy-five souls, until World War II drew off all but a handful of whites and a sprinkling of Native families.

Irving McK. Reed reported after a mining survey in 1937 that "the upper Koyukuk region as a whole is gradually reverting to wilderness" (1938, 165). Lacking new gold strikes within a few years and government help on a road from the Yukon, he foresaw an end to mining in the region. This progression was far along when the wartime ban on gold mining came into effect.

Closing of the school and departure of teacher George Rayburn in 1941 symbolized the end of Wiseman's effective contact with the institutions of the outside world. Pleas and petitions of Wiseman's people to keep the school and teacher Rayburn failed when the student population dropped to a half dozen children. The ensuing institutional vacuum was never filled (Wiseman School District file, Alaska State Archives).

• • •

During this transitional period, the upper Kobuk's Shungnak mining district followed a pattern similar to that of the upper Koyukuk. Except for a few experienced, equipped, and in-residence miners, mining was on the wane. In the early 1930s, attempts to bolster the district with outside capital—fronted by big-name mining engineers and managers from Fairbanks' failing fields—went the way of the Detroit Mining Company on Hammond River. High hopes pushed by speculative fever grounded on essentially the same logistical and geological reefs: high costs of transportation, low-grade gold deposits, and very late ice on Kotzebue Sound, which frustrated ocean transportation and cut the season to only a few weeks.

World War II drained the upper country of all but a few whites. Young miners entered the armed forces. Natives were recruited as scouts in the Territorial Guard. With the wartime ban on gold mining, older miners of the upper-country camps sought war-related jobs in Fairbanks, Nome, and other towns close to military bases, including the airfields that helped

ferry Lend-Lease planes to Soviet Russia. The upper Koyukuk was particularly hard hit, for mining, no matter how marginal, had remained the core of its economy, the reason for its settlements. The exodus forced closing of the Wiseman store, and Bettles almost became a ghost town.

Native villages on the upper Kobuk, with established populations and a broader resource base for traditional subsistence living, weathered the war better and even benefited from some of its spin-off. The influx of military personnel revived the market for furs and Native handicrafts. Government services and communications improved. A short-lived attempt to mine asbestos in the Dahl Creek area in the late war years provided some employment for Eskimos of Shungnak and nearby villages as equipment operators, supply haulers, and ore miners (Foote 1966; Naske 1986; U.S. Army 1969).

• • •

The passage of years and the war nearly wiped out Bob Marshall's Wiseman altogether. After the war, what was left of the old-time cadre, both those who had stayed through the war years and those who came back from war jobs, joined with a few newcomers to perpetuate the Koyukuk camp, whose population varied with the seasons between twenty-five and fifty souls. Mining continued on a small scale on most of the proven creeks in the Wiseman vicinity and at a few isolated sites. Importation of Cats and other earth-moving equipment soon made open-cut mining the principal mode of operation. Deforestation to fuel the old boilers had stripped the country of timber for miles around, so old-style drift mining was impossible except in isolated sites that had escaped the woodcutters. Marshall had noted this deforestation and also the effect it had had upon water supplies for sluicing. The quick runoff over barren ground had shortened the sluicing season several weeks by the time he got there (Marshall 1991; Harry Leonard pers. comm. July 16, 1982).

The postwar generation of newcomers represented the third wave of Koyukuk miners and settlers. The stampeders of the '98 Gold Rush and the first years of the century had been the first. Then came the people of the 1910s, 1920s, and 1930s. Despite Marshall's forebodings, enough old-timers survived into the 1940s and 1950s to pass on the essential traditions of the country, and in time even the postwar generation would join the parade of pioneers. These are the people who overlapped much of the past. They and the more recent immigrants they have tutored remember the historic people and places—which are still worked by today's miners, for the old prospectors knew their business. This historical narrative owes much to the memories of these latter-day survivors and recruits. Their still-vital traditions and sense of being members of a century-old historical community recall those earlier days.

Brooks Range in Anaktuvuk Pass District. J. C. Reed photo 884 of 1949. USGS Historical Photo Library, Denver.

Chapter Seven

STILL A HOMELAND

Walter Johnson, whose association with the upper Koyukuk goes back to the 1930s, is a reflective man. He sees the long span of history in the region in terms of cultural perspectives: the land as viewed and used by aboriginals, by miners and traders, by conservationists and preservationists. He has distilled these perspectives to primary terms: game, gold, athletics/esthetics. During the historic period these categories blended somewhat and crossed cultural lines. But throughout, the archetypes remained: the Native hunter, the miner after gold, and, in the latter days, the wilderness adventurer/philosopher—embodied by Bob Marshall and his followers. It is to the evolving yet stable perspective of historic-period Native people that we now turn. In the life histories of two men, and in the history of Anaktuvuk Village, we shall see how steady the Native perspective has been despite the buffetings of recent history and the eagerly grasped opportunities provided by the coming of the white man.

Joe Sun

Joe Sun, preeminent elder of Shungnak, kin of the prophet Maniilaq, was born January 3, 1900, at Coal Mine near the Kobuk River village of Kiana. This was his mother's village. His father descended from upriver people, with some distant Indian antecedents centered around the historic settlement of Qala (Kalla), near the Pah River. When three or four years old, Joe moved with his family to Sun Camp, ten miles down the Kobuk from present Shungnak. He grew up in the traditional Eskimo way, moving between seasonal camps in the Kobuk Valley. Early in his life he began working at gold mines in the Shungnak district. During World War II he worked as a carpenter in Nome, and some years later as a miner in the Fairbanks area. In recent years, concerned about the erosion of traditional life and language, he became active in the cultural revitalization efforts of the Spirit Program, sponsored by NANA, the Native regional corporation based in Kotzebue (Kassler 1984).

Until very recent years, when age forced Joe Sun to slow down, he divided his time between two worlds, able and competent in both: the world of the white man and that of the traditional Eskimo. His knowledge of his hunting territory in the upper Kobuk and Noatak rivers is profound and one of a kind in today's world. With the aid of his daughter-in-law Susie Sun and ethnohistorian David Libbey, he has done his best to convey that knowledge to his people and to the rest of us.[1]

Joe Sun became a tradition bearer by virtue of an early life nearly devoid of contact with white people and their manufactures until he was well into his teens. His early memories recall Native foods, seasonal camps that responded to hunting and fishing cycles, journeys by dog team, and trading with Native partners. In the sod houses and bark shelters of his boyhood days, he absorbed not only the stories of the elders but also the language and rhythms of oral culture. His tutelage in hunting, travel, and survival followed the organic educational pattern of mimicry—accompanying his father, learning by observation, then being pushed to the front to try it himself. Constant critique by his father perfected his methods. His mother taught him how to snare small game. His father helped him set his first muskrat trap, then showed him how to dispatch the trapped animal with a stick before removing it from the trap. After learning to stalk game with a bow and arrow, requiring knowledge of animal behavior and perfection of stealth, he was given an old, single-shot .22 rifle and one bullet a day. When he finally shot a duck, early one morning, he waited outside camp until his parents awoke, then came in bearing his game. His father taught him how to make everything—snowshoes, sleds, survival camps, deadfalls, fishtraps. His recounting of these exciting times, when he tapped into a venerable tradition and became one of its functioning members, is full of phrases that tell the how, when, where, and why of employing natural things to carry on a life integrated with nature. On field trips to the old sites, he made old-style deadfalls. He named places on the map and sketched shelters made of snow, willows, and skins.

While still a boy, he graduated to long trapping trips by himself, often for several months at a time. Because the family had only one set of dogs, he would depart in the fall, transporting his gear with the dogs to his distant base camp; then he would return them for his father's use and backpack out to his camp. In spring, after winter trapping, he would hike back home to get the dogs so he could retrieve his outfit.

After his marriage in 1927, he got his own dog team. Then Joe, his wife, and later his children began the annual cycle of long trips to the upper Noatak, leaving in the fall and returning in March. When his children started school, he would take them out for a short time in the fall, then bring them back for school. As winter progressed he brought caribou and sheep meat back to his family, then returned to the trapline on the Noatak.

Until he was in his mid-sixties, Joe continued the seasonal journeys to trap and hunt in the Nunataaq (upper Noatak) country. As late as 1982 he ran a trapline near Shungnak.

As a mine laborer, heavy-equipment operator, and carpenter, Joe had adapted to the white man's world. He had visited and lived in cities and successfully raised his family in the new socioeconomic network of stores, schools, and modern transportation and communications systems. Yet, each year he left that modern world for extended periods and renewed his association with the older world known and conveyed to him by his ancestors.

Ernest S. Burch, Jr., has studied the cultural revitalization movement among northwest Alaskan Eskimos. This movement is large in scope, involving legal, psychological, economic, political, and land tenure factors. The overall objective of the movement is a culturewide adaptive response to change that artfully blends sustaining traditional ways (language, hunting and

I've gone out there and spent the whole year with people, elders born before me, and learned about the area from them. That's how I know that area out there. That's why white people come to me and ask for advice about how to go about living out there (Joe Sun 1985, 26–27).

Village of Shungnak. P. S. Smith photo 533 of 1910. USGS Historical Photo Library, Denver.

Jesse Ahgook shows how the old timers used to dress and hunt. His parka and boots are made from caribou skin. His old-fashioned rifle has no scope, so he uses a telescope to spot game. Photo by John Martin Campbell, courtesy Simon Paneak Museum, Anaktuvuk Pass, Alaska.

domestic skills, sharing patterns, homeland integrity) with those selected elements of modern society that benefit the evolving Native culture yet do not destroy continuity with the past. Control of land and the pace and direction of cultural evolution by the Natives themselves is the essence of the movement. Joe Sun's life—his choices and blendings—provides an individual and familial exemplar relevant to the larger cultural objective. He is, by the example of his life, a bearer of both tradition and the new code for cultural survival.

Joe Sun's life was not intentionally shaped for such high purpose. It was simply his way. When Willie Hensley of NANA first asked him to participate in the Elders Conference, he did not fully understand its purpose. But in time, the idea of the elders helping young people perpetuate their Inupiaq identity—countering the pervasive influences of modern society—became a moving force in Sun's life. He later became president of the Elders Conference. The elders' meeting place, a cluster of cabins on the Noorvik River, is called Sivunniugvik, "a place where you plan before you start going further ahead on your future" (Sun 1985, 111).

The Elders Conference itself is an adaptive form of ancient practice. Always the elders have met and counseled the next step in the future of the people. They gather now by invitations over the radio rather than having them delivered by fleet-footed messengers as in old times. The results of their deliberations are broadcast across the land by radio, TV, or tape cassette rather than in the intimacy of the community house. But the purpose is the same. Such adaptations to a changing world are nothing new. The Eskimo people of the Kobuk Valley have faced change and the need for choice many times before. They have been here a long time.

• • •

Arctic John Etalook

Arctic John Etalook was the last old-time survivor of a lost band of mountain Eskimos, the Ulumiut. The center of their historic territory was the Ulu Valley ("Oolah" on USGS maps) in the upper reaches of the Itkillik River. The early people had probably moved eastward across the north face of the Brooks Range during the mid-nineteenth century, coming from the Noatak-Colville headwaters area. They were part of the migration toward better caribou hunting grounds that brought Eskimos into conflict with western Gwich'in Athapaskans, forcing the Indians southeastward across the divide into Chandalar country. Into the vacuum thus created filtered Nunamiut bands to occupy the river valleys of the northern Endicott Mountains.

In 1981, anthropologist Grant Spearman realized the value of documenting the history of the Ulumiut—and the urgency of doing so, for Etalook was then very old. Previous studies of the Nunamiut had mentioned the Ulumiut band only in passing. Almost nothing was known about them. Their cultural geography—camps, hunting and fishing sites, sacred

Arctic John Etalook and Lucy Sackett at Wiseman. Robert Marshall photo. Courtesy of the Bancroft Library, University of California, Berkeley.

places, landmarks, and place names—was represented by only a scattering of names. With the help of Etalook's daughter Louisa Riley, Spearman began a series of interviews and mapping sessions with Etalook, lasting well into 1982. He also consulted with Ben Kavik Aguk, an Anaktuvuk Pass elder who had been a member of the Ulumiut band during its last days in the period 1938–1942. Later, overflights of the Ulumiut territory with Etalook pinpointed historic sites and allowed Spearman to ground-proof them on foot. The results of all this were published in a preliminary report that catalogues 243 historic Ulumiut sites and localities, most of them identified as to resources and uses important to the band (Spearman et al. 1982).

Etalook, adopted son of Aqsiataaq, began life toward the end of the nineteenth century during a period of profound change in the life of northern Eskimos. Declining caribou populations; the attractions provided by whalers, traders, and explorers on the Arctic coast; and death-dealing new diseases caused hardship and disruption among the people. Many of them died from starvation and epidemics loosed upon hitherto isolated populations with no immunity. One of Etalook's earliest memories was the summer 1903 measles epidemic, brought by the ships, which swept away his grandparents and many others who had gone to the coast to trade. When the survivors returned upriver in the fall, the sickness spread to more of the inland people.

Even with its dangers, the coast still attracted families from the Ulumiut and other inland bands. The dearth of caribou meant hard times, even starvation, for those who stayed upriver. For a while, jobs as crewmen on whaling ships or as hunters of fresh meat for overwintering whalers sustained the migrant Eskimos. As the whaling industry faded after 1900, trapping for arctic fox took its place in the economy of the displaced inland people. Trading posts along the coast bought their furs and provided the manufactures and staples they craved.

In the fall of 1913, the fur trade brought Aqsiataaq and his family to the coast where explorer Vilhjalmur Stefansson and anthropologist Diamond Jenness visited their camp that fall. Jenness stayed on to study the Eskimos who had come to the Colville delta area to trap, living part of the time with Aqsiataaq's family. His descriptions of lanky, 18-year-old Etalook drew a picture of a self-reliant, skilled young man, already a superior trapper. Jenness noted that the inlanders were viewed as country cousins by the coastal Eskimos, whose contact with white men went back many years. One of Jenness's problems was the spartan diet in Aqsiataaq's household. Fresh meat and fish were not plentiful, and Utuyok, Etalook's mother, was frugal with the biscuits and other store foods that supplemented the wild-food diet. She made no compensation for the relative lack of nourishment in the store foods, as compared to the high energy in the normal meat and fat diet of the Eskimos (Jenness 1957).

By the 1930s, the fur trade had faltered and the caribou were coming back to the inland foothills and mountains. Aqsiataaq and Etalook had spent time in the Colville's mountain tributaries beginning in the 1920s, on occasion drifting down to the Wiseman mining district. Etalook and his brother took long winter hunting trips in the high valleys, discovering plentiful caribou and furbearers. Based on this news, some of the inland families began the return from the coast. Small groups of families filtered into the north-face valleys, from the Killik River on the west to the Sagavanirktok on the east. In time Aqsiataaq became headman or *umealik* of a group centered in the Ulu Valley.

Reconstitution of the Ulumiut band lasted only a few years. Aqsiataaq and Utuyok were very old, there was pressure from territorial authorities to enroll children in school, and some of the young people were attracted to Fairbanks. Coming of the war made resupply of store goods and ammunition difficult for isolated groups. By 1942, some of the Ulumiut had gone to Wiseman, others to Fairbanks. Etalook and his family split the difference. They had a cabin in Wiseman but spent most of their time at a camp on Nugget Creek to the north, where they continued hunting and fishing in the traditional manner. Finally, age caught up with them, too. In 1970 they moved to Anaktuvuk Pass, then to Fairbanks in 1972 (Walter Johnson, pers. comm. June 16, 1984; Spearman et al. 1982).

Bob Marshall had known the Aqsiataaq (Oxadak) family in Wiseman during his 1930–1931 residency. He described Etalook (Itashluk) as a surly-looking Native of perhaps thirty-five years. "He seems solemn and morose, and this impression is accentuated by his very dark skin, the other Eskimos being as light as dark complexioned Whites. He dresses exquisitely, mostly in furs, and seems to take great pride in his personal appearance" (Marshall 1991, 86).

Walter Johnson, who knew and hunted with Etalook in the 1940s, seconded Marshall's comments about Etalook's always immaculate dress. His dignity was impressive. When Johnson returned seasonally to Wiseman from school, a ritual of reacquaintance ensued: Etalook waited a day, then sent his daughters to Walter's cabin with an offering of sheep liver. Only after another day had passed would Etalook himself formally call, attired in fancy furs for the occasion. Johnson interpreted this as part of a larger village-life ritual that buffered and made indirect the relationships of few people living in isolated proximity. Another example of this social cushioning was the care taken not to box people in with direct questions or requests. If Etalook needed to borrow an axe, he did not pose a direct question. Instead, he would casually remark that he seemed to have misplaced his axe. Johnson could respond with a loan if he felt like it, or simply note the remark.

Other stories seem to confirm Marshall's early judgment that the young Etalook may have been difficult to get along with. But fifteen years later, Johnson knew a man composed and gracious. He was also capable of joviality. During Wiseman dances in the 1940s, when folk and round dances grew tiresome, Etalook ("Arctic John" to his Wiseman friends) would bring out the drums and lead Eskimo dances until dawn (Walter Johnson, pers. comm. Jan. 6, 1984, and June 16, 1984).

Both Walter Johnson and USGS geologist W. P. Brosge recorded that Etalook; his wife, Esther; and his daughter continued to live at Nugget Creek as traditional hunters and trappers, avoiding too much integration into town life. Brosge's observations date from 1959 when Etalook was well into his sixties.

The lives of Joe Sun and Arctic John Etalook spanned a time whose early years reached back toward the dawn of human history in northern Alaska. As traditionalists—initiated by elders who would have been at home with their ancestors of a thousand years before—they have seen and experienced Brooks Range landscapes in ways that more modern men can never know. Consider the richness of their visions: compounded of ancient knowledges and skills, conveyed by evolved language and thought processes attuned to practical and spiritual realities beyond the range of our dulled and ignorant sensitivities. The fragments of these realities gathered by Libbey and Spearman and other workers in these fields give only a hint, an incalculably valuable hint, of the gestalt visions that such a cultural background could provide. We can see but dimly and partially through the eyes of the ancient people. And those whole visions become yet fainter as their beholders grow old and die and fold into icy graves. Worlds are lost this way; whole species of human perception go to ground.

In remote Alaska villages where significant dependence on wild resources persists, where the seasonal imperatives of hunted animals still name the passing months (October translates as *nuliagvik*, caribou breeding time), critical elements of those older visions still shape Native perceptions. What is now called the subsistence way of life, but was always before simply the lifeway of hunters and gatherers, "still links the village in many ways with its past, . . . informs the present, and . . . is the means whereby the village can survive in the future. The land, of course, provides the resources and remoteness on which this way of life depends" (Berger 1985, 53).

Some people view this way of life as an anachronism, a residual thing in the last spasm of phase-out. But traditionalist Natives of all ages reject this dismissive idea, this linear progression toward cultural oblivion concocted by outsiders. These traditionalist people speak of ancestors learning to live in a land of strong winds and cold temperatures, sharing to survive, teaching the young to carry on. They look at the land as source and sustainer of their lives. In Western civilization they see dollar signs but little spirituality. For them, profit is the good life derived from land and sea. Land is the heritage, and what they do on that land—as communities, families, and individuals—is their culture.

Amazing as it may seem, these traditionalist people want to continue being what they are. They do not want to join the rest of us. Being Indians or Eskimos, they believe, is what they were created to be. They conceive the passing on of this identity to their children—with the knowledge, skills, language, and land base to sustain it—as their preeminent cultural duty. Subsistence living, in this view, is more than survival. It is life itself. It is the only worthwhile way to live.[2]

In our study region, a century of the growing influence of Anglo-European culture—including both imposed and chosen elements—has irrevocably altered the bases of traditional Native life. Imported technology, social and educational programs, missionary efforts, and the economic, governmental, and political forces that have created new land-tenure systems and industrial developments, have swept like giant waves over the societies and cultural landscapes of upper-country Natives. Erosions have occurred, but rimrocks and hard cores have resisted and still hold. An evolved way of life—part old, part new—is the result of this transition. In practical terms, this evolution can be described as a mixed cash and subsistence economy. More profoundly, it is a cultural high-wire act that strives to maintain the essence of ancient values in an environment already much changed and still accelerating.

Objectively, given the arrayed forces of modern times, the prospect for survival of indigenous people and cultural pluralism in arctic Alaska seems bleak. But the history of these people is a history of survival. For generations and millennia they have proved their steadfastness in a demanding environment. During the period of recent history, since about 1850, they have seen wave after wave of outsiders come into their world, extract something from it, and leave. Traditionalists are confident that the current inundation—largely oil-and-mineral based, partly sport-and-recreation based—is similarly transient, at least as a major, disruptive force. Their sense is that as long as environmental wisdom and sociocultural equity are guides to the future, they can survive this wave also. During a time like this one, they see the need to exert themselves strongly upon both the external forces that threaten their homeland and the disintegrative forces within their own societies that have been spawned by recent change. Daily they face the dilemma of being both effective modernists to protect their homeland and sustaining traditionalists to preserve their culture.

The village of Anaktuvuk Pass exemplifies the will to survive these stressful times. Its history and its current outlook on the world offer a window into the experiences and perspectives of a people caught in the intersection where the old and the new have only recently met.

The country around Anaktuvuk Pass is one of austere beauty. Crenelated cliffs rise to the west. Wide valleys of the Anaktuvuk and John rivers fall away gently to the north and south. High mountains march eastward. Narrower valleys and canyons channel side streams and dry courses toward the main rivers, lacing the rugged terrain with narrow vistas that bend out of sight between the mountain buttresses guarding their secrets. Past these walls and bends, high ridges trend east-west, their flanks cut by headwater streams that step down toward distant valley floors. Lakes large and small dot valleys and isolated plateaus. In the watered places clumps of willow nod a few feet above the dense tundra mat. Great boulders stand alone or in groups where glaciers left them. Scree and surges of rock debris mark the transition to barren slopes and steeps, whose nakedness is barely tinged at lower elevations by lichen colors.

In the midst of this panoramic country, at the point where a gust of wind determines whether rain drops flow to the Arctic Ocean or the Yukon

Simon Paneak, from a slide taken by Benedicte Ingstad in the Anaktuvuk Pass area, ca. 1950. Courtesy Grant Spearman.

River, stands a cluster of buildings bordering a gravel airstrip. It seems incongruous. Who could live here? In winter, when all hint of green is gone and wind drives veils of snow over darkened, treeless expanse, that question gets urgent.

Yet people have lived here for thousands of years. This writer had a chance to visit a few of the old sites with Grant Spearman and archaeologist Jack Campbell in summer 1985. First we went four miles northeast of Anaktuvuk Pass village to the Tuktu Site, situated on a well-drained glacial terrace. Notched projectile points and other artifacts found here have been dated to 6,000 years B.P. The assemblage identifies a people who hunted big game, people who could move from forest to tundra to coastline as the seasons' offerings came around. They were probably people of the Northern Archaic Tradition, ancestral to the Athapaskan Indians, who came into the Brooks Range passes to hunt caribou. At an adjoining site, artifacts possibly 10,000 years old have been found.

Next we visited a spit jutting into Natvakruak Lake, about fifteen miles north of the village. Here, scattered over an extensive site, were the remains of an ancient occupation of about 4,000 years ago. Microblades and cores, and thousands of tiny flakes indicate an inland Denbigh Flint Complex site. The people who left these small tools may have been ancestors of the Eskimos.

We then moved southeast to Tulugak Lake, about twelve miles northeast of the village. On the ridges above this lake we saw great stone meat caches excavated out of scree slides. When stocked with caribou or sheep meat, they were covered by corbelling flat rocks over the top. Below, in the valley leading toward Tulugak Lake, we retraced the wings of an old caribou surround, first shown to Campbell by Anaktuvuk Pass elder Simon Paneak in the 1950s. Cairns of stone forty feet apart marked the fan-shaped wings leading to the killing site. To these cairns, willows were lashed, giving the visual effect of a person standing there. Other cairns, or *inuksuk*, bordered the side hills to keep the caribou from breaking toward high ground. (In later years, Simon told Campbell, the Eskimos inserted strips of toilet paper in the rock cairns: their wind-blown motion animated the *inuksuk*.) Tulugak Lake is ringed by ancient and historic-period sites, for it has long been a favored camping place, with fish in the lake, caribou trails nearby, and good access to sheep. The nearby scree provided excellent meat storage, a critical necessity for people whose seasonal hunts during times of abundance supplied meat for periods of scarcity. When the inland Eskimos returned from the coast beginning in the Thirties, Tulugak Lake again became a main camp. In 1949 a number of small bands merged here. Later they would move to the present village site in Anaktuvuk Pass.

At a ridge site southwest of Anaktuvuk Pass, high on the east side of John River valley, we found an impressive stone ring, which probably served two functions: as a wind shelter for spotters who signalled the approach and direction of caribou to hunters in the valley below, and as a spotting blind for sheep hunters. On down the ridge, other works of stone included more shelters and cache boxes.

Finally, with Anaktuvuk Pass elder Elijah Kakinya (born 1895; died 1986), we flew west to visit the Chandler Lake area, where Kakinya and Grant Spearman traced the geography and events of the last traditional kayak caribou hunt conducted by the Nunamiut in 1945. The Chandler Lake environs, as those at Tulugak, had been the center of a band territory, with access to game and fish the compelling attraction. On the flight back to Anaktuvuk Pass, over the lake and across the intervening mountains via the canyons of Kollutarak Creek, Kakinya and his interpreter, Anna Nageak, carried on animated discussion in the Inupiaq language, with Kakinya pointing out old hunting sites, camps, travel routes, and locations of historic events. We poked around the mountains at his direction to see the sheep he knew would be there. It had been many years since Kakinya had last traversed that landscape on the ground, but he remembered, it seemed, every rock in it.

Establishment of Anaktuvuk Pass

Beginning in the mid-1930s, we have a picture of inland people returning from the coast, the fur trade there down, the wildlife in the mountains resurgent. Remnants of the old bands trickle back to their ancestral territories—Killik River, Chandler Lake, Ulu Valley. For a decade and more, their lives revert to an approximation of traditional times. It is not quite the same, for they have rifles, they periodically travel south to Koyukuk and Kobuk villages to trade furs for store goods, they have a touch of white man's religion. But they are more rather than less dependent on the old ways and the old landscapes and resources. They are still doing some communal hunting, storing their meat in the old caches, roaming the known places. Until the mid-1940s they see few white men, at least in their home territories.

Pilot Sig Wien did fly in ammunition and other supplies during the war, trading them for wolf hides and other furs. In 1945, a party of USGS ge-

ologists poked around the Chandler River looking for oil. In 1947, Wien convinced the Chandler Lake band to relocate in the Anaktuvuk Valley, promising improved air service and the possibility of schooling for the children. This led, in 1949, to the band consolidation at Tulugak Lake. Through the winter of 1949–1950, Helge Ingstad, a Norwegian explorer, lived with the Nunamiut. His book about them brought these old-style Eskimos to world attention, starting a train of scientists toward their little settlement. Also during this turning-point time, trader Pat O'Connell staged up from the Koyukuk to Hunt Fork and finally Anaktuvuk Pass, where he built a log store. In 1951 came a post office, located in a tent at postmaster Homer Mekiana's hunting camp. Thus did Anaktuvuk Pass, with its store and post

Kobuk Eskimos on hunting trip to Noatak River, using pack dogs. P. S. Smith photo 764 of 1911. USGS Historical Photo Library, Denver.

This is the kind of sled still used by the Nunamiut to hunt, trap, and travel. Snowmobiles have replaced the dogs shown here. Photo by Don McCune, courtesy Simon Paneak Museum, Anaktuvuk Pass, Alaska.

Above: Lunch stop on the trail. Elijah Kakinya historical photo collection.

Below: Nunamiut men at a trading post entertaining people with an Eskimo dance. Elijah Kakinya historical photo collection.

office, become a base camp for resupply. In 1958, Presbyterian missionaries came to the pass from Barrow. The Nunamiut went down the John River to good spruce timber at Hunt Fork, cut logs, hauled them to the pass, and built their own church. The church doubled as a school until 1960, when a permanent school was started with full-time teachers.

With school attendance mandatory, Anaktuvuk Pass became a permanent village. The clincher came when an airline-company Cat walked up from

A Nunamiut hunter using pack dogs on a summer hunt. His rifle is protected by a caribou-skin case. Grant Spearman historical photo collection.

the oil-exploration base at Umiat (on the Colville River) and dragged out a landing strip along the creek. The progression of domiciles during this period reflected the changing times: from the caribou-skin tents of a hunting camp, to wall tents, to permanent houses made of spruce logs covered with sod (Gubser 1954; Spearman 1979, 1982).

Glimpses of these changing times come from the writings of the Nunamiut themselves and of the scientists and observers who visited them. Census enumerator Ethel Ross Oliver hired Simon Paneak in 1950 as interpreter and guide while she visited the remote Nunamiut camps. Entranced by the stories he told, she encouraged him to write of the days when the inland people came back from the coast (Paneak 1960).

Simon and his family, along with the families of Elijah Kakinya and Frank Rulland, migrated to the Killik River in summer 1940 after the coastal fur trade broke down. By this time trader Jack Smith at Beechey Point was nearly broke. In trying to carry the Eskimo trappers through hard times "he let out credit too much to his customers, away behind in

Winter hunting camp. Photo by Don McCune, courtesy Simon Paneak Museum, Anaktuvuk Pass, Alaska.

[The tent's] floor, about a foot thick, was composed of willow twigs, which provided not only insulation from the permafrost underneath, but a ready supply of fire wood. This twig floor, when carpeted with caribou skins was resilient, soft, and warm. The overhead frame of the house was formed by about twelve willow poles stuck in the frosted ground at more or less regular intervals around the perimeter of the house. These poles from long usage had become permanently bent, each pole joining its opposite to form a low arch. To the under side of the skeletal dome formed by these poles, the Eskimos fastened caribou skins, fur side down. Outside and over the skins and the frame, the Eskimos draped a large piece of canvas, analagous to the flies over our own tents and to the poplin outer parkas that the Eskimos wore in cold weather over their inner fur ones. The insulation against cold provided by such a structure was impeccable (Metzger 1983, 52–53).

his book." Word had got out that there might be a market for marmot skins for parkas, so Simon and his partners headed for the mountains. Simon's father, Tonngana, knew the Killik country from boyhood days. But Elijah's father, Poyah, hailed from the Anaktuvuk Pass–Ulu Valley–Itkillik–upper Koyukuk country. So Tonngana would guide them to good marmot country in the Alatna–Hunt Fork headwaters.

The families used pack dogs on their trip. They hunted as they traveled, and one night May Kakinya grabbed a 30/30 and shot a grizzly that intruded their camp.

Simon's only weapon was a .22 bolt-action rifle. He wrote that it could kill any animal in the mountains if it were hit in the right place with the first shot. He proved it by killing a grizzly that had found his meat cache. He used three "little bullets" to do it. From 100 yards he hit the bear in the ear with the first shot, which knocked him down, but "make him mad," so he rolled and roared and charged. The second bullet knocked him down again, but he sprang up and ran to the side, giving Simon a shot at the shoulder blade, which dropped him for good.

The younger men hiked into the high country and used stone deadfalls to get the marmots. Every few days they brought back a load of heavy, greasy skins for the women to clean and dry. The old men hunted near camp for meat.

After the summer's marmot hunting, with about 300 skins taken, Simon and Elijah decided to go down to Sam Dubin's store in Bettles to trade. They had exhausted all store-bought supplies and were living on meat and meat broth only. No tea, tobacco, "no every things." Loading up ten pack dogs, the two men hiked down Hunt Fork to the John River, which had plenty of water to float a boat. They made a skin boat from bull caribou and ram sheep skins fitted over a spruce frame and lashed with willow roots. They had to watch carefully for riffles and rocks because these skins would rip easily. They tied the dogs so they would not move around. Simon steered.

Along the way they killed a bull moose, because they knew that Bettles
people needed meat. With their marmot skins and meat, they had something to trade. A few poor summer wolf pelts were good for bounty money. Downriver they ran into Big Charlie Suckik. He had killed two moose
and was building a raft to get his meat to Bettles. He needed something
to trade because Dubin was not extending any more credit. After leaving
Big Charlie, Simon and Elijah got another wolf, which stood and looked
at them from a sandbar.

From upper Hunt Fork it took them two and a half days to get to Bettles.
They stayed three or four days trading furs for store goods, which Simon
noted were reasonably priced. Then, packing up the dogs, they walked
home. Nine and a half days later, after spotting beaver, muskrat, grizzlies,
and lots of moose, they got back to home camp. "It take us little less than
twenty days round trip. Everybody glad see us" (Paneak 1960, 55).

Homer Mekiana's camp and
post office at Anaktuvuk Pass,
about 1950. Don McCune
historical photo collection.

Simon's account is priceless. So many old and new things come together here: Knowledge of the land and the bear's vulnerable anatomy when using "little bullets." The mix of rifles and stone deadfalls. Speed and assurance in travel—for subsistence resources and for trade. Family division of labor. Hankering for store goods. Cashing in on all opportunities for trade or bounty.

Notable is the major shift from the white-dominated coastal trading economy back to the subsistence-based mountain life, with trapping and trading a sideline for acquiring essential ammunition and a few luxuries. This ability to swing with the boom-and-bust cycle, going back to the homeland-hunting life when opportunities in the white economy slacken, illustrates a critical adaptive strategy still employed.

These combinations of the old and new are further developed in representative historic sites near Anaktuvuk Pass. With Johnny Rulland, son of Frank in the above account, Grant Spearman visited a number of these sites, with concentration on two of them: Puvlatuuq, to the south in the John River valley just inside the margin of the spruce forest, and Kungomovik, alongside the creek by that name a few miles north of the village.

Puvlatuuq is a place of seasonal occupation in the forest zone, south of the Continental Divide and within the winter range of caribou. A nearby salt lick attracts sheep. And Puvlatuuq is a good base for trapping forest-dwelling furbearers.

Kungomovik, in a lush willow grove providing wind-shelter and fuel, has long been a gathering place for festive and trading activities. Nunamiut from

The people of Anatuvuk Pass built this log church in 1959 and still use it today. They traveled more than thirty miles to Hunt Fork of the John River to cut the logs, then hauled them to the village with dog teams. Stephen C. Porter historical photo collection.

other mountain bands and trading partners from the Kobuk and Noatak, as well as Athapaskans, could join here under truce conditions at appointed times. At this place occurred the initial falling out between Nunamiut and Gwich'in Athapaskans that precipitated the nearby Battle of Itikmalakpuk, which drove the Indians southeastward. As well, the nearby terrain of narrow creek valleys funnels migrating caribou to intercept-hunting sites ideal for close-in killing. The upper Kungomovik Creek drainage is a favored summer hunting area for fat caribou bulls, and provides a base for sheep hunting in the surrounding mountains.

Dwellings at these sites track the evolution of house styles, from traditional caribou-skin tents, *itchalik*, and moss houses, *ivrulik*, to more modern sod houses and log cabins.

Artifacts and debris combine the bones of hunted animals and adaptive uses of all manner of white man's packaging and cast-off goods. A sled runner shoe is made from metal strips cut from coffee cans. Chunks of metal have been fashioned into a homemade stove. Sections of old oil drums and five-gallon cans were used to make dog food cooking vats and feeding bowls.

These sites, with archaeological components reaching far back in time and with historic components of the recent past—identified as to individual

Sod house and meat racks at Anatuvuk Village. Stephen C. Porter historical photo collection.

families of the ongoing village—"serve as living links and stabilizing ties" between today's people and their cultural heritage. The strategic locations of these sites, proximate to the resources of game, timber, shelter, fuel, and good water, provide a communication with the past and an educational base for the future. Here, in favored parts of the natural environment chosen by their ancestors, village elders can instruct young people in the skills and activities of those who hunt to live (Spearman 1979).

In summer 1945, USGS geologist George Gryc led a survey party that descended Chandler River from Chandler Lake to the Colville (Detterman et al. 1963). This was one of four parties that year exploring and doing stratigraphic work in the Naval Petroleum Reserve. The cook in Gryc's party, Charles R. Metzger, was then a student and later became a professor of English at the University of Southern California. Some years after the expedition, Metzger turned his notes and observations into a narrative recollection of Arctic adventure (Metzger 1983).

> As the caribou came within range still upwind of us, each Eskimo lever ejected from his carbine the cartridge case left from the most recent shot he had fired, presumably in most instances only a few days before. Leaving the spent case in the breach after firing was a very effective safety precaution (Metzger 1983, 73)

Soon after, the scattered Eskimo bands of the Nunamiut started shifting to the permanent base camp and eventually the village of Anaktuvuk Pass. This move resulted in part from increasing scientific interest in the area, which brought with it more airborne contact centering on the pass. Geologists, botanists, zoologists, and anthropologists entered the Nunamiut world to study the people and their environment. They brought new technology and opportunities for employment as guides and informants. The pace quickened with establishment of Pat O'Connell's store and the post office, which led to weekly air service. Visiting hunters, government officials, teachers, and preachers followed. Old people began

to move from the distant camps to the easier and more secure life of the village. Families came in with their children for school and the religious and social ties of the church (Spearman 1979).

Traditional sod house at Anaktuvuk Pass, built by "Old Hugo." Grant Spearman photo, 1979.

Homer Mekiana, Anaktuvuk Pass hunter and first postmaster, kept a diary throughout this transition period, from May 1950 to April 1964 (Mekiana 1972). The diary records the incongruities of an isolated world of hunters suddenly thrust into the twentieth century. Helicopters, airplanes, and the new landing field compete with notes about wolf hunters and the sighting of 2,000 caribou north of the pass. "Snowshirts," men wearing business suits, sit in council with skinclad Eskimos. Families with pack dogs head down the John River or to Kungomovik to hunt and live in skin tents as a C-46 transport drops supplies, including a gas drum that smashes flat—"no parachute." As hunters gather in a distant tent to exchange information about caribou herds and the price of marmot skins, a radio blares forth news of the world. "Still war on in Korea" is followed by this Stone Age comment: "I ground some bones with stone hammer. Our fat to eat. About two pots full of grinding bones" (Mekiana 1972, entry of Jan. 14, 1951).

In the early 1950s, Anaktuvuk Pass was still more a base camp than a village. During most of the year, many families were out at camps on creeks and lakes, coming back to the pass for resupply then going out again. People like Homer, tied to village-based jobs and responsibilities, still went out nearly every day to hunt or check traps. This latter pattern became the norm as time went on and more people became sedentary because of the school and other ties. Even "village" families, however, went out to camps

The old airfield at Wiseman with Wien's Fokker airplane and Joe Ulen's truck. Robert Marshall photo. Courtesy of the Bancroft Library, University of California, Berkeley.

when school and village affairs slackened seasonally. Men without family responsibilities and families without young children continued to range the country. These hunters brought back meat to share with families stuck at the pass. Village men would go out to help haul in the meat. Homer, who talked to everyone who came in between hunting trips, passed on information about animal movements and concentrations to the next group coming through. Thus evolved a division of labor between those who ranged and those who mainly stayed home. These and other adaptive responses, such as rapid transit to and from distant hunting places, set the scene for a primarily village-based lifestyle that still depended heavily on far-ranging hunting for livelihood.

These social responses joined with environmental, technological, and economic ones to create a veritable sea change in the life of the people. Villagers restricted to short trips for meat soon depleted resident species in the near environs of the pass. To go far, yet be back in time for work or school, hunters needed machines. By 1970, the dogs that had admirably served a slowly but constantly shifting nomadic people were all but gone. Snowmachines in winter and ATVs (all terrain vehicles) in summer provided the rapid transit needed by village hunters (Hall 1972; Hall et al. 1985).

These changes reduced the amount of meat needed for feeding dogs. But they brought on a whole new set of pressures on the people. Machines and their maintenance and fuel cost money. This meant that jobs and cash flow became central to the hunting way of life—perhaps the most difficult to understand of the compounding sets of changes brought by a twentieth century running rampant. In the landlocked, mountain-stream country of the central Brooks Range, costs and complications became intense. Given the lack of coastal or riverine waters accessible by small boat and motor, summer trips in a village that could no longer depend on working dogs required cross-country vehicles.

One upshot of these progressions was a wedge into the integrity of family life and insulating remoteness. Some people went out for jobs, leaving their families. At Anaktuvuk Pass, this phenomenon was not as pronounced as in many other Alaskan villages, because with the onset of big-time oil development on the North Slope in the 1970s, money, construction, and jobs came to the village.

The transportation revolution, dictated by permanent village living, produced many more short- and long-term effects. One of these, totally unforeseen at the time of inception, arose from the summer use of ATVs across fragile arctic landscapes. It would become an environmental issue a few years later, related to the new land-tenure system that overlaid a national park on the central Brooks Range homeland.

Beginning in 1959 with Alaska's achievement of statehood, a series of momentous events, interlocking and reinforcing one another, would sweep across the far north. Together, the discovery of oil at Prudhoe Bay, the settlement of Native land claims, and the Alaska Lands Act of 1980 would create entirely new systems of governance, land management, and development in the region. The old days of intermittent visits and quick exits by outsiders were over. Within 20 years, the remote village of hunters at Anaktuvuk Pass would become part of the world.

As the pieces fell in place for these later developments, Homer Mekiana and his fellows continued their busy lives, becoming, in a sense, dual persons living two kinds of lives—partly in the new age, partly in the old. During January and February 1951, the families were scattered to the south and to the north, from Hunt Fork to Tulugak Valley and on many creeks between. A few weeks later Mekiana took his first airplane ride, going to Fairbanks for medical examinations at Ladd Field's Aeromedical Lab, which was studying Eskimo physiological adaptations to arctic conditions. At the army base he saw a jet fighter—"fast" (entry of Apr. 5, 1951). A few days later Mekiana was packing caribou meat back to the village with his dogs. The next year wolf-pup hunters had a tough season because small-plane hunters from other places were beating them to the dens. In July 1952, a number of hikers and recreational floaters (down the John to Bettles) visited the village. On the 25th a photographer from *Life* magazine flew in, snapped a few shots, and flew out to Bettles.

In 1968, pushed by the Prudhoe Bay oil discovery, the Alaska Department of Highways punched a winter road—called the Hickel Highway after Alaska Governor Walter J. Hickel—from the Yukon, across the Koyukuk, up the John River, through Anaktuvuk Pass, and across the Arctic Slope to Sagwon, where it joined an existing trail to Prudhoe. For a few weeks huge trucks rushed tons of backlogged freight to the developing oil field.

An observer at Anaktuvuk Pass noted that the Eskimos watched silently as the construction tractors moved through the pass. For the first time Anaktuvuk Pass was connected by road to the rest of the world.

The Hickel Highway symbolized the frustration of an undeveloped frontier state. Finally, with discovery of the giant Prudhoe oilfield, Alaska would realize its destiny as a mineral trove for the nation. But federal regulations and ownership of land had threatened to choke off oil development. Sea and air logistics were inadequate to the task. A freeze on federal land transfers, including rights-of-way, pending settlement of Alaska Native land claims, further complicated matters. Eventually, under pressure from oil and trucking companies and through the active intervention of the state, the winter-road construction was allowed over federal land administered by the Bureau of Land Management. Speed of construction doomed the road with the next thaw. Essentially an ice road lacking the thick insulating gravel base of advanced permafrost road construction, the freight track melted and gullied in 1969's summer sun. Exposed permafrost, its tundra mat scraped off by the tractors, turned to muck. Grades became canals (Coffey 1969).

The truck invasion of Anaktuvuk Pass was short-lived. But the mucky road and the pressure for oil development and land disposition, of which the road had been symptomatic, precipitated hot debates and big decisions. In Alaska and nationally, conservation groups were galvanized by the ill-advised road, which had scarred the nation's last great wilderness and provoked crisis at Anaktuvuk Pass. Larger questions about arctic conservation and development, licensing and right-of-way for a proposed trans-Alaska oil pipeline, and settlement of Native land claims clamored for solution. Ultimately, the political and economic forces generated by Prudhoe Bay helped to break the land-freeze and license logjams. With great speed the way was opened for oil development and transport via pipeline, resumption of federal land transfers to the State of Alaska as provided by the Statehood Act of 1958, settlement of Native land claims, and conservation of large tracts of wilderness. Resolution of such vast issues could flow from only one source, the U.S. Congress. The central instrument that would allocate for these many purposes Alaska's lands—nearly all federally owned at that time—was the Alaska Native Claims Settlement Act of 1971.

The act was the pragmatic product of a strange alliance. Native land claims had been talked about but had been politically stymied for years. When state land selections under the Statehood Act began to impinge on Native homelands in the early 1960s, the Natives mobilized politically to protest. In partial response, in 1966 Secretary of the Interior Stewart Udall instituted a freeze on further land transfers until Native land claims could be resolved. Immediately the State of Alaska sued the federal government, jamming the issue in the courts. It was the pressure to deliver newly discovered oil via pipeline from the North Slope to a warm-water port in south Alaska that lent urgency to congressional consideration of land-claims bills already drafted. To the Natives' plea for justice had been added the potent persuasions of the oil industry, backed by a state desperate for oil-royalty revenues (the state owned the Prudhoe Bay oilfield). With passage of the Settlement Act, the right-of-way for the pipeline and the oil-development haul road could be carved out of the public domain. The route through the Brooks Range traversed Atigun Pass, some 90 miles east of Anaktuvuk.[3]

Meanwhile, back at Anaktuvuk Pass, the people reacted ambivalently to the new state of affairs brought about by oil and the spotlight of national concern. Correspondent Jane Pender of the *Anchorage Daily News*, while preparing a 1969 series of articles entitled "Crisis on the North Slope," visited Anaktuvuk Pass to find out how the winter road had affected the village. She found that consternation at the massive intrusion was qualified by practical considerations. In 1962 the Anak-tuvukers, having exhausted their nearby willow-fuel supply, had considered moving to Umiat—leaving school, church, and homes. They were saved from this by emergency provision of oil and oil stoves by government agencies. But they were still on the margin. Generally, the village people—despite the yearnings of anthropologists for continuation of the old culture—wanted some sustaining mix of the good life, as provided by cash jobs and modern conveniences, and the old ways on the land.

Pender's interviews with traditionalists like Charlie Edwardsen, Jr., of Barrow showed that the Eskimos feared oil-development pressures on the land. The old culture of free use of the land was in jeopardy. Arctic Slope Native Association attorney Frederick Paul, himself a distinguished Native activist, commented ruefully that the oil companies were coming in and nobody could stop them: "No one cares that this is your homeland" (Pender 1969). A sense of foreboding was pervasive. The temptation of jobs, access, and affordable goods battled with qualms about restrictions on land use, destruction of subsistence resources, and the social problems that would surely accompany an industrial invasion. All of this was happening suddenly. There was no time for job training and acculturative staging. Where would the people be in a few years? Would they benefit? Or would they be left on the sidelines, watching others tear up their homeland?

The Settlement Act not only cleared the way for oil development. It also focused the attention of environmentalists and conservationists on the central Brooks Range. The Native people would be wooed by both developers and preservationists. On the one hand, jobs and material progress were promised to the Natives under a regime of environmentally sound development. Environmentalists countered with concern over fragile arctic ecosystems, oil spills, and wildlife depredations. Given the technical problems of arctic development, they urged that national policy in the Arctic should emphasize setting aside wilderness areas and wildlife habitat in parks and refuges. This would preserve for the nation the region's recreational and esthetic values and at the same time protect the homelands of traditional peoples.[4]

The Settlement Act also brought a new way of life to the Natives. Statewide, some 44 million acres of land would be conveyed to Native corporations at village and regional levels. Typically, each Native became a shareholder in both a village and a regional corporation. A cash settlement of close to $1 billion would be distributed to the corporations and the shareholders. Suddenly, homelands became property and caribou hunters became executives. Both land ownership and management of business enterprises were alien concepts for most Native people in isolated villages. These new responsibilities, with their legal and administrative burdens, would further disrupt and dilute the subsistence way of life.[5]

Thus, in rapid succession oil discovery and development, the conservation movement, and the Settlement Act avalanched on Anaktuvuk Pass. On a less structural level was the increasing traffic of casual visitors: day-tourists, hikers, floaters, and hunters. On the good side, these people bought the caribou-skin masks made by the local people—a welcome source of cash. But the seasonal flurry of air traffic was often disturbing. Far worse was the slaughter and waste of game by trophy hunters, who thus took meat from village tables. The synergy of these new forces raised the pace of change to new levels. "Snowshirts" with their briefcases and scenario charts descended in droves on the village. To some extent, to protect their interests, Natives themselves had to join the briefcase brigade. The leaders chosen to represent the village at meetings locally, around the state, and in Washington, D.C., were often the very ones most admired for traditional skills and prowess. Time on the land for these leaders and tradition bearers became a luxury. Under the prevailing circumstances of stress and disruption, absence or distraction of village leaders from traditional affairs could not help but detract from the social cohesion of the village.

Capital improvement programs funded by taxes on the Prudhoe Bay oil operation soon followed. Construction of new houses and public facilities in the village under sponsorship of the arctic region's municipality, the North Slope Borough, increased the villagers' dependence on costly fuel, maintenance services, and other imports from the outside world. Certainly, by any conventional measure, these projects improved the standard of living in the village, and they were welcomed both for their material results and for the infusion of jobs and cash flowing from construction projects. Along with electric power and modern communications came television and other diversions, also welcomed by people increasingly co-opted by a world that only a few years before had been a distant mystery.

To top it off, the caribou hunters of Anaktuvuk Pass—and such they largely remained despite the radical changes—were visited by more and more scientists. Anthropologists crowded in to extract the diminishing base of traditional knowledge before the elders' final slide to mortality. Sociologists recorded the impacts of the changing lifestyle. Natural scientists tapped the remaining fund of traditional science and historical knowledge about animal behavior, cycles, and other phenomena.

More ominous than these innocent seekings were the radiation ecology studies conducted by Los Alamos and other national scientific laboratories. Radioactive elements from worldwide weapons testing descended from arctic skies to concentrate in the slow-growing lichen eaten by caribou. The caribou hunters of Anaktuvuk Pass contained significant concentrations of these elements in their bodies.

Truly, this little village, which entered the period of rapid change with barely a hundred souls, this last outpost of inland Eskimo culture, had come into the world, and the world had come into it (Arctic Environmental Information and Data Center 1978).

From the beginning of scientific inquiry at Anaktuvuk Pass, foreboding about the future of this relict culture group has been expressed. In 1954, when the process of change was still largely "taking place within the framework of traditional Nunamiut culture," Nicholas Gubser predicted:

> A generation hence, most Nunamiut activity, including future change, will take place in an already acculturated context. The Nunamiut of Anaktuvuk Pass will become another typical small north Alaskan native town (Gubser 1954, 27).

In 1972, Ed Hall noted that hunting peoples were disappearing the world over. Turning to Anaktuvuk Pass, he wondered what change would do.

> Certainly these Eskimos are acquiring a new view of the world, along with a new technology. Their desire for education and the other apparent riches offered by Western civilization continues unabated. I do not know if the combination of newly available material goods and a growing awareness of other possible lifeways will be the end of the caribou hunters of Anaktuvuk Pass (55).

Seven years later Grant Spearman (1979) tabulated all of the forces for change noted above, plus a few more:

- Oil and mineral development in the neighboring National Petroleum Reserve.

- Interdiction of caribou movements by the oil pipeline.

- Easy public access via the haul road into the eastern perimeter of Nunamiut hunting and fishing territory.

- Village population increase (215 people in 1982), causing more hunting pressure on wildlife.

- Creation of a new, surrounding national parkland that, among other things, invites still more visitors to intrude into the cultural privacy of the villagers.

He urged Park Service planners and managers to take careful account of this need for privacy, for, "with any society in the process of acculturation, a large influx of outside influences (in this case, visitors) can easily upset the balance of the community" (Spearman 1979, 138).

As earlier noted, the prospect for survival of cultural pluralism in arctic Alaska may seem bleak. But the tool kit of the professional survivors at Anaktuvuk Pass contains a multitude of implements, including tenacious ties to the past and hard-headed ideas about the desired future. Fortunately for their cause, Inupiat leaders had foreseen the coming massive change. During a conference of village leaders at Barrow in 1961 called the Peoples' Heritage, they defined the problems they must solve: "(1) Aboriginal land and hunting rights. (2) Economic and social development" (Arctic Environmental Information and Data Center 1978a).

When the Settlement Act was passed, the Anaktuvukers had already plotted the main outlines of lands they must have to perpetuate their village life. With the aid of resource advisors such as David Hickok, a major contributor to the 1968 Federal Field Committee for Development Planning in Alaska study *Alaska Natives and the Land* (1968) and under the direction of their own land chief, Riley Morry, the Anaktuvuk people prepared the maps and other documents needed to make their land selections.

Hunting areas for various species were defined, their travel routes were illustrated, the places of wood harvest, berry picking: all were indicated. Also, the people noted other knowledge of oil seeps, coal outcrops and mineral occurrence, and springs and gravel sources.

To their own knowledge was added the input of legal counsel on the potential effects of land classification over lands they used, the impact of selection regulations, and the portent of the alleged highway right-of-way through Anaktuvuk Pass. Resource advisors investigated surface and subsurface land values, and it was all put together. The Arctic Slope Regional Corporation and the Nunamiut Corporation of Anaktuvuk developed a joint land selection strategy with its first priority of retaining the people's subsistence way of life, and second priority to maximize potential opportunities for economic reward and progress within their value system (Hickok 1974).

By virtue of their early planning and systematic approach to the land selection requirements of the Settlement Act, "the Nunamiut of Anaktuvuk Pass became the first village in all of Alaska to completely file their village land selections on November 14, 1973" (Hickok 1974, 11).

Special negotiations were undertaken with the secretary of the interior to assure that critical areas at ancestral sites marked for inclusion within the proposed Gates of the Arctic National Park, would be available for Native selection or, failing that, would be recognized as Native-use areas under established subsistence patterns. Among other safeguards sought at this time was elimination of any proposal for a transportation corridor through Anaktuvuk Pass.

At a higher level of strategy, the Arctic Slope Regional Corporation and the Nunamiut Corporation of Anaktuvuk Pass proposed a Nunamiut National

Park that would be jointly managed by the Native people and the federal government to assure protection of both local subsistence and national interests. This proposal and later variations on it did not survive the legislative process that created Gates of the Arctic National Park and Preserve, but the documentation of traditional subsistence-use areas incident to that proposal continues to bear on management of the parkland, which, under the terms of the Alaska National Interest Lands Conservation Act of 1980, allows subsistence activities to continue in traditional-use areas within the park (Hickok 1974).

Consistently, since passage of the Settlement Act in 1971 and on through the creation and early management of Gates of the Arctic National Park and Preserve, the people of Anaktuvuk Pass have accommodated new plans and developments when they could and sharply contested them when they could not. In their relationships with the larger world—state and federal agencies, development interests, and their own regional corporation and municipality—they have won some and they have lost some. The struggle for cultural integrity and sustaining land uses goes on. So too do negotiations and agreements for land uses that assure access to key subsistence areas. Because of the dynamics of land, prey, and people, it is a continuing colloquy between the people of the village, the National Park Service, and other interested parties. The task before all parties is to find common ground and build amity upon it, for in truth, no matter how divergent the interests that converge at Anaktuvuk Pass may seem, no matter how intricate the boundaries of land tenure and jurisdiction that wind through its environs, this is one geography comprising both a homeland and a wilderness park.

Some years ago, the noted conservationist Raymond Dasmann, reflecting on the relationship between indigenous people and national parks around the world, said this:

> National parks must not serve as a means for displacing the members of traditional societies who have always cared for the land and its biota. Nor can national parks survive as islands surrounded by hostile people who have lost the land that was once their home (1976, 166).

These words still offer fresh counsel.

• • •

For all the learned commentary and the often pessimistic analyses of societal and psychological impacts brought by these years of rapid change, the pragmatic people of Anaktuvuk Pass continue to go their own way. Through the long winter—when cold and darkness reign and visitors taper off—hunters and trappers go out in the country as they always have, camping at the old sites, pursuing the same animals, though with easier access through motorized technology. During holiday breaks from school, families trek to the camps to join the hunters. In summer the tent camps can be seen scattered through the country at the lakes and along the creeks. In systematic fashion, a cadre of young people is being coached in the skills of living off the land (Calkins 1982).

There is an awareness in the village that the heyday of construction projects and wage employment is over, that another boom has crested and that older dependencies on the land and its wild resources are coming to the fore again. It is an old rhythm. A study of village subsistence economies in Alaska demonstrates that those communities far from urban centers, not connected by roads to urban areas, with lower immigration, and with lower household incomes must for survival continue to depend heavily on wild harvests (Wolfe and Walker 1987). These criteria apply with special force at landlocked Anaktuvuk Pass as the construction-based flirtation with the wage economy cools.

In a study of Anaktuvuk Pass subsistence strategies and adaptive responses through time, Edwin Hall has summarized the current view of the villagers:

> For the Anaktuvuk Pass Inupiat, the subsistence issue remains basic to life itself. They continue to teach their children, through word and example, the tenets and techniques of the subsistence quest, though most, always seeking survival alternatives also emphasize the importance of securing marketable skills through formal education. They are continually made aware that subsistence as a means of survival today balances on the razor edge of politics. They know that the contribution of subsistence activities to their everyday existence cannot fall below a certain critical level, given the economic realities of today's world, without rendering their traditional relationship with the land untenable.
> . . .
> The present subsistence quest is inextricably intertwined with that of the past, woven, from the threads of antiquity which both fashioned and constrained a world view that derives from a holistic understanding of the Arctic environment and encompasses a wide range of alternative strategies focused on survival in the most comfortable and rewarding fashion possible. Still, the present Anaktuvuk Pass Inupiat subsistence quest is a unique response to the circumstances of the present. Even so, as long as subsistence hunting remains part of the Anaktuvuk Pass Inupiat lifeway, the adaptive responses chosen in the future will reflect the lessons of both the present and the past. Experience is not only the teacher, the guide, but also the body of today's existence and the spirit of tomorrow's hope. Innovation, experimentation, shifts in emphasis, fluctuations in the

relative importance of particular resources, the importance of specific areas, and the importance of specialized techniques will all continue to interplay with the accumulated wisdom of the past as the Inupiat struggle in the future to retain their unique adaptation. Mobility, recognition of alternatives, and access to resources will remain the key concepts of that quest, all directed towards the provision and the promise that the land will continue to provide (Hall et al. 1985, 89).

Oil exploration supplies lightered to beach at Barrow during Barrow Expedition of 1947. J. C. Reed photo 913. USGS Historical Photo Library, Denver.

Chapter Eight

CREATION OF THE PARK

Since World War II, Alaska's Far North has undergone amazing changes. From being a region barely known or noted by the world at large, it has become a focal point of international interests: geopolitical, industrial, and conservationist. The instruments of modern society have come to the far places. They have shrunk the distances that made these places remote from the outer world and from each other.

Individual episodes spurring the recent progression—military installations, statehood, acts of Congress, oil and mineral discoveries, the oil pipeline, and emplacement of a bewildering array of lines on the map— have aggregated into a more profound and revolutionary change: For at least 10,000 years people dwelt in these landscapes subject to the natural forces around them. The fate of travelers depended on the sufferance and succor of local people. Now all this is reversed, with the greater part of the shift occurring in the last 40 years. Natural forces have been largely tamed, at least temporarily, by modern transport and imported technologies. And the fate of local landscapes and people depends to an extraordinary degree on decisions made elsewhere.

In many discussions with local people, this writer has heard one sentiment more than any other: the heartfelt wish that things had not changed. The people who call the upper country home remember a vast and mainly vacant public-domain commons whose few inhabitants were governed almost without exception by customary rules. They all knew each other, and they had enough time and room, usually, to dissipate their occasional conflicts. They didn't ask for much, nor were they given a lot of things that they hadn't asked for—like new laws and regulations or suddenly appearing roads through their settlements and villages. But these things have come unasked in recent years.

When they came, a dichotomy developed. Local people divided over the two generic prospects for their future offered them by outsiders. As writer John McPhee has observed, this division

> produced a tension that underlay much of what was happening in the state. It was tension over the way in which Alaska might proceed. . . . It was the tension of preservation versus development, of stasis versus economic productivity, of wilderness versus the drill and the bulldozer, and in part it had caused the portentous reassignment of land that now . . . was

altering, or threatening to alter, the lives of everyone in the state (1977, 83).

Signs and portents of changing times began with the war and accelerated thereafter. A big landing field was built five miles upstream from Bettles in 1945 to support petroleum explorations in the Naval Petroleum Reserve north and northwest of the central Brooks Range. A new town of Bettles Field grew up there, sheltered partly in buildings moved from what had become Old Bettles. Large-scale air freighting could now commence. Ex-Spring Creek miner Al Withrow, the elder, ran the radio beacon there. A companion Indian village, Evansville, grew up at the north end of the runway in response to job opportunities (Al Withrow, pers. comm. summer 1985).

In the 1950s, the Kennecott Corporation renewed its interest in the Bornite copper deposits on Ruby Creek near Shungnak. Another big airstrip, development roads, and increased barge traffic resulted. Should commodity markets improve, a mine employing up to 600 people and a community of thousands was forecast (Foote 1966).

Increased air access to the Brooks Range periphery encouraged a minor boom in guided hunting into areas heretofore known only to Natives, prospectors, and geologists. Old-style guides like Hal Waugh, Bud Helmericks, and Bernd Gaedeke established camps and lodges on the forested south flank of the Brooks Range at such fly-in sites as Iniakuk Lake, Walker Lake, and Takahula Lake. Hal Waugh, honored as the first master guide in Alaska, believed with passion in the principles of fair chase. He fought the growing trend of fast-in, fast-out hunting guides, for whom numbers of hunting parties and big bucks were the objectives of guiding. He warned his clients that the old ways—getting on the ground, taking time, and sweating for an animal in its own terrain with no guarantees of kill success—would govern any hunt he guided. He took only a few parties each year, screened by these standards, to participate in what he believed was a profound human experience when conducted ethically. He and his peers deplored the cheaters and lamented "the end of old Alaska," which, since the war, had fallen under the sway of "Industrial Religion" (Keim 1977).

While groups of old-timers huddled around campfires and cabin stoves remembering better days, the big world kept coming. Conveyance of Prudhoe Bay's potentially rich oil lands from the federal government to the state opened the way for major oil discoveries. Soon followed the push for roads and pipeline. Jet airliners began service to Barrow, Deadhorse (Prudhoe), and Kotzebue (Pender 1969).

Meanwhile, the conservation movement had been busy. Beginning in 1950 and for several years thereafter, the National Park Service fielded an Alaska Recreation Survey team headed by George Collins. Among the published recommendations was a preliminary concept for an arctic wilderness park. Collins encouraged Olaus and Mardy Murie's expedition to

the eastern Brooks Range in 1956, which was supported by a consortium of scientific and conservation groups in Alaska and across the country (Theodore R. Swem, pers. comm. Jan. 28, 1987). Partly as a result of the Muries's expedition, the Arctic National Wildlife Range was established by Public Land Order in December 1960. While stumping around the country for Brooks Range preservation, Olaus, then president of the Wilderness Society, urged that some vestiges of Alaska's backcountry be saved for all the people before "progress" claimed them. He carried this message in full recognition that land withdrawals of any kind were controversial in Alaska. As an honorary member of the Pioneers of Alaska, he urged that designated wilderness areas would provide the last refuge for Alaska's traditional Native and pioneer lifestyles. Far from locking up the land, such areas, properly adapted to the needs of their neighbors and inhabitants, would perpetuate frontier Alaska's beauty, scientific values, social and cultural integrity, and access for the people at large (Murie n.d.).

This argument succinctly framed the conservationists' position for the years ahead. Places and details would vary. But the lines drawn then would continue to define the intellectual, esthetic, and emotional ramparts of a struggle dedicated to thwarting open season on arctic Alaska by any version of Progress that would be destructively exploitative. In addition to the basic wilderness preservation idea were two complementary elements of the largely homegrown Alaska conservation movement: concern for the preservation of traditional Alaskan lifeways, both Native and frontier American; and protection of fragile, frozen landscapes from industrial projects conceived in ignorance or for narrow economic reasons. These concerns resulted, on the one hand, in alliance of conservationists and traditionalists, and on the other, in a strong environmental emphasis that, for example, blocked early pipeline construction plans whose design and engineering principles were ill-adapted to the problems of permafrost.[1]

The first Seebee camp at Umiat on the Colville River. This camp helped inaugurate modern oil exploration on the Arctic Slope. R. M. Chapman photo 130 of 1946. USGS Historical Photo Library, Denver.

Oil exploration at Umiat, 1947.
J. C. Reed photo 876. USGS
Historical Photo Library, Denver.

The national interest in a balanced program of development and conservation for Alaska was formally recognized in the Alaska Native Claims Settlement Act of 1971. The act directed federal agencies to study outstanding areas for possible designation as national conservation units—parks, refuges, forests, and wild and scenic rivers. In part because of Robert Marshall's well-publicized adventures in the Brooks Range, as well as the writings of his cohorts and followers, the Gates of the Arctic region had long been viewed as a potential national park. During the 1960s the National Park Service had conducted its studies of Alaska's natural and cultural landscapes. During this period the central Brooks Range came to the fore as a premier parkland candidate. For example, in January 1965, George Collins, chairman of the Park Service's newly formed Alaska Task Force, recommended study of a Brooks Range and Arctic Slope zone as a potential park; it included the eastern part of the later Gates of the Arctic National Park and Preserve (T. R. Swem, pers. comm. Jan. 28, 1987).

In 1966 the fruits of these early studies were brought together in an informal study report that recommended for preservation, among other proposals, certain areas in the central Brooks Range: the Anaktuvuk Pass environs as a significant cultural, geological, and wildlife corridor between the Koyukuk and Colville rivers; and the western part of the Endicott Mountains inscribed by the upper Alatna and Kobuk rivers. These headwater areas contained, according to Roger Allin,

> the most rugged, spectacular, fearsome and awe-inspiring
> mountains in all of Alaska—and the most remote. While they

Freighter SS Jonathan Harrington caught in ice off Point Barrow, part of the supply operation for oil exploration in the Naval Petroleum Reserve in 1945. J. C. Reed photo 897. USGS Historical Photo Library, Denver.

rise only to elevations of 8,000 to 9,000 feet, the vertical drop between peak and valley floor and the exposure of jagged, bare granite peaks, the isolation of the small lakes, which are ice-free only a few weeks out of the year, formed within the glacial cirques add to the appearance of desolation and the feeling of aloneness one experiences in this last region of true wilderness within the United States. . . . While in this part of Alaska nature is a tough and unforgiving adversary, here also she is beautiful beyond all description—remote, pristine, undiscovered and unspoiled (Allin 1966, 7, 13–14).

In an October 1967 meeting in Juneau between Alaska's Governor Walter J. Hickel and National Park Service Director George Hartzog, Hartzog endorsed a proposal by Federal Field Committee chairman Joseph Fitzgerald for a joint NPS–State of Alaska study of the Alatna–Kobuk region to see if it qualified for possible addition to the National Park System. The Brooks Range study would be part of a larger NPS–State cooperative effort across Alaska to set aside park and recreation areas in anticipation of major acceleration of the state's economic development (Mattes 1969).

Meanwhile, the national organizations of the Sierra Club and The Wilderness Society, joined by Alaskan members and supporting groups, had added their endorsements to the idea of Brooks Range preservation. In 1963, a Wilderness Society conclave at Mount McKinley passed the following resolution:

> It was the consensus of the [Wilderness Society] Council that the staff explore informally with the Secretary of the Interior a suitable form of wilderness type classification for an appropriate area in the Upper Koyukuk-Endicott Mountains region of the Brooks Range (Mattes 1969, 2; Jack Hession, pers. comm. Mar. 31, 1986).

Air-freighted supply cache for later use by USGS oil-exploration field teams. J. C. Reed photo 917 of 1947. USGS Historical Photo Library, Denver.

By 1964, the Bureau of Land Management (BLM), then the federal agency in charge of almost all of Alaska's public domain, was inventorying the south slope of the Brooks Range for recreation sites that should be reserved from destructive forms of commercial or industrial development. Within a few years, under pressure from the Alaska chapter of the Sierra Club and the Alaska Conservation Society, the BLM was preparing a land classification plan that would treat major scenic and recreation sites in the central Brooks Range as wildlands "to prevent the loss of irreplaceable public values." Richard J. Gordon of Juneau was a workhorse in the conservationists' efforts to protect the central Brooks Range. His letters of advocacy and his analyses of the region's resources and values, beginning in the late 1960s, contributed strongly to the development and defense of expansive conservation proposals that foreshadowed the scope of the eventual parkland.[2]

In June 1968, the NPS unilaterally began the field study of the central Brooks Range endorsed earlier by Director George Hartzog. It occurred in a context of gathering urgency, for the State of Alaska's proposed Arctic Transportation Corridor through the Brooks Range, the recent oil discoveries, and the new tourist invasion of the Arctic via commercial airlines had taken the wraps off the remote mountains.

The field reconnaissance was directed by Merrill Mattes, a historian, with the invaluable flight assistance of chief pilot Theron Smith of the U.S. Fish and Wildlife Service. The three-man team included Bailey Breedlove and Richard Prasil, providing a balance of cultural, landscape architectural, and natural history disciplines. The team's impressions of the country—its flora, fauna, geology, scenery, and scattered humans—recall those of Marshall, except for the decline of population in the upper country (the Wiseman-Nolan camp now comprised only eighteen souls). At Wild Lake, a bearded man—doubtless a disciple of homesteader Fred Meador, self-appointed protector of the lake and its creatures—chased the party's taxiing amphibious plane in a rowboat to protest this noisy disturbance of Eden. At Anaktuvuk Pass the visitors were welcomed by patriarchs Elijah Kakinya and Simon Paneak, and the Eskimos' sod houses and meat-laden drying racks were noted. Kobuk village seemed "a quiet peaceful place" compared to the Outside's civil rights and anti-Vietnam War strife (Mattes 1969, 4).

The team's recommendations took account of the state's plan for an Arctic Transportation Corridor—presumably via the John River and through Anaktuvuk Pass—proposing a two-part parkland. The small east section centered around Mount Doonerak and included upper North Fork and the Gates themselves; the larger west section comprised the Alatna-Kobuk headwaters, including Arrigetch Peaks, Mount Igigpak, Walker Lake, and the Kobuk canyons. The park was conceived as undeveloped, roadless, and wild, supporting Marshall's idea of the ultimate wilderness. Subsistence hunting by Natives would continue under this proposal (Mattes 1969).

These modest recommendations struck a middle ground between a larger Alaska Wilderness Council proposal and a restricted lake–recreation site concept pushed by Alaska miners. The preservationists would extend the west section of the parkland north of the Arctic Divide to protect important caribou range and preserve a transect of North Slope tundra. Mining spokesman Jack McCord envisioned a state–federal cooperative program that would develop recreation sites and floatplane landings along selected lake shores, plus pack trails radiating from the landings into the hinterlands where government-built cabins would support mineral exploration by mining engineers.[3]

Shortly after the NPS Kobuk-Koyukuk field-study team returned from Alaska, nearly a year before the June 1969 publication of its report, chief planner Theodore R. Swem of the service's Washington office had supervised preparation of an extended four-million-acre Gates of the Arctic proposal. It was part of a larger package conceived by Secretary of the Interior Stewart Udall (T. R. Swem, pers. comm. Jan. 28 1987). In the closing months of 1968, Udall presented the package to President Lyndon B. Johnson. The secretary urged that the Gates of the Arctic and other key Alaskan and Lower 48 areas totaling seven million acres be proclaimed national monuments as Johnson's parting conservation gift to the nation in the last days of his administration. Anticipating congressional distress at

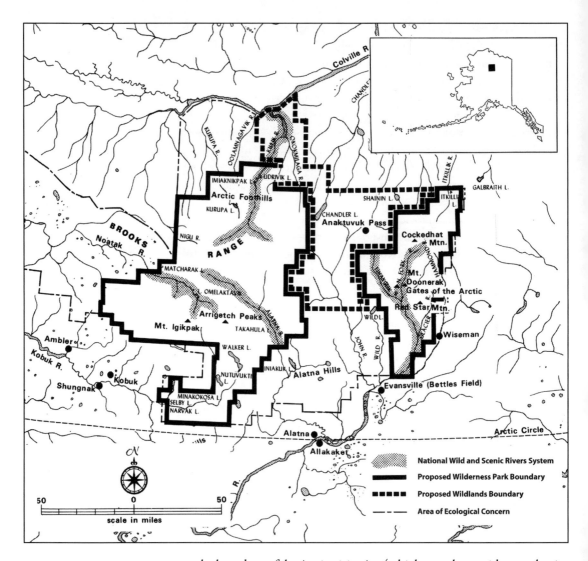

The map legend:
- National Wild and Scenic Rivers System
- Proposed Wilderness Park Boundary
- Proposed Wildlands Boundary
- Area of Ecological Concern

The original National Park Service Gates of the Arctic parkland proposal, from the Merrill Mattes Kobuk–Koyukuk reconnaissance of 1968.

such a broad use of the Antiquities Act (which gave the president authority to proclaim national monuments), and angry at Udall's maneuvering to achieve this last-minute coup, Johnson balked and refused to sign the Gates of the Arctic and other large-acreage proclamations. Not until after passage of the Settlement Act in 1971 would the Gates proposal be revived.[4]

•••

The nine years between passage of the Alaska Native Claims Settlement Act of 1971 (ANCSA) and passage of the Alaska National Interest Lands Conservation Act of 1980 (ANILCA) telescoped historic decisions and events whose counterparts had taken a century in the trans-Mississippi West. The overriding result of this fast-motion Alaskan replay was the disposition by Congress of Alaska's 375 million acres, almost all of which had been owned by the federal government. Through ANCSA, Congress lifted the land freeze that had safeguarded Native land-claim options. Alaska Natives were authorized to select forty-four million acres. The State of Alaska could now resume selection of the balance of 104 million acres authorized by the Statehood Act of 1958. And, after a titanic struggle that tested the nation's political processes, ANILCA established 106 million acres of new conservation units.

One of these new conservation units is the eight-million-acre Gates of the Arctic National Park and Preserve. As finally defined by the statute, the parkland stretches nearly two hundred miles from the Koyukuk's North Fork country westward to include the upper reaches of the Kobuk and the Noatak. North of the divide it captures the north-flowing streams and arctic valleys tributary to the Colville—from Itkillik on the east to Killik on the west. Excepting blocs of Native-selected lands in the Anaktuvuk Pass vicinity and scattered private tracts, the parkland comprises an integrated geographic region that extends from the ridgeline of the central Brooks Range to its eaves. Abutting it on the west is the Noatak National Preserve. And on the east, beyond the Dalton Highway corridor through Middle Fork and Atigun Pass, the expanded Arctic National Wildlife Refuge stretches to the Canadian border. The Gates park acts as keystone for this vast reservation of virtually the entire Brooks Range.

Seven million acres of the Gates parkland were designated national park; one million acres in two sections were designated national preserve. The southwest or boot section of the preserve on the upper Kobuk contains a congressionally reserved right-of-way that would, if needed, allow surface transportation between the Alaska Pipeline Haul Road (now Dalton Highway) and the Ambler Mining District north of the Kobuk River (bornite and other mineral prospects). The northeast section of the preserve on the upper Itkillik contains acreage whose subsurface mineral rights are held by the Arctic Slope Regional Corporation. Sport hunting is allowed in the preserve; otherwise it is managed as though it were part of the national park. Excepting private tracts and Native corporation lands within the park boundary, the entire national park was designated wilderness by ANILCA.[5] Under that law's provisions, the national preserve lands are also being studied for wilderness suitability.

During the 1970s, two latter-day pilgrims, John Kauffmann and Ray Bane, traversed the Gates region summer and winter—learning its secrets and mingling with its people. Kauffmann, a writer and park planner, had been appointed by the National Park Service to steer the Gates proposal through the years leading to its establishment—first by presidential proclamation as a monument in 1978, then by an act of Congress as a park and preserve in 1980. A seasoned wilderness trekker, Kauffmann was also a poet and romantic. He was attuned, as Marshall had been, to the lure of the central Brooks Range. Bane, his assistant, was an ex-teacher in Arctic Coast villages and an anthropologist. His years of arctic experience, during which he and his wife, Barbara, had several times circuited the country by dog team, had prepared him for local residence and extended surveys through the region.

In gathering the data that described the park proposal and informed congressional decisions, these men reinforced their already strong

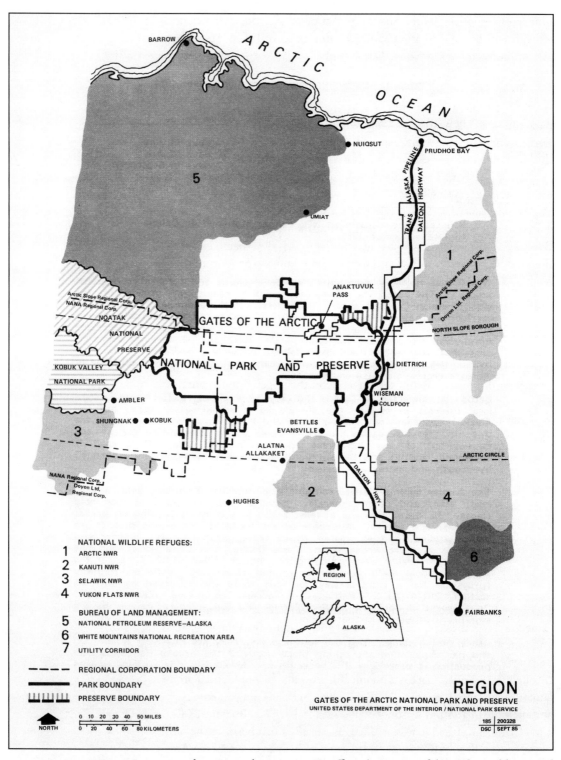

GATES OF THE ARCTIC NATIONAL PARK AND PRESERVE
UNITED STATES DEPARTMENT OF THE INTERIOR / NATIONAL PARK SERVICE

185 | 20032B
DSC | SEPT 85

This map shows boundaries of conservation units established by the Alaska National Interest Land Conservation Act of 1980 and depicts the preserved lands across the Brooks Range.

attachments to the country. Kauffman's concept of the park would respond to Robert Marshall's plea to keep northern Alaska largely a wilderness.

Kauffmann believed that the central goal of the National Park Service at Gates of the Arctic should be to retain the land in its present untrammeled condition. Later, this purpose was given statutory sanction in ANILCA when Congress declared that "the park and preserve shall be managed . . . to maintain the wild and undeveloped character of the area" (Public Law 96-487). Given the special nature of the Gates landscape, Kauffmann urged a protective but unobtrusive management regime, with no in-park developments that would alter wilderness qualities. "While other proposed parks in Alaska and existing parks in the Lower 48 states offer a wider range of modern recreational opportunities, Gates of the Arctic would be available for the experiences that only wild, untouched country can provide" (Kauffmann 1976).

Ray Bane became the first resident representative of the Park Service at the Gates. He and his wife, Barbara, had the experience and the tools to start the tradition envisioned by Kauffmann.

As an on-site anthropologist, Ray became the intermediary between a known past and an unknown future, between the Park Service and the people of the scattered camps and communities who wondered how the new parkland would change their lives. He later explained his role in these words:

> The work of numerous researchers, of which I am but one, has revealed a complex interrelationship between what many have called a wilderness and the people who have and continue to draw upon these environments for their basic subsistence needs. Recognizing its responsibility to avoid placing undue hardship on established rural Alaskans, the Park Service has pioneered research efforts into subsistence and attempted to develop new management regulations and policies to permit the continuation of this ancient lifestyle.
>
> My personal role in the N.P.S. subsistence effort has been varied ranging from actually living among active subsistence based Native peoples to helping these same people to understand and reply to proposed subsistence regulations. Along the way I often find myself assisting in environmental studies, identifying cultural sites, acting as a liaison between N.P.S. and village councils, explaining N.P.S. policies and regulations to miners, trappers, big game guides, and others, assisting visitors to the new parklands, etc. Utilizing a small aircraft, dog team, and boats, I visit numerous remote villages and scattered homesites. My office is my home, a small log cabin in the village of Bettles Field near the Gates of the Arctic National Monument (Bane n.d.).

In late 1978, the Alaska Lands bill jammed in Congress. The ANCSA-imposed deadline for congressional action on this issue was rapidly approaching. Fearing that the proposed conservation units would be lost through Congress's inaction, President Jimmy Carter and Secretary of the Interior Cecil Andrus joined in a massive withdrawal of these proposed areas: the president proclaiming seventeen national monuments, including Gates of the Arctic; Secretary Andrus withdrawing thirteen

A ranger's vehicle will be his airplane, canoe, dogsled— or his boots. He may heat his cabin with wood he has cut, while his wife draws water with a bucket. He must accept arctic dark and cold, few amenities, and the sometimes delicate relationships of small-village living. It is to be hoped that local hire provisions in the legislation will allow the Park Service to alloy experienced NPS supervisors with skilled local residents strong to the life of the arctic and loving of the area that is to be preserved in their care. Such a management team, thriving on the hardscrabble life, can grant Bob Marshall's plea, keeping true the faith that somewhere in America there will always be . . . wild country of adventure, a park for discoveries—beyond the ridges and within ourselves (Kauffmann 1978).

potential refuges by public land orders. This action held the conservation units in trust, giving Congress more time to resolve its differences. And it reinforced the need for congressional action, for the national monuments would have to be managed much more restrictively than the parklands proposed in the Alaska Lands bill. The bill had been crafted to blend the national interest with the needs of local people for access, cabin privileges, subsistence use, and sport hunting. The proclamations brought into play general federal regulations only marginally adaptive to Alaska conditions (Williss 1985).

Predictably, all hell broke loose in the hinterlands. Ray and Barbara Bane, still the only resident field representatives near the proposed northern parklands, received the full brunt of resentment in their community. Years of patient work—explaining the proposals, relaying local viewpoints, countering rumors, establishing trust—went down the drain, except for the understanding of a few staunch friends (Ray and Barbara Bane, pers. comm.).

This response was felt across Alaska by Park Service people, as large segments of the public and press waxed furious at what they perceived to be an unconstitutional application of the Antiquities Act and public land laws.

Recognizing that the proclamations and withdrawals represented a holding action pending congressional action, the Park Service in Alaska—now headed by John Cook—approached management of the 41-million-acre national monument accession with caution. Lacking funds, manpower, and public acceptance, Cook determined that the principles of protection, presence, and persuasion, rather than aggressive management and enforcement, should prevail. By hook and by crook he and his cohorts throughout the Park Service assembled a temporary-duty Ranger Task Force that provided a thin line of custodial care for the new parklands during the two-year national monument period. It was a kind of interregnum, bridging the gap between congressional acts. For both the managers and the carefully chosen rangers in the field, it was a balancing act between opposite public perceptions that criticized Park Service aggressiveness on the one hand and its lassitude on the other.

Despite these criticisms, and instances of threat and vandalism, the handful of task force rangers carried out their sensitive assignments at Gates and other areas. They established a presence, greatly restricted illegal hunting, and absorbed much hostility. In time, particularly after some ugly episodes of plane tampering and arson by disgruntled individuals, the great majority of Alaskans who came in contact with them accepted the rangers as people, despite unwavering opposition to the monuments and other withdrawals. A number of the rangers would come to Alaska on permanent assignment after ANILCA was passed (Williss 1985).

Passage of ANILCA in December 1980 gave the congressional stamp of approval to the new parklands. The Park Service inaugurated permanent staffing, began legally mandated park planning, and started to develop steady operational relationships with neighboring individuals and communities. The pioneering phase of Park Service activities during the proposal and national monument periods had largely vindicated the management principles of gradualism, persuasion when at all possible, and day-by-day integration with park landscapes and neighbors that had long been advocated by the service's Alaska employees. At Gates of the Arctic and in the other new areas, small field staffs—most of them remotely situated in communities that only grudgingly acquiesced to the new system of land tenure and authority—went about the business of setting up their parks. At Gates, the ultimate wilderness park, the main task would be to allow Nature to rule these landscapes in its own way, with managers intervening in authorized human activities only as necessary to conform them to the natural regime.

As John Kauffmann predicted, this task has not been easy. The initial planning process, now mercifully ended, had forced both the park staff and its neighbors to contemplate the full range of problems that might possibly occur. On the one hand were the fears of park neighbors over potentially arbitrary and capricious administration. On the other was the fear of administrators over potential worst-case violations of law covering a wide range of complex issues—subsistence, access, cabins, sport hunting—that distinguish wilderness parklands in Alaska from parklands in the Lower 48. Acculturation under ANILCA's provisions has become a two-way street: local people facing another large dose of change that threatens their traditional patterns; Park Service people required to adapt their own venerable traditions of stewardship to new modes of management flexibility under a law that deals almost as much with neighbors as with natural landscapes.

In contrast to the fearsome systemic levels of concern forced by the planning process, day-to-day operations deal with specific cases. To the credit of park neighbors, there have been remarkably few premeditated violations of law and regulation, and on the whole, in the gray areas created by the law's complexity, moderation and going halfway have marked the efforts of both park staff and park neighbors to respond rationally to the new realities.

A working example of such efforts in the 1980s is described in *Gaunt Beauty . . . Tenuous Life,* by William E. Brown (1988). The park's Subsistence Resource Commission, made up mainly of local people, is working with the park staff to develop a subsistence hunting plan for the park that will satisfy both park managers and subsistence hunters on matters of eligibility, traditional-use zones, and access—all touched upon by ANILCA, but requiring detailed resolution in the specific park context. One phase of this work relates to the problem sketched in Chapter 6—access of Anaktuvuk Pass villagers to summer hunting and fishing sites by ATVs. Existing access easements across park lands are unsatisfactory to the villagers because of bad terrain, yet summer ATV traverse across park lands outside of the easements is prohibited by law

Noatak Valley becomes progressively more scenic as one travels into its upper reaches. The mountain walls become higher and more precipitous. Mt. Igikpak's dark granite face and needle-like peak stands above its lesser snow blanketed mates like a beacon luring the traveler toward even greater natural grandeur (Bane 1981).

because of potential damage to vegetation. The Park Service and the villagers are exploring the possibility of a land exchange or, as a last resort, a legislative adjustment to accommodate both park protection and the villagers' subsistence requirements. This is a tough problem: both park protection and subsistence needs are weighty concerns, as reflected by provisions in ANILCA. "Winning" the negotiation is not the point. The people of Anaktuvuk Pass are limiting their access requirements to an area of demonstrated heavy subsistence use. The Park Service has averred that it will go to every legitimate length to respond in as helpful a way as possible. And indeed, in a landmark land exchange, an ATV access corridor to Chandalar Lake was created so the older folks can get to their traditional fish camps.

• • •

In historical perspective, the problems and controversies of these first years of park establishment can be viewed as a shakedown cruise. Throughout history the laying on of new land-tenure systems has been painful. Parklands, though they are dedicated to holding intact the diminishing spaces of yesteryear landscapes, are part of Alaska's new land-tenure system—and are therefore resented. The bugs and contradictions in a law as lengthy and broad in scope as ANILCA—a product of nine years of heated debate and political compromise—were to be expected. The fact that all of this is occurring in a larger context of change besetting Alaska could only contribute to stress and turbulence. In this light, for most of the immediately affected people, the transition from an unfenced local commons to a partially fenced national commons shared by local people is progressing remarkably well. In the long run, for those older denizens and their younger followers who wish that things had not changed, creation of the Gates of the Arctic Park and Preserve will be seen as a conservative act. In this place, whatever changes occur around it, the landscapes and lifeways of a more innocent age can be perpetuated.

Epilogue

For the writer, coming to the end of this history after two and a half years of immersion in it is both a relief and a sad leaving of unforgettable friends and places. My partners in bush-whacking field adventures to the old sites will be missed, as will the pilots and park people who got us out to our base camps. The people who welcomed us to mining camps and far communities, even though we did represent the National Park Service, recall the hospitality and helpfulness of an older Alaska—thank God, not dead yet. And from the writings and anecdotes of those long dead, whose footsteps we had the good fortune to follow for awhile, grew a distant friendship and present admiration that surmounted the Great Divide, over which, in awhile, we will follow them once more.

Memories of people and places crowd the tapestry of these two and a half years:

- A river float from Walker Lake through the canyons of the Kobuk, with Cantwell's notes at hand.
- Our camp on Glacier River under the loom of Blue Cloud Mountain, a score of old cabins nearby.
- The Ernie Creek–North Fork junction, with Marshall's Doonerak and Gates of the Arctic in view.
- Elijah's old eyes scanning Chandler Lake for signs of that last great caribou hunt.
- Arctic John's sod-house ruin in the angle of Nugget Creek and the haul road, trembling with the passage of heavy trucks.
- Vern Watts' discovery claim on Hammond River, the boiler cabin still standing, sunbeams shafting through the broken roof.
- The deserted dance hall at Old Bettles, crowded by willow and alder, its lights and laughter gone, melting into the ground.
- Fourth of July at Wiseman, still calling the folks in for games and food and frolic.

At Wiseman, where we spent some weeks recording the old structures, a special relationship grew. Harry Leonard showed us his cache of old pictures and documents, his museum of mining machines. It was a trove of history illumined by a memory that reached back half a century in this place.

Walter Johnson, owner with Bill English, Jr., of the old Wiseman store, showed us the old sites and told of his days as Alaska Road Commission foreman in the 1940s. When Vern Watts died in 1946, Walter and George

Miscovich, then working with a Cat on the Hammond River road, placed their friend in a sluice box and lashed it to the Cat blade for the trip to Wiseman. Before they started back, they sat for a moment in Vern's cabin to bid him goodbye with the last of his whiskey.

Gentle philosopher Ross Brockman—when we met him, completing his eighteenth year without leaving Wiseman—had tried prospecting during his early years of residence. He told us that he knew of many places in these mountains where there was no gold.

Charlie Breck, who prospected the North Fork with trader Pat O'Connell in 1947, keeps very cold beer in his permafrost-chilled cellar. He showed us around the Linda Creek drift mining site, telling us how the old system worked and allowing that he had never fancied underground mining because he would be underground soon enough. When we proposed to Charlie that we should record all decipherable data from the fading markers in the Wiseman Cemetery, he acquiesced: "I don't hear many of those stiffs complaining, but go ahead—they won't mind."

• • •

And so the tales go on. There is an integrity in these people and places that makes being a historian a joy. Perhaps in no other site did that integrity so strike us as on the upper reaches of Spring Creek off Wild Lake. Here Austin Duffy's old boomer dam and cabin stood untouched except for nearly a century's exposure to the elements. The crafted, salvaged implements, the leaning remains of cabin and dam, the laboriously piled rocks at the side of the creek had brought him no return in gold. Yet one suspects in such a place—alone with the wind and the creek tumbling through slotted mountains to the lake glimpsed far below—that Austin Duffy probably got what he came for.

END NOTES

CHAPTER 1: LAND OF TRADITIONAL TIMES
1. The above description applies in general to neighboring Chandalar country, with the major difference that salmon do not enter the upper forks of Chandalar River (Alaska Department of Fish and Game, 1978, I, Map 126-1). McKennan (1965, 17) states that lack of this food source sets off the mountain-dwelling Chandalar Gwich'in from their more riverine neighbors to the south.

CHAPTER 2: EARLY EXPLORATION, 1700–1900
1. The role of the Revenue Marine Service (precursor of the Coast Guard) in north Alaskan waters is summarized in Nielson (1979). Its responsibilities included law enforcement, civil administration, navigation aids and rescue, medical services, transportation, mail, and supply. As an arm of government and link to the outside world, the revenue cutters "were sources of law, comfort and security for Native and white alike" (Nielson 1979, 12).
2. The expedition log (ship's log of the USS *Explorer*) is in Record Group 24, National Archives; the rough maps are in the National Archives map section, Alexandria, VA.

CHAPTER 3: EARLY MINING AND KLONDIKE OVERFLOW
1. One account of Bremner's killing, based on the perspective of an experienced Russian Creole, blamed the Native doctors or medicine men. They warned the Indians that too many white men were coming into the country and would scare away the game; maybe killing a few of them would keep them out. Plunder of Bremner's outfit seemed also to have been a motive. See Case (1947, 153).
2. Schneider (1984) summarizes the wise and heroic control exercised by Captain Ray and Lt. W. P. Richardson in 1897–98, when they provided the only United States authority on the boiling Yukon frontier. It also details Captain Ray's significant influence on subsequent events and reforms made necessary by the gold rush: exploration for an all-American route to the Alaska gold fields; establishment of army posts along the Yukon to both regulate and assist the hordes of miners flooding the country; regulation and inspection of Yukon River transportation and supply to prevent starvation, disorder, profiteering, and steamboat disasters; and the need to provide assistance to Indians, whose dependence on trading posts for their own supplies was by this time critical. The reports of Ray and Richardson are found in *Compilation of Narratives of Explorations in Alaska* (1900).

CHAPTER 4: FAR NORTH CAMPS AND COMMUNITIES, 1900–1930
1. Original field notebooks are on file at the Alaska Geology Branch technical library, USGS Western Regional Office, Menlo Park, CA.
2. Brooks (1953) used the name Arctic Mountains. After his death in 1924, they were renamed the Brooks Range. (Orth 1967, 162.)

CHAPTER 5: THE CIVILIZATION OF THE NORTH
1. Marshall's table from pp. 37–38 shows the periods of boom and decline in the Koyukuk camp:

Year	Permanent White Population	Prostitutes	Gold Production (Dollars)
1898	200	0	n/a
1899	120	0	n/a
1900	270	2	$ 107,000
1901	320	6	173,000
1902	350	10	200,000
1903	300	7	301,000

1904	210	0	200,000
1905	220	1	165,000
1906	160	0	165,000
1907	120	0	100,000
1908	240	6	220,000
1909	230	5	420,000
1910	190	8	160,000
1911	160	5	130,000
1912	230	9	216,000
1913	250	8	368,000
1914	270	13	260,000
1915	300	14	290,000
1916	250	12	320,000
1917	200	7	250,000
1918	150	2	150,000
1919	130	2	110,000
1920	119	0	90,000
1921	107	0	78,000
1922	101	0	132,000
1923	97	0	37,000
1924	92	0	54,000
1925	88	0	50,000
1926	93	0	68,000
1927	98	0	78,000
1928	90	0	46,000
1929	83	0	32,000
1930	77	0	31,000
1931	71	0	27,000
Total			$5,028,000

2. A detailed account of upper-country roads, trails, shelter cabins, and communities is found in Joseph Ulmer's 1923–34 Log of a Reconnaissance Survey, Fort Gibbon to Kobuk and Koyukuk Rivers, performed for the Alaska Road Commission (Joseph Ulmer Collection, Box 10, University of Alaska Fairbanks, Archives).

CHAPTER 6: ROBERT MARSHALL'S KOYUKUK

1. As indicated by early Wiseman store and commissioner's records, the old-country spelling of Yale was Yehle. By Bob Marshall's time, Yale was standard usage for man and cabin.
2. In addition to *Alaska Wilderness* (1970), see Marshall 1930; "The Wilderness Society," a 1935 prospectus defining reasons for and objectives of such a society, in Robert Marshall Collection, Bancroft Library, University of California, Berkeley; and various letters in the Robert Marshall Collection, including especially Marshall to Ickes, Feb. 14, 1935, Marshall to Oberholtzer, Feb. 28, 1935, Marshall to Grosvenor, Mar. 1, 1935, Marshall to Yard, June 17, 1938, memorandum to Ickes, Apr. 25, 1935, and report to society members, Feb. 24, 1937.
3. Wilderness Society resolutions draft attached to June 27, 1938, letter to Yard; letter to Strauss, Nov. 1, 1938, both in Robert Marshall Collection, Bancroft Library, University of California, Berkeley.

CHAPTER 7: STILL A HOMELAND

1. The account that follows is based on Sun (1985). Logistical support during the field survey with Joe Sun was provided by the National Park Service, with special help on site visits and overflights from Ray Bane.
2. For recent expressions of these views, see Berger (1985), subsistence photos and quotations following 47; Chap. 2.
3. See Berry (1975) and Arnold, et al. (1978) for details of these major developments. David M. Hickok, who served on the Federal Field Committee for Development Planning in Alaska (FFC) during these critical times, cautions against attributing the passage of ANCSA solely to oil-development pressures. He notes that an FFC report to President Lyndon B. Johnson in 1965 recommended no further economic development in Alaska pending settlement of Alaska Native land claims. This report sparked renewed interest in Congress on this subject. It led to the drafting of bills on the land claims issue well before oil was discovered at Prudhoe

Bay. In a critique of my draft language on this subject he states: "It is a myth that the pipeline forced congressional action on ANCSA. Bills were already in various stages. The FFC's *Alaska Natives and the Land* [a 1968 publication that provided the critical database for congressional committees dealing with the land claims issue] was already finished, etc., before Prudhoe Bay was discovered. What Prudhoe Bay did was (a) provide urgency and (b) jack up the price of compensation" (pers. comm. October 9, 1986).

4. The development/preservation controversy generated a huge literature, with subtopics such as the fight over environmental safeguards for pipeline construction filling large sections of libraries. Samplings of various viewpoints can be found in the following sources: "Alaska Strikes It Rich" (1968); Cantwell (1969); Main (1969).

5. The Alaska Native Claims Settlement Act (ANCSA) is another vast subject. The pros and cons of its effects, particularly as it affects the Native land base and the chances for perpetuation of traditional life ways, are hotly debated at the time of this writing. Many corporations are in financial trouble and the corporation-owned lands (individual Natives do not own lands conveyed under ANCSA), often selected for commercial rather than subsistence values, could soon be alienated from Native ownership through taxation or sale of stock. A number of Native groups seek amendments to the act that would safeguard Native land ownership and restructure the law in favor of traditional institutions for land control and governance. See Arnold et al. (1978), Berger (1985), and Mitchell (2001) for broad coverage of these issues.

CHAPTER 8: CREATION OF THE PARK

1. Weeden's *Alaska, Promises to Keep* (1978), esp. Chaps. 4–6, gives an excellent overview of the conservationists' developing doctrine in response to the oil boom. A special "Alyeska project" edition of *Oil & Gas Journal* published in 1974 traces the environmental safeguards built into pipeline construction. In later years, industry spokesmen commented that the conservation injunction spurred improvements in pipeline construction technology that proved of great benefit in the operational stage. Seminal sources on development trends and impacts include Hickok (1970), Strong (1977), and Kaye (2006).

2. BLM Recreation Specialist Wayne Boden memorandum of Oct. 21, 1964, "Inventory of the South Slope of the Brooks Range"; letter from BLM Fairbanks District Office Manager Robert C. Krumm to Nancy Hundt, Juneau Group, Alaska Chapter of the Sierra Club, Mar. 28, 1969. Many other conservationist groups and individuals were involved during this formative period of urgency when the imminence and the subsequent fact of major oil discoveries loomed as a threat to Alaska's arctic wilderness. See Cahn (1982) for a full account of groups, people, and actions. For a general review of these developments from the NPS perspective, see Williss (1985, 29–93). A select file of Richard J. Gordon's papers has been deposited in the history collection of Gates of the Arctic National Park and Preserve.

3. Letter from Bailey Breedlove to Chief, Office of Resource planning, SSC, April 8, 1969; Sierra Club, Alaska Chapter, Alaska Conservation Society broadside, Gates of the Arctic National Park proposal, printed in Juneau, 1969; McCord quoted in letter from Sen. Ernest Gruening to Secretary of the Interior, Feb. 19, 1964. All letters in Gates of the Arctic National Park and Preserve history file.

4. Williss (1985, 56–59). See Crevelli (1980) for administrative history of the proclamations episode. By personal communication of Jan. 28, 1987, T. R. Swem clarified the sequence of events that resulted in the Udall-inspired National Monument proposal, which anticipated both the study team's published proposal and the conservationists' proposal of March 1969.

5. T. R. Swem notes that the original proposals to Congress in 1973 by then-Secretary of the Interior Rogers C. B. Morton would have designated the Gates of the Arctic an "instant" wilderness. That designation was blocked by the president's budget office, but Morton, in a press conference, vowed that he would push the idea with Congress (Swem, pers. comm., Jan. 28, 1987).

BIBLIOGRAPHY

"Alaska Strikes It Rich." 1968. *U.S. News & World Report*, December 9, 48–53.

Allen, Henry T. 1887. *Report of an Expedition to the Copper, Tanana and Koyukuk Rivers, in the Territory of Alaska in the Year 1885*. Washington, DC: U.S. Government Printing Office.

Allin, Roger W. 1966. "Alaska, A Plan for Action." Typescript report. Washington, DC: National Park Service. Roger Allin 1966 Report file, Box #6, Ted Swem Collection, Denver Public Library.

Anderson, Douglas D. 1981. "The Kotzebue Basin." *Alaska Geographic* 8(3).

Arctic Environmental Information and Data Center (Alaska). 1978. National Petroleum Reserve in Alaska, 105(c) Study, Socioeconomic Profile. Anchorage: U.S. Department of the Interior.

Arnold, Robert D., Emil Notti, and Janet Archibald. 1978. *Alaska Native Land Claims*. Anchorage: Alaska Native Foundation.

Bane, Ray. 1981. *Winter Field Trip into the Upper Noatak Valley, March 16–26, 1981*. William E. Brown Collection, Archives, Alaska and Polar Regions Department, University of Alaska Fairbanks.

———. n.d. (ca. 1980). *Tasks and Objectives of Subsistence Coordinator in Northwest Alaska*. Bane file, William E. Brown Collection, Archives, Alaska and Polar Regions Department, University of Alaska Fairbanks.

Bearss, Edwin C. 1970. *Proposed Klondike Gold Rush National Historical Park Historic Resource Study*. Washington, DC: National Park Service.

Berger, Thomas R. 1985. *Village Journey: The Report of the Alaska Native Review Commission*. New York: Hill and Wang.

Berry, Mary Clay. 1975. *The Alaska Pipeline: The Politics of Oil and Native Land Claims*. Bloomington: University of Indiana Press.

Berton, Pierre. 1974. *The Klondike Fever*. New York: Alfred A. Knopf.

Bettles, Gordon C. 1941. "First Surgery on the Koyukuk." *Alaska Life*, July, p. 5.

Brooks, Alfred Hulse. 1953. *Blazing Alaska's Trails*. College, AK: University of Alaska and Washington, DC: Arctic Institute of North America.

———. 1923. *Geology and Petroleum Resources of Northern Alaska and Plans for Survey of Naval Petroleum Reserve No. 4*. Menlo Park, CA: Technical Data Library, USGS.

Brown, William E. 1988. *Gaunt Beauty . . . Tenuous Life: Historic Resources Study, Gates of the Arctic National Park and Preserve* (2 volumes). Alaska: National Park Service.

Burch, Ernest S., Jr. 1972. "The Caribou/Wild Reindeer as a Human Resource." *American Antiquity* 3(3): 339–68.

———. 1975a. *Eskimo Kinsmen: Changing Family Relationships in Northwest Alaska*. St. Paul, MN: West Publishing.

———. 1975b. "Inter-Regional Transportation in Traditional Northwest Alaska." *Anthropological Papers of the University of Alaska* 17(2):1–9.

———. 1976a. "The 'Nunamiut' Concept and the Standardization of Error." In *Contributions to Anthropology: The Interior Peoples of Northern Alaska*. Ottawa: National Museums of Canada.

———. 1976b. "Overland Travel Routes in Northwest Alaska." *Anthropological Papers of the University of Alaska* 18(1):1–10.

———. 1979. "Indians and Eskimos in North Alaska, 1816–1977: A Study in Changing Ethnic Relations." *Arctic Anthropology* 16(2):124–29.

———. 1981. "Studies of Native History as a Contribution to Alaska's Future." Typescript lecture paper, 32nd Alaska Science Conference, Fairbanks, AK.

Buskin, Evey, ed. 1984. "Letters to Lizzie: A Koyukuk Gold Seeker Writes Home." *Anchorage Daily News*, May 6, "We Alaskans" magazine section.

Cahn, Robert. 1982. *The Fight to Save Wild Alaska*. Washington, DC: National Audubon Society.

Calkins, Annie. 1982. *Puvlatuuq*. Barrow, AK: North Slope Borough School District.

Cantwell, John C. 1902. *Report of the Operations of the U.S. Revenue Steamer* Nunivak *on the Yukon River Station, Alaska, 1899–1901*. Washington, DC: Government Printing Office.

Cantwell, Robert. 1969. "The Ultimate Confrontation." *Sports Illustrated*, March 24, 67–76.

Case, Will H. 1947. *Reminiscences of Captain Billie Moore*. Kansas City, MO: Burton Publishing.

Caswell, John E. 1956. *Arctic Frontiers: United States Explorations in the Far North*. Norman: University of Oklahoma Press.

Coffey, Raymond R. 1969. "Oil Boom Cuts Deep Scars into Alaskan Wilds." San Francisco *Sunday Examiner & Chronicle*, September 14, A26.

Cole, Terrence. 1983. "Early Explorers and Prospectors on the Koyukuk." In *Up the Koyukuk. Alaska Geographic* 10(4):26.

Crevelli, John P. 1980. "The Final Act of the Greatest Conservation President." *Prologue: The Journal of the National Archives* 12(4):173–91.

Dall, William H. 1870. *Alaska and Its Resources*. Boston: Lee and Shepard.

Dasmann, Raymond F. 1976. "National Parks, Nature Conservation, and 'Future Primitive.'" *The Ecologist* 6(5):164–67.

Detterman, Robert L., Robert S. Bickel, and George Gryc. 1963. *Geology of the Chandler River Region, Alaska*. USGS Prof. Paper 303-E. Washington, DC: Government Printing Office.

English, Shirley. 1983. "Tishu's World." In *Up the Koyukuk. Alaska Geographic* 10(4):40.

Federal Committee for Development Planning in Alaska. 1968. "Alaska Natives and the Land." Washington, DC: U.S. Government Printing Office.

Fitzgerald, Gerald. 1951. *Surveying and Mapping in Alaska*. Circular 101. Washington, DC: USGS.

Foote, Don Charles. 1966. "Human Geographical Studies in Northwestern Arctic Alaska: The Upper Kobuk River Project, 1965." Montreal: Geography Dept., McGill University.

Gal, Robert, and Edwin S. Hall Jr. 1982. "Provisional Culture History (National Petroleum Reserve in Alaska)." *Anthropological Papers of the University of Alaska* 20(1–2):3–5.

Giddings, J. L. 1952. *The Arctic Woodland Culture of the Kobuk River*. Philadelphia: University Museum, University of Pennsylvania.

———. 1961. *Kobuk River People*. Fairbanks: Department of Anthropology and Geography, University of Alaska.

Goddard, Elizabeth Hayes. 1934. *Diary of Koyukuk River Journey Aboard the Episcopal Mission Boat* Pelican (typescript). Elizabeth Hays Goddard Collection, Box 1, 101–2, Archives, Alaska and Polar Regions Department, University of Alaska Fairbanks.

Greeley, A. W. 1970. *Handbook of Alaska, Its Resources, Products, and Attractions in 1924*. Originally published in 1925 and reissued by Kennikat Press, Port Washington, NY.

Gruening, Ernest. 1954. *The State of Alaska*. New York: Random House.

———, ed. 1966. *An Alaskan Reader, 1867–1967*. New York: Meredith Press.

Gubser, Nicholas J. 1954. *The Nunamiut Eskimos, Hunters of Caribou*. New York: W. W. Norton.

Hall, Edwin S. Jr. 1972. "The Caribou Hunters of Anaktuvuk Pass." *Alaska Magazine* 38(11):6–7, 53–55.

———. 1975. "Kutchin Athapaskan/Nunamiut Eskimo Conflict." *Alaska Journal* 5(4):248–52.

———. 1976. "Noatak Eskimo Tool Bag." *Alaska Journal* 6(4):230–34.

———. 1977. "A Memento of the Northern Alaska Naval Exploring Expedition of 1885–86." *Alaska Journal* 7(2):81–87.

———. 1984. "A Clear and Present Danger: The Use of Ethnohistoric Data for Interpreting Mound 44 at the Utqiagvik Site." *Arctic Anthropology* 21(1):137.

Hall, Edwin S., Jr., S. Craig Gerlach, and Margaret B. Blackman. 1985. *In the National Interest: A Geographically Based Study of Anaktuvuk Pass Inupiat Subsistence Through Time*. Barrow, AK: North Slope Borough.

Healy, Michael A. 1889. *Report of the Cruise of the Revenue Marine Steamer* Corwin *in the Arctic Ocean in the Year 1884*. Washington, DC: Treasury Department.

———. 1887. *Report of the Cruise of the Revenue Marine Steamer* Corwin *in the Arctic Ocean in the Year 1885*. Washington, DC: Treasury Department.

Hickok, David M. 1970. "Developmental Trends in Arctic Alaska." Typescript presentation paper, 1 July. Available at Arctic Information and Data Center, Anchorage.

———. 1974. "Nunamiut Experience and Current Approaches to Subsistence Harvest Problems by the People of Anaktuvuk Pass." Address before the Federal-State Land Use Planning Commission for Alaska, February 5, 1974.

Hinckley, Ted C. 1968. "Reflections and Refractions: Alaska and Gilded Age America." In Robert A. Frederick, ed. *Frontier Alaska: A Study in Historical Interpretation and Opportunity*. Anchorage: Alaska Methodist University Press.

Huey, George. *Alaska Weekly,* Nov. 4, 1927, p. 5.

Hunt, John Clark. 1973. "The Adventures of the Iowa Gold Seekers." *Alaska Journal* 3(1):5–6.

Ingstad, Helge. 1954. *Nunamiut: Among Alaska's Inland Eskimos*. New York: W. W. Norton.

Jenness, Diamond. 1957. *Dawn in Arctic Alaska*. Minneapolis: University of Minnesota Press.

Kassler, Katrina. 1984. *Discussion Guide to "The Oral Tradition: A Film Series on Three Alaska Native Elders."* Fairbanks: Alaska Native Heritage Film Project, University of Alaska Museum.

Kauffmann, John. 1976. "Gates of the Arctic National Park Briefing Statement. Kauffmann file, Gates of the Arctic National Park and Preserve files.

———. 1978. "Draft Management Concept." Kauffmann file, Gates of the Arctic National Park and Preserve files.

Kaye, Roger. 2006. *Last Great Wilderness: The Campaign to Establish the Arctic National Wildlife Refuge*. Fairbanks: University of Alaska Press.

Keim, Charles, comp. 1977. *Alaska Game Trails with a Master Guide*. Anchorage: Alaska Northwest Publishing.

Kunz, Michael. 1977. "Athapaskan/Eskimo Interfaces in the Central Brooks Range, Alaska." In *Prehistory of the North American Sub-Arctic: The Athapaskan Question*. Calgary, Alberta: Archeological Association of the University of Calgary.

Kunz, Michael L., ed. 1985. "Cultural Resource Survey and Inventory of the North Fork Koyukuk, Middle Fork Koyukuk, Glacier, and Upper Itkillik River Drainages." Draft National Park Service report, Fairbanks.

Leffingwell, E. 1919. *The Canning River Region, Northern Alaska*. USGS Prof. Paper 109. Washington, DC: Government Printing Office.

Lopez, Barry. 1984. "Story at Anaktuvuk Pass." *Harper's Magazine,* December, 49–52.

Madison, Curt, and Yvonne Yarber. 1979. *Moses Henzie, A Biography: Allakaket*. North Vancouver, BC: Hancock House.

———. 1980. *Frank Tobuk, Evansville: A Biography*. North Vancouver, BC: Hancock House.

Main, Jeremy. 1969. "The Hot Oil Rush in Arctic Alaska." *Fortune,* April, 120–25, 136–42.

Mangus, Marvin D. 1980. "A History of the Exploration and Development of North Slope Oil and Gas Reserves." In *Mining in Alaska's Past*. Pub. No. 27, Office of History and Archeology, Alaska Division of Parks.

Marshall, Robert. 1929. Journal, North Fork of the Koyukuk trip, Alaska—July 22–Aug. 16, 1929. Robert Marshall Collection, Bancroft Library, University of California, Berkeley.

———. 1930. "The Problem of Wilderness." *Scientific Monthly* 30(2):141–48.

———. 1991 [1933]. *Arctic Village*. Fairbanks: University of Alaska Press.

———. 1934. "Reconnaissance of the Northern Koyukuk Valley." USGS Bulletin 844-E. Washington, DC: Government Printing Office.

———. 1939. Field journal and notebook, "North Doonerak, Amawk and Apoon." Robert Marshall Collection, Bancroft Library, University of California, Berkeley.

———. 1970. *Alaska Wilderness: Exploring the Central Brooks Range*. 2nd edition, George Marshall, ed. Berkeley: University of California Press.

Martin, Calvin. 1980. "Subarctic Indians and Wildlife." In Kai T. Erikson, *American Indian Environments: Ecological Issues in Native American History*. Syracuse, NY: Syracuse University Press.

Mattes, Merrill. 1969. "Kobuk-Koyukuk, a Reconnaissance Report." Typescript report. San Francisco: National Park Service.

McFadyen Clark, Annette. 1974. *Koyukuk River Culture*. Ottawa: National Museums of Canada.

McKennan, Robert A. 1965. *The Chandalar Kutchin*. Montreal: Arctic Institute of North America.

McPhee, John. 1977. *Coming Into the Country*. New York: Farrar, Straus and Giroux.

Mekiana, Homer. 1972. *This Is the Story about Anaktuvuk Pass Village*. Barrow, AK: Naval Arctic Research Laboratory.

Melchior, Herbert R., ed. 1976. *Biological Survey of the Proposed Kobuk Valley National Monument.* Fairbanks: National Park Service.

Mendenhall, Walter J. C. 1902. *Reconnaissance from Fort Hamlin to Kotzebue Sound, Alaska, by Way of Dall, Kanuti, Allen (Alatna), and Kowak (Kobuk) Rivers.* USGS Prof. Paper No. 10. Washington, DC: Government Printing Office.

Metzger, Charles R. 1983. *The Silent River.* Los Angeles: Omega Books.

Mitchell, Donald Craig. 2001. *Take My Land, Take My Life: The Story of Congress's Historic Settlement of Alaska Native Land Claims, 1960-1971.* Fairbanks, AK: University of Alaska Press.

Murie, Adolph. 1961. *A Naturalist in Alaska.* New York: Devin-Adair.

Murie, Olaus J. 1935. "Alaska-Yukon Caribou." *North American Fauna,* No. 54. Washington, DC: U.S. Dept. of Agriculture, Bureau of Biological Survey.

——— .1973. *Journeys to the Far North.* Palo Alto, CA: Wilderness Society and American West Publishing.

——— . n.d. "Dr. Murie Reports on Wilderness Study of Impressive Brooks Range." Unsourced newsclipping (presumed to be from *New York Times,* late 1956), in Murie Collection, Archives, Alaska and Polar Regions Department, University of Alaska Fairbanks.

Naske, Claus M. 1986. *Paving Alaska's Trails: The Work of the Alaska Road Commission.* Lanham, MD: University Press of America.

Nelson, Richard. 1977. "Preliminary Report: Subsistence Activities in Proposed Alaskan Parklands." Typescript report. Anchorage: National Park Service.

Nelson, Richard K. 1973. *Hunters of the Northern Forest.* Chicago: University of Chicago Press.

——— . 1983. *Make Prayers to the Raven: A Koyukon View of the Northern Forest.* Chicago: University of Chicago Press.

Nelson, Richard K., Kathleen H. Mautner, and G. Ray Bane. 1982. *Tracks in the Wildland: A Portrayal of Koyukon and Nunamiut Subsistence.* Fairbanks: Cooperative Park Studies Unit, University of Alaska.

Nichols, Jeannette Paddock. 1963. *Alaska: A History of Its Administration, Exploitation, and Industrial Development During Its First Half Century Under the Rule of the United States.* Cleveland: Arthur H. Clark Co., 1924; reprint, New York: Russell & Russell.

Nielson, Jon M. 1979. "Conduct Most Becoming: The Revenue Marine Service in Alaska." *Alaska Journal* 9(3):12–13, 91.

North Slope Borough Commission on History and Culture. 1980. *Qiniqtuagaksrat Utuqsanaat Inuuniagninisiqun: The Traditional Land Use Inventory for the Mid-Beaufort Sea.* Barrow, AK: North Slope Borough Commission.

Orth, Donald J. 1967. *Dictionary of Alaska Place Names.* Geological Survey Professional Paper 567. Washington, DC: Government Printing Office.

Osgood, Cornelius. 1971. *The Han Indians: A Compilation of Ethnographic and Historical Data on the Alaska-Yukon Boundary Area.* New Haven, CT: Department of Anthropology, Yale University.

Oswalt, Wendell H. 1979. *Eskimos and Explorers.* Novato, CA: Chandler & Sharp.

Paneak, Simon. 1960. "We Hunt to Live." *Alaska Sportsman* 26(3):12-13, 55.

Price, A. Grenfell, ed. 1971. *The Explorations of Captain James Cook in the Pacific as Told by Selections of His Own Journals, 1768–1779.* New York: Dover.

Pender, Jane. 1969. "Crisis on the North Slope: Last of the Caribou People." *Anchorage Daily News* 4, Mar. 5.

Ray, Dorothy Jean. 1975. *The Eskimos of Bering Strait, 1650–1898.* Seattle: University of Washington Press.

Ray, P. H. 1900. *Compilation of Narratives of Explorations in Alaska.* 56th Cong., 1st Sess., Senate Rep. 1023, pp. 501–02 and 552–53. Washington, DC: U.S. Congress.

Reed, John C. 1958. *Exploration of Naval Petroleum Reserve No. 4 and Adjacent Areas, Northern Alaska, 1944–53.* Part I, *History of the Exploration.* USGS Prof. Paper 301. Washington, DC: Government Printing Office.

Reed, Irving McK. 1938. "Upper Koyukuk Region, Alaska." Dept. of Mines, Territory of Alaska, typescript report.

Richardson, W. T. 1900. *Compilation of Narratives of Explorations in Alaska.* 56th Cong., 1st Sess., Senate Rep. 1023, pp. 504–07. Washington, DC: U.S. Congress.

Schneider, William. 1984. "Capt. P. H. Rayon: The Alaskan Frontier in the Fall of 1897." Typescript report, Fairbanks.

Sherwood, Morgan B. 1965. *Exploration of Alaska, 1865–1900.* New Haven, CT: Yale University Press. Reprint, Fairbanks: University of Alaska Press, 1992.

Smith, Philip S. 1926. "Memorial of Alfred H. Brooks." *Bulletin of the Geological Society of America* 37.

Smith, Philip S., and J. B. Mertie Jr. 1930. Geology and Mineral Resources of Northwestern Alaska, USGS Bulletin 815. Washington, DC: Government Printing Office.

Spearman, Grant. 1979. *Land Use Values through Time in the Anaktuvuk Pass Area.* Fairbanks: Cooperative Park Studies Unit, University of Alaska.

———. 1982. *Nunamiut History.* Barrow, AK: North Slope Borough School District.

Spearman, Grant, Arctic John Etalook, and Louisa M. Riley. 1982. "Preliminary Report to the North Slope Borough's Inupiaq History, Language, and Culture Commission of the Ulumiut Territorial Land Use Inventory." 3 December.

Stein, Gary. 1978. "History of the Northwest Arctic." Typescript report prepared for Cooperative Park Studies Unit. Fairbanks: University of Alaska.

———. 1981. "Ship Surgeon on the Yukon." *Alaska Journal* 11:232.

Stern, Richard O. 1980. *Eskimos, Reindeer and Land.* Agricultural Experiment Station, Bulletin 59. Fairbanks: University of Alaska.

Stoney, George M. 1974. "Explorations in Alaska." In U.S. Naval Institute Proceedings, September and December 1899. Seattle: Shorey Reprint.

Strong, B. Steven. 1977. *The Social and Economic Impact of the Trans-Alaska Oil Pipeline upon the Alaska Native People.* Montreal: McGill University.

Stuck, Hudson. 1920. *A Winter Circuit of Our Arctic Coast.* New York: Charles Scribner's Sons.

Sun, Joe. 1985. *My Life and Other Stories.* From transcripts translated by Susie Sun and compiled by David Libbey. Kotzebue: NANA Museum of the Arctic.

Ulmer, Joseph. 1923–34 Log of a Reconnaissance Survey, Fort Gibbon to Kobuk and Koyukuk Rivers, performed for the ARC. Joseph Ulmer Collection, Box 10, Archives, Alaska and Polar Regions Department, University of Alaska Fairbanks.

———. n.d. "Historical Sketch of James Bender." Joseph Ulmer Collection, Archives, Alaska and Polar Regions Department, University of Alaska Fairbanks.

U.S. Army. 1969. *The Army's Role in the Building of Alaska.* Seattle: Headquarters, U.S. Army, Alaska, Pamphlet 360-5.

U.S. Bureau of Outdoor Recreation. 1977. *The Iditarod Trail (Seward-Nome Route) and Other Alaskan Gold Rush Trails.* Anchorage: Bureau of Outdoor Recreation.

U.S. Congress. 1904. *Conditions in Alaska.* 58th Cong., 2nd Sess., Senate Rep. 282 4570, Washington, DC.

U.S. Geological Survey. 1899. *Maps and Descriptions of Routes of Exploration in Alaska in 1898.* Washington, DC: Engraving and Printing Division, USGS.

VanStone, James W. 1974. *Athapaskan Adaptations: Hunters and Fishermen of the Subarctic Forests.* Chicago: Field Museum of Natural History.

Vecsey, Christopher. 1980. "American Indian Environmental Religions." In Kai T. Erikson, *American Indian Environments: Ecological Issues in Native American History*, p. 21. Syracuse, NY: Syracuse University Press.

Webb (Grauman), Melody. 1977a. "A Historical Overview of the Seward Peninsula–Kotzebue Sound Area." Typescript report. Washington, DC: National Park Service,.

———. 1977b. *Yukon Frontiers.* Fairbanks: Cooperative Park Studies Unit, University of Alaska.

Webb, Melody. 1985. *The Last Frontier.* Albuquerque: University of New Mexico Press.

Weeden, Robert. 1978. *Alaska, Promises to Keep.* Boston: Houghton Mifflin.

Wells, E. Hazard. 1900. *Compilation of Narratives of Explorations in Alaska.* 56th Cong., 1st Sess., Senate Rep. 1023, pp. 511–13. Washington, DC: U.S. Congress.

Whymper, Frederick. 1871. *Travel and Adventure in the Territory of Alaska, Formerly Russian America—Now Ceded to the United States—and in Various Other Parts of the North Pacific.* New York: Harper & Brothers.

Will, Susan M. 1982. "Coldfoot, an Historic Mining Community on the Middle Fork of the Koyukuk River, Alaska." Fairbanks: Yukon Resource Area, Bureau of Land Management.

Williams, Howell, ed. 1958. *Landscapes of Alaska.* Berkeley: University of California Press.

Williss, G. Frank. 1985. *The National Park Service and the Alaska National Interest Lands Conservation Act of 1980.* Denver: National Park Service.

Wiseman School District letter file, Alaska State Archives, Juneau.

Wolfe, Robert J., and Robert J. Walker. 1987. Subsistence Economies in Alaska: Productivity, Geography, and Development Impacts. *Arctic Anthropology* 2:56–81.

Index

Page numbers in *italics* refer to illustrations.